TRUE CRIME

Mass Murderers

BY
THE EDITORS OF
TIME-LIFE BOOKS
Alexandria, Virginia

Mass Murderers

Deadly Rage

Criminologists label the people who kill several victims in a single short and bloody episode mass murderers. And, say the experts, these lethal criminals are increasingly common: Mass murder is not strictly a 20th-century phenomenon, but theorists believe that a breakdown in social controls during the past three or four decades has undermined the inhibitions that ordinarily keep a person from acting on the impulse to kill. Some authorities mark the dawn of the new age of mass murder as September 6, 1949, the day that Howard Unruh gunned down 13 people during a 12-minute walk through Camden, New Jersey *(pages 58-59)*.

From this notorious pioneer on down to the 1990s, mass murderers have proven similar enough to one another for experts to sketch out a typical profile. The mass murderer is almost always male. He's probably white and over 30 years old. He loves weapons and usually owns at least one gun. He's a loner—at best a man with acquaintances but no real friends, at worst a drifter with no fixed address, no job where someone counts on him, no family he can depend on. He probably has no criminal record, nor has he been treated for any serious psychiatric disorder.

But he has a festering store of real or imagined grievances, frustrations, disappointments, and outrages done to him by others over a long period of time. At some point this hateful burden of resentments reaches critical mass and explodes as murderous rage. The trigger is often an obvious blow, such as losing a job or being spurned by a woman. The killer usually sets out to strike back at the people he blames for hurting him, but he has a way of spreading that blame to irrational lengths. The mere fact that a person works in a place where the murderer has suffered some insult may be reason enough to mark that individual for death.

Mass murder so grossly violates social and moral norms that it seems those who commit it must be insane. In some cases this is so; Howard Unruh, for instance, was diagnosed a paranoid schizophrenic and committed to a hospital for the criminally insane for life. But criminologists consider the majority of mass murderers to be both medically and legally sane; however ugly their reality, they haven't lost their grip on it. Their behavior cannot be explained away by calling them lunatics. Until they kill, they are far more ordinary than most people may want to think.

An individual's chances of being killed by a mass murderer are infinitesimally small. But the very fact that mass murders occur rouses in many the dreadful suspicion that life is a crapshoot: Any one of us can run fatally afoul of a man who is consumed with rage and compelled to act it out.

The University of Texas tower from which Charles Whitman shot 13 people dead on August 1, 1966, looms beyond a shop window pierced by bullets.

Yeah, I killed them. I stabbed them and I choked them.

RICHARD SPECK

1

Loser

The convict's body lay chilling on a morgue slab at Silver Cross Hospital in Joliet, Illinois. He'd been remarkably ugly in life, and death did nothing to improve his looks. Lank, gray-brown hair surrounded his slack face and feathered over his prominent ears, and his long nose projected like a weathered crag from acne-pocked cheeks. His face looked crumpled, slept in, and if it had any expression, it was one of eternal exhaustion. The man had died of a heart attack.

His body weighed 220 soft and doughy pounds. Once muscular, it had fallen into ruin under a regimen of prison food, limited exercise, chain-smoking, and moonshine whiskey. Only the enormous hands seemed to have survived the dissipation. Even in death, they looked hard and powerful—the hands of a laborer or a fighter. Or a killer.

Aside from its uncommon homeliness, the cadaver looked fairly unremarkable as it lay awaiting cremation that cold December day in 1991. It did, however, sport one notable feature: an intricate complex of tattoos that scrolled intermittently along the torso and arms. Some of the artwork was defaced with scars, implying that the wearer had tried to obliterate a sentiment here and there. This was the case, for instance, with the tattoo above the elbow on the right arm. But despite the scarring, "Richard and Shirley" was still faintly legible, the remnant of a bad marriage that started young and ended early. The names conveyed no particular hostility, but certain other markings did. On the right forearm a serpent coiled around a dagger, oozing menace. And on the left arm, just above the wrist, was the most telling tattoo of all: the words Born to Raise Hell.

The motto had been a prophecy, and it served just as well as an epitaph. In a way, Richard Speck's life was written on his body.

Speck had died one day shy of his 50th birthday, but for many of those old enough to remember his name, he'd lived 25 years too long. He was the man who, on a sultry Chicago night in the summer of 1966, strangled and stabbed to death eight young nurses. His ghastly crime stunned the nation and charged the term *mass murderer* with a dreadful new meaning.

Even the birth of Richard Speck seemed ill-starred. He was born December 6, 1941—the day before the Japanese bombed Pearl Harbor and thus drew the United States into World War II. But the working-class Speck family seemed far removed from such world-shaking events. Richard's father, Benjamin Speck, worked as a potter in the western Illinois town of Kirkwood. He and his wife, Mary Margaret, had eight children, five girls and three boys. Richard was the seventh child. Years later Martha Speck Thornton recalled that her little brother had seemed an ordinary kid, if on the sickly side. He was the apple of his father's eye, she said, and followed him around "like a shadow."

A shadow of an unhappy kind began to dog Richard when he was only five: He experienced the first of the head injuries that would befall him so often over the years that they probably impaired his mental functioning. Richard was playing in a sandbox, trying to pull some nails out of a board with a claw hammer. He somehow lost control of the hammer, and it smashed into his head and knocked him out. On another occasion, he fell out of a tree and lay unconscious for an hour and a half. His younger sister, Carolyn, found him, still unconscious but twitching and foaming at the mouth. Years later doctors theorized that the boy suffered brain damage in that accident. When Richard was 15 he ran full tilt into the steel support rod of a storefront awning and was knocked out again. Speck sometimes pointed out a patch of lighter hair where the rod had penetrated his scalp and half-jokingly said he believed that it must have driven straight into his brain.

In 1947, the year after the sandbox incident, Benjamin Speck died. The family was then living in Monmouth, Illinois, but something impelled Mary Margaret to move to Dallas, Texas, with her two youngest children, Richard and Carolyn. The trio landed in Fair Park, a tough, dreary neighborhood on the east side of Dallas. There was never

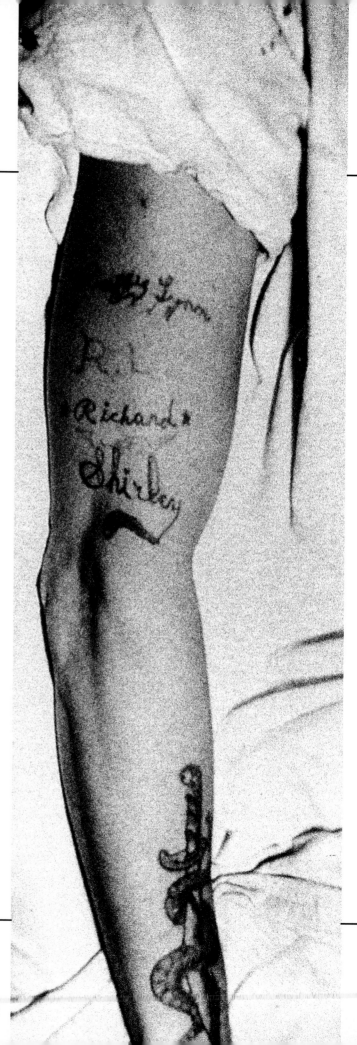

enough money, but Mary Margaret did her best to pamper her boy, and little Carolyn followed her mother's example. Neighbors later reported that the two females consistently gave in to Richard and ignored, forgave, or covered up his bad behavior. In their eyes he could do no wrong.

The situation was very pleasant for young Richard, but it didn't last long. It ended when his mother, whom he adored and depended on, got married again. The boy loathed his stepfather, an insurance man named Lindbergh who drank too much, disappeared often, and provided neither stability nor guidance to his wife's children. His flaws were real enough, but they weren't the main cause of Richard's resentment. Mostly he loathed his stepfather because Lindbergh could never replace Richard's beloved real father.

Some experts have theorized that Mary Margaret Speck's remarriage marked the point where Richard's attitude toward women began to take an ominous twist. It's possible that the child became deeply and permanently angry at his mother because she had, in his view, abandoned him and betrayed his father by marrying another man.

Speck began to turn inward in his teens. Undisciplined and none too bright, the young loner did poorly at school. He read comic books, not textbooks. He was not well-liked, and he fought frequently with other students. An eighth-grade teacher remembers him as "sort of lost. It didn't seem like he knew what was going on. I wasn't able to teach him anything. I don't think I ever saw him smile. He seemed to be in a fog, sort of sulky." The teacher recalls, "He didn't have any friends in class. Kids who sat next to him would ask to be moved." All in all, school was hell for Speck, and he dropped out when he was 16. He was in the ninth grade.

Whatever the impact of his unhappy family life and schoolboy frustrations, alcohol made things worse, turning Speck from a difficult adolescent into a dangerous one. He started drinking at the age of 12 and by 15 was boozing heavily. (He would drink this way all his life, even in jail; only death could come between him and the bottle.) Drinking added new possibilities for head injuries. Although he was still enough of a kid to get knocked unconscious in a bicycle accident and in another fall from a tree, by the age of 16 he was also being beaten up in barroom brawls and billy-clubbed when police were called in to break up fights. He began to suffer headaches so fierce that he sometimes reeled dizzily from the pain. The headaches would plague him all his life, and they made him drink more.

The year after his first drink there was another first for Speck: his first arrest. He was busted for trespassing. This event was far less alarming, however, than the new habit he acquired to go with his teenage drinking. He started carrying a knife. Patty Cox, the wife of his friend Jerry Lynn Cox, tried to explain what amounted to Speck's obsession with knives: "He had to feel important," Cox said. "He carried that knife and wanted people to look up to him." In retrospect it seemed to her that Speck was constantly "fooling with that knife, chunking it in the floor, opening it and standing up and swishing it like he was going to cut somebody. And cleaning his fingernails with it. He had a thing about knives, all right. I never saw him without one." He used it for more than cleaning his fingernails, according to what a friend of Cox's told her. "This cat ran by," she said, "and he caught it and whipped out that knife, cut it in the back like you skin it, and he skinned it right there."

Cats weren't his only targets. When Speck was 18 he was at a swimming hole with Jerry Lynn Cox and another friend when a gang of boys showed up and started a fight—a mistake on their part. In addition to drinking, Speck also took drugs. Before the fight that day at the swimming hole he'd already downed three or four yellow jackets—the street name for sodium amytal, an addictive barbiturate that can cause hallucinations and bizarre behavior. "I had a barbecue knife I stole someplace and went after them with it, just swinging away," Speck reminisced years later. "They really ran. We laughed like crazy."

Sober, Speck had a chance of controlling his savage temper; he could, in fact, be "nice and polite," according to Patty Cox and others. But he wasn't sober very often, and violence was deeply ingrained in his nature. When he was 18 he flew into a rage at his mother and beat her up. The incident shamed him; he did have his rules, after all. You didn't hit your mother, for instance, and you didn't hit cripples. Even though he despised his stepfather, Speck went for years without attacking the man. He restrained himself because Lindbergh had a peg leg and used crutches as the result of a car accident. But all bets were off when Speck drank, and one day he finally hit Lindbergh, who was himself drunk and brandishing a crutch at his stepson.

Patty Cox observed that when he was drinking Speck would talk "very dirty," and he was also prone to "beat up the women." Speck admitted mistreating women and even boasted about it. He laughed, for instance, about the time he took a woman into the countryside and then drove off, leaving her stranded. Women deserved no better, he seemed to be saying. They were tramps and cheats who always let a guy down. They deserved whatever they got.

At 19 Speck went to a tattoo parlor with some friends and walked out with his trademark inscription. "We all had something different—a skull, a heart, a girl's name," he recalled. "I couldn't think of nothing to have on my arm, so I asked the tattooer if he had any ideas. He suggested all kinds of things, slogans and stuff, and one of them was BORN TO RAISE HELL. That sounded kinda good, so I let him put that. Didn't mean anything special to me."

Perhaps it was true that this off-the-shelf motto meant nothing to Speck. But there is another possibility. When the tattooer rattled off that item on his list, Speck may have had a flash of recognition, knowing that it summed up his life in a way that he was too unreflective or too dull to articulate himself. Whatever the truth, by the time he died, his name and Born to Raise Hell were uniquely and forever connected in the public mind, as if he were the sloganeer's muse.

For the hell-raiser, work was a sometime affair. He was fired from a job as a driver for a meat company, for instance, because "he'd knock down awnings with the trucks, hit a corner of a building, I don't know what all," according to his ex-boss. Off the job, he was constantly in trouble. By 1962 he'd been picked up by police 36 times for such offenses as drunkenness, criminal trespass, and burglary. He was jailed once, briefly, for burglary, but most of his run-ins with the law were for misdemeanors, and they cost him no more than inconvenience and a small fine.

On the whole, Speck's résumé in 1962 did not qualify him as a very eligible bachelor. Still, something about the rake-hell youth caught the attention of an attractive, dark-haired 15-year-old named Shirley Annette Malone. The couple married and moved into Speck's mother's asbestos-shingled cottage, a shabby-looking place with broken furniture on the porch, on Fair Park's Terry Street. Richard's sister Carolyn and her husband, Buddy Wilson, were also living there, but by then Lindbergh had moved out.

Speck found a job with the Dallas Park Department in November 1962, but it didn't last. He also worked as a construction laborer, baker's helper, and trucker's helper, but only for brief periods. The Specks were chronically down-and-out; they owed money to the neighborhood grocer. Richard kept drinking, and soon he and Shirley were quarreling. It was a corrosive existence, but there was one bright spot: The couple's daughter, Robbie Lynn, was born July 2, 1963. The proud father immediately went out and had her name tattooed on his arm.

But a baby was not enough to stabilize the rocky marriage. Speck had begun to suspect that Shirley was seeing other men. The suspicions only aggravated his contempt and distrust for women. Shirley was a slut, he concluded, and the idea made him furious. Her cheap behavior, if such it was, reminded Speck of his mother's disloyalty to his dead father. A cheating woman was lower than dirt—Speck always thought so, even when he was the object of the cheater's attentions. Once, when a workmate of his was jailed, Speck accompanied the man's wife to another city to help raise bail money. They stopped for beers, got a little high, and went to a motel, where she made sexual advances to him. Speck was horrified. "I told her she was nothing but an old whore," he recalled later. "First chance I got I lifted a hundred bucks from her."

If Shirley was in fact cheating on her husband, Speck's behavior was also reprehensible. Among other things he wrote bad checks and committed a number of burglaries. Three months after Robbie Lynn's birth he was arrested for forgery and burglary and sentenced to three years in Huntsville State Prison. Speck served 14 months before being paroled on January 2, 1965. When he got out he was convinced that Shirley had been fooling around while he was away in prison. The thought drove him wild.

Speck had been free only a week when he accosted a slender, attractive brunette named Sarah Wadsworth in the parking lot of her East Dallas apartment house and put a 17-inch carving knife to her throat. She screamed and a neighbor came outside, scaring Speck off. He was caught three blocks away, and Wadsworth identified him in a line-up. Speck, who admitted that he'd been drinking, told police that he'd only intended to rob the stranger. Whatever his motive, however, the crime was more ominous than any he'd previously committed. He wasn't just playing with a knife anymore; this time he'd made a murderous move with one—against a woman resembling his wife.

After his assault on Wadsworth, Speck was sent back to Huntsville Prison. When he was released in July, he returned to Dallas and tried to patch things up with Shirley. She wanted nothing to do with him. Furthermore, his brother-in-law ordered him to leave Terry Street and warned him

not to come back. Shirley filed for divorce in January 1966.

Hardly anything had gone right in Richard Speck's young life up to that point. Nothing would ever go right again.

The year 1966 found Speck stewing in black emotions and dire circumstances. He was jealous, angry, lonely, broke, and addicted to drugs and alcohol. Drinking and doping harder than ever, he flashed his knife in bars and threatened to get revenge on Shirley and on the stepfather who'd stolen his mother. Jerry Lynn Cox later maintained that Speck had changed radically. "When Richard came back from prison I saw that he was lots wilder," Cox said. "It had made him an outlaw. He was tough." Speck's divorce became final on March 16. Two days later Shirley married another man.

Speck's criminal behavior began accelerating. Wanted for questioning in a March 5 burglary, he left Dallas and headed for Monmouth, his childhood home in Illinois. His brother William, a carpenter, still lived there; the two hadn't seen each other for 14 years. Speck rented a room and stayed for six weeks. With his brother's help, he got work as a carpenter and apparently boosted his income by breaking into houses. He spent a lot of time in bars, where he boasted about his sexual conquests, vented his rage against Shirley, and shot pool. One fellow drinker would later remember that Speck showed him "a picture of a real nice-looking gal. He said she was his wife, and he was going back to Texas and kill her if it was the last thing he ever did."

Unable to stay out of trouble, a drunken Speck was arrested after a knife fight in late March and jailed overnight. He also began paying unwelcome attention to the barmaid at a Monmouth tavern he frequented. She was a slender, attractive brunette named Mary Pierce, and she had no interest at all in Speck. She made that clear to him. On April 9 Pierce left the bar shortly before midnight and vanished. Her body was found five days later in a shed behind the tavern. She'd been killed by a blow—or a kick—to the stomach. Although her underwear was in disarray, she'd not been raped. Speck had been in the bar the night she disappeared. He would eventually claim to be innocent of Pierce's murder, which remains unsolved.

A little over a week after Pierce was killed, someone broke into a house in Monmouth, robbed a 65-year-old woman, and raped her at knife point. Speck matched the description that the victim gave of her assailant, but before police could

SHERIFF DEPT
101978
10 5 61
DALLAS TEX

Speck sat for a mug shot after being arrested for burglary in 1961 *(above)*. Making light of his numerous arrests, he posed playfully in a sham jail cell at the 1963 Texas State Fair *(left)*. Before the year was out, Speck was behind bars again, this time for burglary and forgery.

question him about the crime he fled to Michigan and got a job on a Lake Superior ore barge.

A week after he signed on, Speck fell ill with stomach pains and was put ashore at Hancock, Michigan. Hospitalized there for an emergency appendectomy, he met a 28-year-old nurse, Judy Laakaniemi. After the hospital discharged him, Speck and the nurse went dancing and swimming several times. He was "very nice" to her, Laakaniemi said later. But she also got a glimpse of his unquenchable anger: Speck told her there were two people in Texas he would kill if he got the chance. He didn't name them, although one was certainly Shirley and the other was probably his stepfather.

By June 27 Speck was well enough to take another job as a seaman. But within a few days he got drunk, picked a fight with a shipmate, and threw coffee in an officer's face. He was fired and put ashore on July 2 in Indiana Harbor, a town on Lake Michigan 50 miles east of Chicago. That same day, three young women vanished from nearby Indiana Dunes National Lakefront Park. Their clothes were found in their car—they'd presumably been wearing bathing suits at the park—but they were never seen alive again nor were their bodies ever found. Later, when his name was in virtually every newspaper in the country, there was a flurry of speculation that Speck was involved in the Indiana Harbor disappearances, but an investigation failed to make a case against him.

On July 10 Richard Speck surfaced in Chicago, where his sister Martha Thornton lived. True to the pattern of women in Speck's family, Thornton went to bat for her brother, giving him $25 to tide him over and driving him to the National Maritime Union (NMU) hiring hall. There he filled out a job application and provided a photograph taken in a coin-operated booth. It showed a homely, big-eared young man with acne scars. His light hair was combed into a flashy pompadour.

I had a barbe-cue knife I stole someplace and went after them with it, just swinging away. They really ran.

For the next three days Speck stayed in a flophouse and tried to get work on a vessel bound for New Orleans. Every day he checked in at the NMU hiring hall. It was located in a middle-class residential neighborhood called Jeffrey Manor on Chicago's South Side.

On Tuesday, July 12, Speck checked out of his seedy room. For the moment New Orleans was not on his mind; he'd been promised a job on a ship in Indiana. He drove there with a sailor friend, only to discover when they reached the ship that the job had gone to somebody else. Depressed and frustrated, Speck returned to Chicago with no job and only a few dollars in his pocket. Drawing a blank at the hiring hall, he talked the manager of a nearby service station into letting him leave his suitcases there. From a bar he telephoned his sister, who said she would get more money to him. It was raining hard, so Speck sought shelter in the basement of a half-completed apartment house. He fell asleep there, using his shoes as a pillow.

The next morning Speck drank a Royal Crown Cola while he waited for the gas station to open. After retrieving his bags, he made his daily trek to the hiring hall, where he got good news for a change: There would be a job in a couple of days. Cheered, he played hearts with other sailors until his brother-in-law showed up with another $25.

After renting a room at a flophouse called the Shipyard Inn, Speck went to a tavern to shoot pool. He did well, winning $10 or $11, and he picked up another dollar by selling a knife he was carrying—a big one. "Really it was a dagger," he said later, "like a bayonet." With a job prospect and a few extra dollars, Speck was feeling pretty good. He drank more beer and took six redbirds—sodium seconals. Like yellow jackets, redbirds are strong barbiturates that can be mind-altering. Speck left to take a walk, but he was back by 3 p.m. and ready to party some more. "I had some whiskey and a pint of wine and got talking to these sailors," he would later recall. "They took me to their room. It was dark. They had this disposable syringe and took this stuff from a bottle and started popping. I tied a handkerchief around my left arm and stuck it in. All the way. Before I had the needle out I could feel, you know, feel—zzzoommm—a buzzing all over me, and I was feeling real, real good."

The evening was warm, and the windows of the yellow brick town house at 2319 East 100th Street, a block from the NMU hiring hall, were open to catch a breeze. The town house was one of three in a complex that South Chicago Community Hospital had leased as quarters for nursing students and foreign exchange nurses. Eight women, all in their early twenties, lived at 2319; five were American senior nursing students, and three were graduate nurses from the Philippines. Among the cheery clutter in the three-bedroom house hung a poster that read "Sleep well tonight, your National Guard is awake."

At 11 p.m. six of the nurses were at home. Corazon Amurao was ready to turn in. She and her roommate, Merlita Gargullo, both from the Philippines, slept in double-decker bunks in the rear bedroom on the second floor. Across the hall were two more bedrooms that overlooked the street. Amurao had locked her door and was about to switch off the light before climbing into the top bunk when Gargullo asked that it be left on until she'd said her prayers. Amurao fell asleep before her friend had completed her ritual.

Four knocks on the bedroom door awakened the two women. Amurao groggily climbed down from her bunk and unlocked the door.

Amurao, Gargullo, and Valentina Pasion, the third Filipino housemate, had been in the United States only two months and were homesick. They got on well with their American housemates, but the three Filipinos, each 23 years old, spent much of their time together. Amurao, one of eight children of a rural teacher, was from a village south of Manila. She was a determined, hardworking student whose diplomas were proudly displayed in her parents' house. Amurao was the practical one, levelheaded and adaptable, blessed with presence of mind. Tonight, these qualities—and a generous measure of luck—would save her life.

Valentina Pasion was the shy one. Also the daughter of a schoolteacher, she sent half her salary home to her family. She had a boyfriend back home, a dentist, and though she claimed the relationship wasn't serious, her friends believed

otherwise. They kidded her about him good-naturedly, and she took the ribbing with equal good nature. Merlita Gargullo, whose father was a doctor, was considered the pretty one of the trio. People were always telling her so and trying to fix her up with dates. She had a wonderful voice and would sing while doing the laundry or the dishes or when she and her friends were out together.

Of the five American housemates, three were at home and getting ready for bed at the time Amurao locked her bedroom door. Twenty-three-year-old Nina Schmale, who planned to become a psychiatric nurse, had been crowned queen of the student nurse dance the previous spring. She had a charmingly carefree, almost careless, style. Her friends remembered that when she bathed her patients, she would casually flip washcloths across them and into a waiting basin without a drop's splashing out. Casual at home as well as at work, Schmale preferred low-maintenance pets—she kept turtles—and she had a rather vaguely defined romantic life. She'd gone out with the same man for seven years, but theirs was an on-again, off-again relationship.

Patricia Matusek, 20, had spent the evening visiting her parents and sister on Michigan Avenue, where they lived above Matusek's Tavern, the family business. She had planned to spend the night there but changed her mind and went back to the nurses' residence. Matusek was engaged to a male nursing student. The previous Sunday the couple had seen *Doctor Zhivago* and, in the afterglow of the romantic film, they'd talked about a wedding date.

Pamela Wilkening, whose friends called her Willie, had worked that day in the hospital's intensive care unit, a high-pressure assignment she especially enjoyed. Wilkening thrived on pressure, and she liked action. She was a class officer, played the piano, and was an avid fan of sports-car racing. Her older brother raced Porsches and Lotuses, and Willie often helped him time laps or watched as he tinkered with engines. She was saving for a sports car of her own.

Suzanne Farris spent the evening with her friends Pat McCarthy and Mary Ann Jordan. The three drove around for a while in Jordan's car, stopped for Cokes, then went back to McCarthy's apartment. Farris enjoyed children and was planning to become a pediatric nurse. It was she who, like a mother hen, kept track of the group of friends and created occasions for them to be together. A few months earlier, for instance, she'd engineered a party where the young women put on roller skates and old bridesmaids' dresses, switched on the hi-fi, pushed back the rugs, and made such a splendid ruckus that the housemother grounded them for a week. Farris had a lot to talk over with Mary Ann Jordan because she was to marry her friend's brother Philip the following June. Four of Farris's housemates were going to be bridesmaids, as was Jordan. They planned to wear yellow dresses.

Mary Ann Jordan was not one of the housemates, even though she knew them all well and visited often. She lived with her family. Mature, responsible, and an exceptional student, she helped look after her mentally retarded 12-year-old brother. Jordan planned to continue in school and earn a bachelor of science degree. Once in a great while, she spent the night at the town house with her friends. Tonight was one of those nights. A little after midnight, Mary Ann Jordan started home with Suzanne Farris.

Gloria Davy, a good-looking brunette, was a woman people noticed. Ambitious, sure of herself, and a little spoiled, she cheerfully bummed cigarettes from her roommates and made it their responsibility to wake her up in the morning.

Gloria Davy was still out on a date when Corazon Amurao heard the four knocks on the bedroom door. Tragically, Davy would come home in time to see Richard Speck—and to have him see her.

From the sailors' filthy room where he'd shot himself up with the unidentified drug, Richard Speck made his way to the house on East 100th Street, about a mile away—why that house, among many possibilities, is unknown. Getting in was easy. The kitchen was on the ground floor at the rear, and a window was open. All Speck had to do was lift the screen out of its frame and climb through.

He walked quietly through the dimly lighted, empty kitchen and into the deserted living room. A staircase led from the living room to the second floor. When Speck reached the landing at the top of the stairs he saw an empty bathroom on his right, its door open. Directly ahead was a door. It was locked, and he rapped on it four times, rousing Corazon Amurao. After she unlocked the door, she later testified, "I started to open it and at once there's somebody who's pushing the door. Then I saw a man."

To the four-foot-ten-inch nurse, the lanky intruder looked very tall. He had watery blue eyes that struck her as somehow gentle, despite the fact that he presented a clear threat. He reeked of alcohol, and in his right hand he held a gun that was pointed at her. Pushing his way inside, Speck

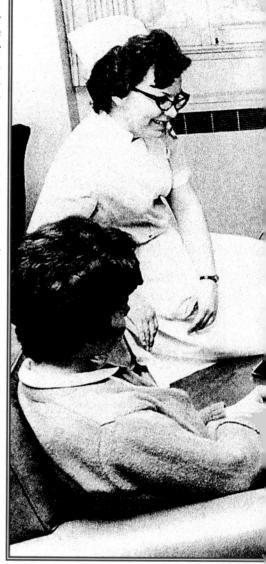

found Merlita Gargullo. Then he went to the other two bedrooms, where he roused Nina Schmale, Patricia Matusek, Valentina Pasion, and Pamela Wilkening. He herded them into the rear bedroom and made them sit on the floor.

"What do you want?" one of them asked.

"I want money," Speck said. "I'm going to New Orleans." By now the women had seen that he had a knife as well as a gun. He didn't have to threaten them or search for money; the nurses readily handed over what cash they had. Speck talked with the Americans, but Amurao couldn't follow the conversation. She had a hard time understanding his East Texas drawl. Using his knife, he cut a sheet into strips and began tightly binding the women's wrists and ankles. He was still at it when he and his captives heard Gloria Davy arriving home from her date. It was 11:20 p.m.

Speck took Davy upstairs to join the others. As he tied her up, she asked him, "Why are you doing this? We're student nurses." "Oh, you're a student nurse," he replied noncommittally, ignoring the question about his motives. Davy's brunette good looks reminded him of someone he knew. He

Four of the women Speck would kill were photographed in 1965 chatting with nurse Judith Dykton *(upper left)*. Seated, left to right, are Mary Ann Jordan, Suzanne Farris, Nina Schmale, and Pamela Wilkening. Until their roommate Gloria Davy *(inset)* came home the night of the murders, Speck seemed intent merely on burglary.

GLORIA DAVY

didn't try to escape, nor did they agree on any plan to overpower the intruder.

Probably no one will ever know for sure why the women acted as they did—or why they failed to act. Chicago homicide chief Francis Flanagan's speculation that they "were completely paralyzed by fear like a bird with a cobra" seems cruelly glib and patronizing. It appears more likely that the women took a calculated risk. Corazon Amurao said later that the three Filipino women, fearing that Speck might have rape in mind, wanted to fight him. The Americans took the position that if everyone remained quiet and calm, the intruder might stay that way himself. Sheer numbers could also have lulled them into a false sense of security. How, they might have reasoned, could one man manage to rape so many women? Moreover, he said that he only wanted money to get to New Orleans, and his manner was not harsh. "Don't be afraid," he assured them. "I'm not going to kill you." Surely they wanted to believe him, and perhaps they chose to do that, to trust

smiled at her in the crowded bedroom, but it was not a friendly smile. From the time Davy got home, Speck's demeanor began changing for the worse.

He'd finished tying up Davy, Schmale, Pasion, and Wilkening and had bound Matusek's ankles when the doorbell rang. Leaving Matusek as she was, with her hands still free, Speck forced Amurao and Gargullo downstairs with him to see who was there. For several minutes the women in the back bedroom were unguarded, giving Matusek the opportunity to remove their bonds. But the moment passed. They

and hope that he'd just take their money and go. After all, which of the nurses, in her worst nightmare, could have imagined the horror that was to come? This was 1966, and gruesome tales of mass murder were not yet part of the public consciousness. Richard Speck was the man poised to change all that, but his victims couldn't have known it. So they waited passively while Speck went to answer the door.

Nobody was there. It would come to light later that another student had come to borrow bread but left when no one came to the door. Luck was with her that night.

Speck went back upstairs and finished tying up Matusek, then bound Amurao and Gargullo with sheet strips. Surrounded by his captives he sat on the floor, smoking cigarettes and toying with his gun and his knife. At one point he asked Gargullo, "Do you know karate?" He seemed to be getting more agitated, and the women didn't understand why. They'd done everything he'd asked. They couldn't possibly have fathomed the impact that Gloria Davy was having on the intruder—dark-haired, pretty Gloria Davy, who looked so much like Shirley Speck that the two could have been sisters.

When Speck finally stood up, the women may have thought with relief that he was about to take the money they'd given him and leave. Instead, with dreadful calm, he untied the strips of sheeting from Pamela Wilkening's ankles and led her out the bedroom door. It was just about midnight. The killing began.

At Richard Speck's trial, the prosecutor asked Corazon Amurao, "After Speck had taken Miss Wilkening from the south bedroom, did you hear anything?"

"After one minute, I heard Miss Wilkening say 'Ah,'" Amurao replied. "It was like a sigh."

"Did you hear anything after the noise you just described?"

"No, I didn't hear anything."

Moments after that soft, chilling sound, Suzanne Farris and Mary Ann Jordan arrived. It was 12:20 a.m. Speck,

MERLITA GARGULLO

VALENTINA PASION

NINA SCHMALE

In the bedroom where Richard Speck stabbed and strangled nurses Nina Schmale, Merlita Gargullo, and Valentina Pasion, a two-piece bathing suit hangs drying beneath a sign from a Wheaton, Illinois, street named after Schmale's family.

gun in hand, directed them to the rear bedroom, where his other captives waited. Almost at once, however, he forced Farris and Jordan back out of the room. Soon the women in the bedroom heard voices and muffled screams. It sounded as if someone was resisting. Whoever it was soon fell silent.

Amurao and the others heard water running in the bathroom, then footsteps approaching the bedroom.

This time Speck took Nina Schmale. Again, after a minute, Amurao heard a sighing "Ah," then the sound of water running in the bathroom. And so went the rhythm of the night: a woman led from the room, a sigh or a groan, running water, the returning footsteps. Each cycle took about 20 minutes.

To the five women still alive, it was becoming appallingly clear what was happening, and when Speck left the room, Amurao, the calm, practical one, begged the others to resist the murderer. She was working at freeing her hands, and she whispered that when they were loose she would try to hit him with the steel bunk ladder.

But the women did not, in fact, ever try to fight. Instead, Amurao, Pasion, Gargullo, Matusek, and Davy—all still bound—tried to wriggle under the beds to hide. It was a pitifully inadequate ploy, and Speck was not deceived. When he returned he pulled Pasion out and took her away. Cowering against the wall, Amurao heard her friend's mortal sigh. It was louder than the others had been.

The water ran in the sink. The footsteps came back. This time Speck chose Gargullo, the pretty one. Five minutes later, for the first time, Amurao heard a word from beyond the bedroom wall. Reverting in her terror to her native Tagalog, Gargullo said, *"Masikit"* ("It hurts").

Amurao lay facedown under the bed, praying that the man would go away. He'd been drinking, perhaps he was drunk and confused, maybe he would forget about her and Matusek and Davy. Or maybe he'd killed enough. But he came back, this time for Pat Matusek. She pled with him, "Will you please untie my ankles first?" That pathetic word: *first. First, before you kill me?* Her plea was ignored. Speck picked her up and carried her away, still bound.

When Speck returned, he didn't look under the bed where Amurao was cowering. Perhaps he was too fixed on Davy, his ex-wife's look-alike. Perhaps he'd methodically disposed

Patricia Matusek was murdered in the second-floor bathroom.

PATRICIA MATUSEK

of the other nurses only in preparation for this one. Whatever the reason—befuddlement, revenge, or Amurao's blind luck—Davy was to be his final victim.

From under the bed, Amurao saw Speck removing Gloria Davy's jeans, then heard him unzipping his pants. She saw him on top of Davy on the bed across the room. Amurao turned away then, pressing her face to the floor, but she heard the bedsprings creak. After a few minutes she heard Speck ask politely, "Will you please put your legs around my back?"

The assault continued for perhaps 20 minutes. When the sounds stopped and Corazon Amurao looked around, Davy and Speck were gone. The house was silent now. Time passed, and the silence remained unbroken. Still she didn't come out of hiding: The man could be there, waiting.

The alarm clock buzzed, as it always did, at 5 a.m. For a time Amurao lay listening. Then she went to work on her bonds. Finally freeing herself, she crept out and got to her feet, unsteady after hours under the bed. In the bathroom and the other two bedrooms, Corazon Amurao found sickening confirmation of her worst fears.

It was now 6 a.m. Pushing out the screen of a front bedroom window, Amurao climbed out onto a narrow ledge and screamed into the still summer morning: "Help me, help! They are all dead! My friends are all dead! Oh God, I'm the only one alive!"

A neighbor out walking his dog heard Amurao's cry and flagged down a police car. The first officer to enter the house was Daniel Kelly, a 25-year-old patrolman. Finding the front door locked, he went around to the kitchen door; it was unlocked, presumably because Speck had used it to make his exit. "I walked into the kitchen but didn't see anything there," Kelly reported that day. "Then I walked into the front room and I found a body on a couch."

The woman was naked. An autopsy would show that she had been raped, sodomized with an unknown object that mutilated her anus, and strangled. It was Gloria Davy, and although Kelly didn't recognize her then, he knew her. He'd dated her in high school just a few years before. It would turn out that his wife, a nurse, knew all of the victims.

In case the killer might still be in the house, Kelly and his partner drew their handguns and went cautiously upstairs. They found the rest of the victims, three in each of the two front bedrooms and one in the bathroom. Kelly coaxed Corazon Amurao in from the ledge, and she collected herself sufficiently to give him a description of the killer. It was flashed to a police communications unit.

The Cook County coroner, Andrew Toman, arrived to inspect the slaughter scene and to try to reconstruct what had happened. Pat Matusek had been thrown onto the bathroom floor and kicked in the stomach. (Some observers were reminded of the similar brutalization of Monmouth barmaid Mary Pierce in April.) The kick had not been fatal, Toman determined; Speck had squatted astride Matusek and strangled her to death.

In one front bedroom were Speck's first three victims. Pamela Wilkening had been stabbed in the chest and strangled with a strip of bedsheet. Suzanne Farris, who'd apparently tried to fight off the killer, had been stabbed 18 times, then strangled. Her underwear was torn to shreds. Mary Ann Jordan had been stabbed through the heart, the neck, and one eye. In the adjoining bedroom were three more victims: Nina Schmale, stabbed in the neck and strangled; Valentina Pasion, with a single deep stab wound in the neck; and Merlita Gargullo. Speck had stabbed Gargullo four times before she fell across Pasion's body, then choked out what life was left in her with his bare hands.

The shaken coroner emerged to describe what he'd seen as "the crime of the century." Within hours not just Chicago but the whole nation was riveted in horror by the murderous details revealed in newspapers and over the air.

The police had the advantage of Amurao's description of the murderer—a tall man with a pocked face, blue eyes, and light hair, a man with a tattoo on his arm that read, "Born to Raise Hell." Bloody fingerprints on the town house walls were another source of hard evidence for investigators. There were also a few more subtle clues—the fact that the women's hands had been tied with the palms together, for instance. Police officers often arrange a suspect's hands this way before handcuffing them, so officers speculated that their man knew something about being manacled. They also suspected that he was a seaman. The murderer had

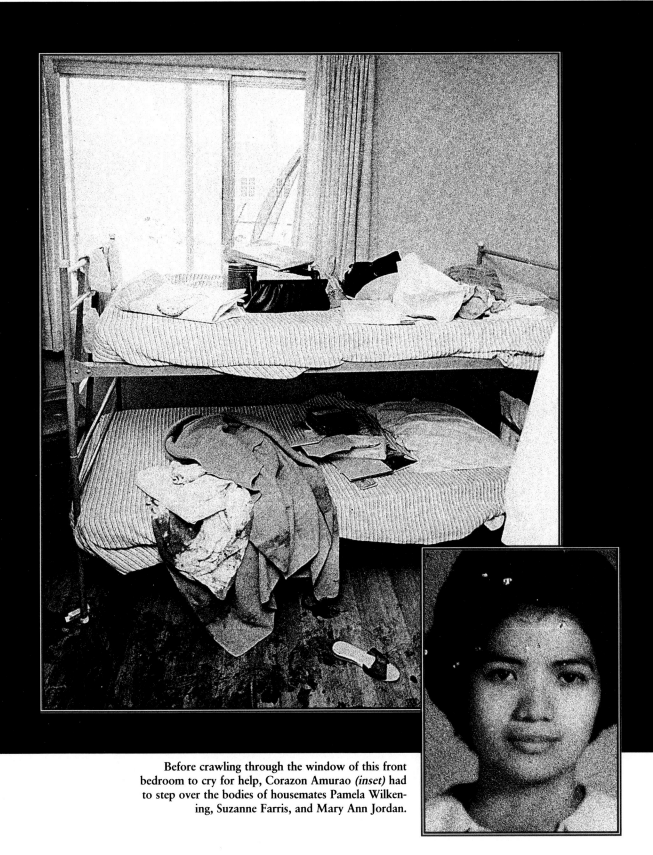

Before crawling through the window of this front bedroom to cry for help, Corazon Amurao *(inset)* had to step over the bodies of housemates Pamela Wilkening, Suzanne Farris, and Mary Ann Jordan.

On the morning after the murders a crowd gathers in front of the nurses' town house. The window screen that Corazon Amurao broke to get out is visible on the second floor.

mentioned going to New Orleans, a major port, and the NMU hiring hall was in the neighborhood.

In their canvass of the neighborhood on July 14, police were told about the pockmarked man who'd left his suitcases at the gas station across the street from the town house two days earlier. At the hiring hall they learned that a pockmarked man had asked about work on a ship to New Orleans. A search of the wastebaskets at the NMU hall turned up the application he'd filled out, then discarded when he found that there were no jobs available. The name on the application was Richard Franklin Speck, and a check of U.S. Coast Guard files produced the photo made on July 10.

When an investigator called the number on the application, Martha Thornton answered. In a ploy to snare the suspect, she was asked to deliver the message that a job was available for her brother on a ship to New Orleans. She agreed: Speck's habitual petty

offenses were one thing, but mass murder was quite another, and she was perfectly willing to cooperate with police. Speck soon called the hiring hall and made an appointment to go there in half an hour. He did not, however, show up.

Meanwhile, Corazon Amurao had been sedated for shock at South Chicago Community Hospital, where she and her dead friends had worked and studied. By the morning of July 15, twenty-eight hours after the bodies were discovered, she was alert enough to look at the photograph from the Coast Guard files. She identified the man positively as the killer. In addition, a match had been made between the bloody

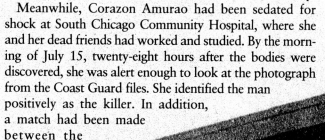

fingerprints and prints on file with the Dallas police. There seemed little doubt that Richard Franklin Speck, 24, was the man the police were after.

Around 8 a.m. on July 15, several hours before Amurao positively identified the photograph of Speck, the manager of the Raleigh Hotel on Chicago's North Side called police to report that a client with a prostitute at the hotel had a gun. Officers found the man in bed in room 306. He said his name was Richard Speck and claimed that the weapon belonged to the prostitute. The officers confiscated the gun, told Speck and the woman not to cause any trouble, and left. The name Richard Speck meant nothing to them yet; police on the South Side had Speck's name and physical description, but the information had not yet spread throughout the city's police districts. Not until that evening did authorities realize that Speck had slipped through their fingers. They rushed back to the hotel, but he'd checked out, apparently in the company of a second prostitute.

Sitting at the bar in the Shipyard Inn on the afternoon of Friday, July 15, Speck heard a radio announcer describe the murders. Months later, in prison, he told a psychiatrist that he turned to the man next to him at the bar and said, "I hope they catch the son of a bitch."

At 2:40 p.m. on Saturday, July 16, the Chicago police announced that Richard Speck was being sought as the nurses' killer. True to form, Speck was in a bar when he heard his name on the radio for the first time. He bought a bottle of cheap wine and left. Under the name of B. Brian, he checked into the Starr Hotel, a 90-cent-a-night flophouse on the West Side. He lay there on a bunk in a grubby five-by-nine-foot cubicle and drank the wine. Around midnight Speck called out, "Come and see me. You got to come and see me. I done something bad." A man in a nearby cubicle, put off by Speck's drunken Texas twang, shouted back, "I don't trust no hillbilly!"

"I'm going to die if you don't come see me," Speck appealed again. When no one came, he staggered out of his room. "Hey!" one of his fellow lodgers yelled to the elevator operator, "This guy's bleeding to death." Speck had slashed his right wrist and the inside of his left elbow with a razor. The desk clerk called the police, and a couple of hotel residents took Speck back to his cubicle. Under his bed was a blood-soaked newspaper with a story bearing the headline "POLICE SAY NURSE SURVIVOR CAN IDENTIFY SLAYER OF 8."

For the second time since the murders, Speck found himself faced with police, but the officers summoned to the Starr Hotel failed to connect him with the suspect whose name and photograph were already on their way to notoriety. Nor did they try to verify whether the bleeding man's name was actually "B. Brian." The lack of thoroughness was, if not pardonable, at least understandable: Drunkenness, mayhem, and suicide attempts were routine on the West Side. In any case, police took Speck to Cook County Hospital's emergency room and left him there in the care of a medical resident, Dr. LeRoy Smith, and a nurse. Fortunately, the doctor was more alert than the police had been. He glanced down at his patient's face, then peered closer.

"I picked up his head and looked at the nurse to see if she'd noticed," Smith said later. "I said to her, 'Get the newspaper.'" Then the physician wet his fingertips and began rubbing at the patient's bloody arm. The letters emerged one by one: $B \ldots O \ldots R \ldots N \ldots$ Smith bent over and asked the patient his name. "Richard," the man whispered weakly. "Richard Speck."

"This is the fellow the police are looking for," Smith told the nurse.

Speck had lost so much blood that he was given a transfusion, and the razor cuts were closed with stitches. That night he was transferred to Bridewell Prison Hospital where, as a potential suicide, he was restrained with leather thongs and sedated. Two days later, on Tuesday, July 19, Corazon Amurao arrived in the company of a detective at the door of the room where Speck was confined. She studied the patient, then told the detective, "That is the man."

The brief hunt was over.

The press called it the worst mass slaying in Chicago history, more terrible even than the Saint Valentine's Day Massacre in 1929, when seven members and hangers-on of the Bugs Moran gang were machine-gunned in a North Side garage by followers of mobster Al Capone. That had been a case of gangsters killing gangsters—a crime both easy to understand and hard to mourn. This was different. Innocents had died, and for no apparent reason.

When authorities began to interrogate Speck, he didn't deny committing the murders—nor did he confess to them. His standard answer to questions was, "I don't know anything more about it than you do." Still wan and haggard from his suicide attempt and from withdrawal from alcohol

A police sketch of Speck *(above, right)* based on Corazon Amurao's detailed description of the killer is strikingly similar to a photograph taken some time earlier. Speck heard on a July 16, 1966, newscast that the police had named him their chief suspect in the slaying of the eight nurses. Later that day he checked into the Starr Hotel *(right)*.

Desk clerk William Vaughn *(above)* summoned the police to the Starr Hotel after Speck slashed himself with a razor. The killer had stuck under his mattress several newspapers reporting the murders, including an issue of the *Chicago Tribune* with front-page photos of the eight dead nurses *(right)*.

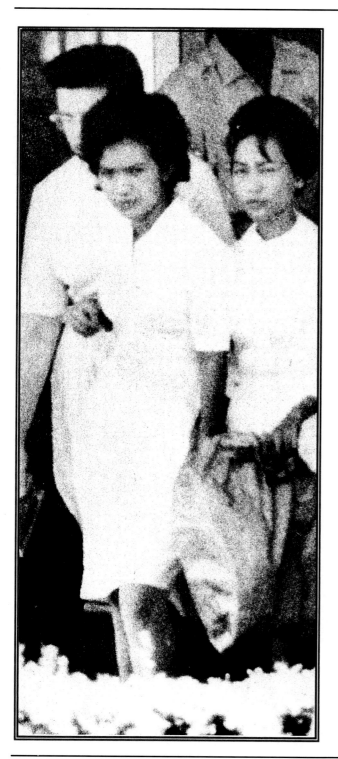

On July 19 Corazon Amurao *(center)* leaves Bridewell Prison Hospital, where Speck was recovering from his suicide attempt. She had just identified him as her roommates' murderer.

and barbiturates, Speck was also suffering from an inflammation of the heart. By July 29, however, he was well enough to be transferred from Bridewell to the Cook County Jail. Marvin Ziporyn, the jail's psychiatrist, was assigned to determine Speck's potential for another try at suicide.

Ziporyn found the prisoner lying on his bunk reading *Look* magazine—or at least looking at the pictures. A large fan hummed in a corner of his cell, making the oppressive heat of the midwestern summer a little more tolerable. Speck was deeply depressed and apathetic. "When I heard what they said I'd done, on the radio, I just felt there was no point in living," Speck told Ziporyn, explaining his suicide attempt at the Starr Hotel. Still claiming ignorance of the crime, he was nevertheless resigned to his fate. "If they say I did it, I did it," he shrugged. When Ziporyn asked him whether he was concerned about his daughter, his mother, or his sister, Speck replied, "Nope, I ain't interested in nothing—don't care about nothing either."

The prisoner was arraigned on August 1, 1966, under tight security. Before his trial began in March of the following year, he would spend more than 100 hours with Ziporyn. The psychiatrist wondered whether a sympathetic connection to another person might allow Speck to reveal more—not only about the murders but also about the psychological and biological factors that had helped cause them. Nominating himself as Speck's confidant, Ziporyn probably came to know him better than anyone else had, including members of the killer's own family.

Doctor and prisoner met every few days. Speck was defensive and reticent at first, but the psychiatrist's steady attention, flattery, and kindness—he sometimes brought presents, such as a radio—eventually won him over. At the psychiatrist's urging, Speck assembled jigsaw puzzles and then took up painting. His depression lifted enough at times for him to show flashes of self-deprecating wit. In the main, however, Ziporyn judged Speck to be a bitter loner who, by the time of the murders, was at the end of his emotional rope. He'd arrived in Chicago feeling rejected, defeated, and profoundly worthless. "He kept on saying how the world wasn't worth anything and he'd be better off dead," his sister Martha told the psychiatrist.

The sessions with Speck were the basis of Ziporyn's book, *Born to Raise Hell,* published in 1967. Far from objecting to his life's being revealed in print, Speck wrote a brief, semiliterate note authorizing the psychiatrist to write the

Looking dazed and exhausted, Richard Speck lies on a cot in
the infirmary of the Cook County Jail after his arraignment on
August 1. He pleaded not guilty to eight charges of murder.

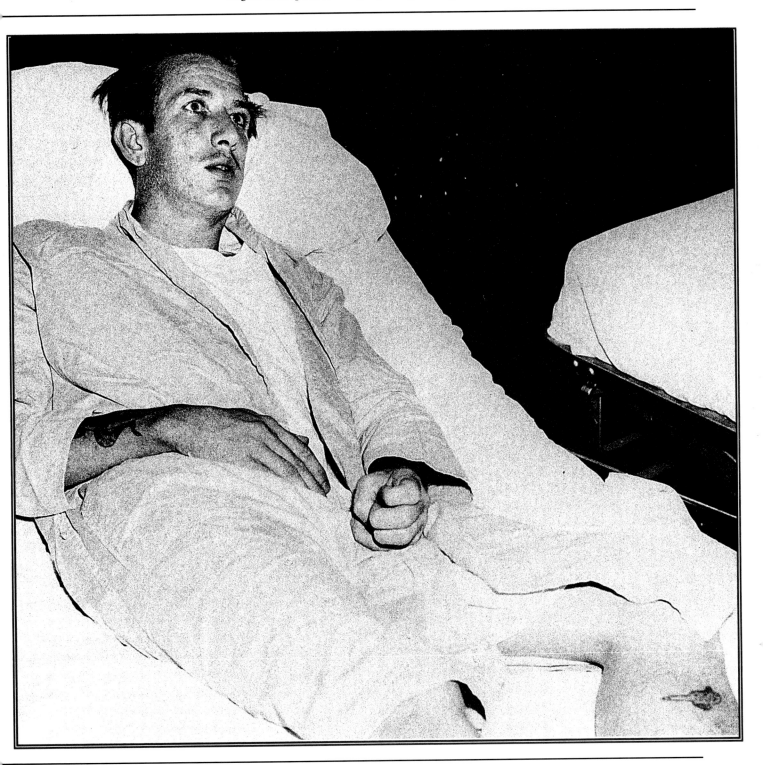

book: "I understand dr. ziporyn is writing a book about me," the note said. "I am glad he is doing this, because he is the only person who knows anying thing about me. I want the world to know what I am really like, and I fell he is the one who can tell about me."

The horrors that Speck would visit on his victims began to take shape, according to Ziporyn, in the killer's early childhood. When he was only three months old, Richard had a bout of pneumonia so serious that he was placed in an oxygen tent; despite this treatment, his brain might have been damaged by oxygen deprivation. His numerous head injuries could also have inflicted permanent brain damage. The severe headaches and dizziness Speck reported suggested that such injury had in fact occurred. As an insidious side effect of his condition, Speck drank or used drugs as an antidote to pain. Of course, such ill-chosen home remedies only aggravated the damage. Speck also undermined himself with a pathetic vanity that prevented his wearing glasses to correct his poor eyesight. His weak, watery blue eyes thus confronted the world uncovered, but eyestrain probably made his chronic headaches worse.

In Ziporyn's opinion, Speck betrayed many typical signs of brain damage: He was impulsive, self-centered, rigid, sulky, quarrelsome, resentful, and willful. He had a low tolerance for drugs and alcohol, and he was given to violent outbursts. Speck reported blacking out, sometimes learning when he regained consciousness that he'd assaulted someone in a frenzy. "There was lots of times when I'd black out like that and not remember a thing," he told Ziporyn. "I get a glassy haze, like when you look into the sun. I get those hazes all the time, had one when I was near my sister's home right here in Chicago a little while back." As the sessions went on, Speck recounted many incidents that kept the vicious cycle of blows to the head and wild behavior going: a gas station attendant whom he'd tried to rob beating him with a tire iron, a policeman pistol-whipping him.

To add insult to injury, an intelligence test administered in prison revealed that Speck was rather dull-witted—dumb as well as damaged. During pretrial maneuverings, attorneys compared his intelligence to that of a 10-year-old. Speck already had evidence that he was not bright; for instance, he'd flunked the eighth grade and been forced to repeat it. But this official assessment of his IQ wounded his pride. "Stupid is one thing," he told Ziporyn. "A 10-year-old mind is another."

Ziporyn concluded that Speck's native dullness and probable brain damage were aggravated by a family that encouraged him to remain childishly insistent on gratifying his whims. His mother and little sister Carolyn had coddled him to excess—Carolyn wading into fights to help him, his mother excusing and explaining away the misdeeds of his boyhood and early manhood. The family became sadly adept at denial, at evading the truth, concealing it from themselves, from one another, and from the outside world. The result, said Ziporyn, was that Speck was never required to take responsibility for himself and his acts. So, the psychiatrist concluded, "The boy never became a man."

Ziporyn also homed in on Speck's pathological view of women, which the psychiatrist viewed as a classic instance of the so-called Madonna-Whore Complex. In this disorder, a man is able to see a woman only in terms of extremes—angel or devil, pure or sluttish. Mothers usually fall into the Madonna category, while most other women—and certainly those available for sex—run the risk of being perceived as Whores. If the psychiatrist was on the mark, Speck viewed women in terms of black and white. To him, no female could be a blend of good and bad. Despite his mother's marriage to the despised Lindbergh, Speck nevertheless made her the model of the Madonna. He thought of her as "the only girl who ever knew me." His sister Carolyn came close to the same chaste, untouchable perfection. Speck also cherished the memory of a girlfriend named Carol. "I never touched her," he said. "She was a nice girl, you know. I had too much respect for her, so I never touched her."

As to the Whores, they filled Speck with disgust and contempt, even when he enjoyed their favors—in fact, perhaps then most of all. If a woman offered herself to him sexually, Speck's perverse logic made him assign her to the Whore category. Given the Madonna-Whore Complex, marriage for Speck was doomed to be an emotional disaster. A good woman must not be defiled by sex; sex was always defiling; so anyone who had sex with him—even his wife—must be a Whore. According to Ziporyn, Shirley Speck didn't stand a chance of escaping her husband's contempt; whether she cheated or not, she was, to him, nothing but a tramp. Shirley once told Speck she wanted him to love her more than he did his mother. His revealing reply: "That will never be." And he didn't merely love Shirley less; he came to hate her. "I think his wife cracked him up," said a friend of Speck's after the murders—as if she were to blame for his crimes.

Six white-uniformed student nurses were among the mourners at the burial service for Gloria Davy at Holy Cross Cemetery in Calumet City, Illinois. Although Speck did not identify his subject, an oil portrait *(below)* that he painted while awaiting trial bears an eerie resemblance to Davy.

One day Ziporyn showed Speck photographs of the victims, handing them over one by one. "They're so young, so pretty," Speck said when he'd studied the faces of Mary Ann Jordan and Suzanne Farris. He was about to take the next photograph when he snatched his hand back.

His eyes wide and his lips trembling, Speck finally took the photograph in both hands. "You know what?" he said. "This is a dead ringer for Shirley." The dead ringer was, of course, Gloria Davy, the nurse killed last and the only one who was raped and sexually mutilated.

Speck would not, or could not, explain his reaction to Davy, even after Ziporyn suggested why she might have been singled out for a particularly brutal death. On the night of the murders, Ziporyn speculated, alcohol and drugs had so eroded Speck's control that it took no more than the sight of Davy's face—so like Shirley's—to destroy the last shred of his inhibition. His raging hatred transformed him from a drunken burglar into a murderer.

"Does any of this ring a bell for you?" Ziporyn asked.
"Nope," said Speck.

Speck was not an introspective man, and the fine points of his motivation might have escaped him. But, according to Ziporyn, the killer could appreciate the horror of what he'd done. Speck would sometimes brood about the murders when he was with the psychiatrist, expressing a self-disgust so profound that he seemed suicidal. Nevertheless, Ziporyn noted, when strangers were present Speck appeared blasé about the crimes. Other psychiatrists concluded after brief examinations that Speck was a psychopath—totally egocentric and devoid of a conscience, a man who perceived others as no more than objects to be used however he liked. But Ziporyn could not accept such a diagnosis. It had taken Speck months, but he'd at length confessed to Ziporyn that he'd once hit his mother when he was high on drugs. It could have been worse, Speck said; he could have killed her. Admitting the deed seemed to shake him to the core. The psychiatrist was convinced that Speck had a conscience—one so strong, in fact, that when the murderer allowed his feelings about past actions to surface, he was at times overwhelmed by guilt. Such feelings, according to Ziporyn, explained why Speck was sometimes suicidal.

Speck, who had trouble reading even faintly complicated prose, was barely able to follow Ziporyn's explanations of the various forces that might have led him to kill the nurses. It was too complex for him to ponder for long, and Ziporyn

would have to sit him down and explain it again and again.

But no one described him as insane. All of the psychiatrists who examined Speck, including Ziporyn, agreed that he was competent to stand trial. Speck accepted the judgment without much reaction. But when the court decided to move the proceedings 150 miles away to Peoria to escape the pretrial publicity that had saturated Chicago, the defendant was upset. He'd come to feel at home in his maximum-security cell in the county jail. There he was surrounded by his radio and his paintings and the cardboard furniture he'd made, and he was visited frequently by an intelligent man who listened thoughtfully to his every word.

Speck seemed to feel that in jail he'd achieved some mastery over his life. He'd even passed a correspondence course in Bible studies, and he proudly showed Ziporyn the diploma on the wall of his cell. "First thing I ever passed," he said with a mixture of pride and amazement. "First goddamned thing I ever passed. Ain't that something? I tell you, I was dumb in school, but dumb. First thing I ever passed."

At midnight on February 14, 1967, Speck was driven to Peoria in a convoy of unmarked cars filled with armed policemen. The trial began five days later. Speck, his face pallid from six months in jail, chewed gum and slumped in a swivel chair, the collar of his ill-fitting blue suit puckered at the back of his neck. He'd gained 25 pounds since his arrest in July and now weighed a fleshy 185 pounds. He seldom glanced at the jury, and his main emotion appeared to be boredom as, fact by fact, prosecutor William Martin built the case against him. Martin had excellent material, including the bloody fingerprints Speck left at the scene of the crime and Corazon Amurao's eyewitness testimony. What he didn't have was Speck's confession, but it scarcely mattered. Although public defender Gerald Getty tried to demote the fingerprints to "smudges" and cast doubt on Amurao's identification, he was fighting a hopeless battle.

Even though his life was at stake, Speck didn't take the stand during his four-week trial. The thought of having to appear in front of strangers stirred up something in him akin to stage fright. Getty didn't press him; the prosecutor's case was overwhelming. The jury took only 49 minutes to find Speck guilty and recommend a sentence of death.

Getty filed the usual appeals to delay Speck's execution. But in the end it was not his lawyerly gifts that saved his client from the electric chair and allowed him to die a nat-

Chained and handcuffed, Richard Speck hangs his head during a 1978 interview in which he said that if one of the nurses had not spit in his face, they would all still be alive.

ural death 25 years later. On June 29, 1972, the U.S. Supreme Court declared a moratorium on the death penalty, and in November of that year Speck was resentenced to eight consecutive terms totaling 400 to 1,200 years—at the time, the longest sentence ever given in the United States.

During his quarter-century at the Statesville Correctional Center at Joliet, Illinois, Richard Speck kept a stamp collection and listened to music. He became known as the birdman—after the movie *Birdman of Alcatraz*—because he made pets of two sparrows that flew into his cell. The loner kept to himself and placidly carried out his work assignment: painting the prison walls and bars. "Everything is 'yes sir' and 'no sir' and a smile on his face," said assistant warden Ernest Morris.

But Speck was too much of an addict to be a model prisoner. He distilled moonshine whiskey and managed to get hold of barbiturates as well. Punishment for these infractions failed to deter him. "How am I going to get in trouble?" he said. "I'm in here for 1,200 years!"

The closest Speck ever came to a full and public confession of his crimes occurred when the *Chicago Tribune*'s Bob Greene interviewed him in 1978: "Yeah, I killed them," Speck said. "I stabbed them and I choked them." But he was still not prepared to take full responsibility, alleging that there had been an accomplice who took part in killing the nurses—a claim that no one took seriously. "I'm sorry as hell," Speck said. "For those girls, and for their families, and for me. If I had to do it all over again, it would be a simple house burglary."

In the opinion of the relatives of the murdered women, justice was served when Speck was rejected for parole seven times. Winning his release from prison apparently ceased to be important to Speck after his mother died in 1985. He told the warden that he no longer had a reason to be on the outside. When Speck died six years later, his survivors, even his once-devoted sister Carolyn Wilson, declined to take custody of the body. The corpse was cremated. The final resting place of the ashes has never been disclosed.

Two days after Speck's death, Corazon Amurao Atienza, 48, now a nurse at Georgetown University Medical Center in Washington, D.C., told a reporter that she still had nightmares about the night of the murders. She couldn't understand how Speck had overlooked her. She could not, even after 25 years, get over her extraordinary good luck.◆

At times it seems as if I am going to explode.

CHARLES WHITMAN

2

The Tower

The limestone clock tower on the University of Texas campus at Austin has long been a popular tourist attraction. Soaring up 307 feet from the university's administration building, it commands a majestic view. From its four-sided observation deck a visitor can see the 232-acre campus, with its vast mall and red tile rooftops, and the Texas capital and its perimeter of lush farmlands beyond. On a clear day the view extends westward to the mist-mantled hills whose purple hue inspired the writer O. Henry to christen Austin the City of the Violet Crown.

Monday, August 1, 1966, was clear and cloudless. At 11:25 a.m. that day, in the gathering Texas heat, a 25-year-old architectural engineering student pulled his black Chevrolet Impala into a slot reserved for university officials near the administration building. He had permission for this impertinence. The guard at the parking lot's entrance had issued a 40-minute parking permit after the Chevy's driver, a nice-looking young blond fellow, explained that he was delivering equipment to a professor. The guard had no reason to question the story. It seemed plausible enough, and besides, the Impala's driver was not the type to arouse suspicion. He looked like a former altar boy or Boy Scout. (In fact, he'd been both.) The gear supposedly destined for the professor rested inside an olive drab footlocker on the Impala's backseat. The locker, left over from the driver's stint in the Marine Corps, was draped with a quilt. Had the gate guard examined it, or had he bothered to look inside the Chevy's trunk, he would have instantly surmised that the contents were not intended for academic use.

The footlocker and trunk held the following items: cans of meat ravioli, Spam, Vienna sausage, peanuts, sliced pineapple, fruit salad, and liquid diet formula; a jar of honey, boxes of raisins, sandwiches, and a vacuum flask of coffee; vitamins, Dexedrine, Excedrin, earplugs, jugs of water and of gasoline, matches, charcoal lighter fluid, rope, binoculars, canteens, a machete, a hatchet, three knives, a transistor radio, toilet paper, a Gillette razor, and a plastic bottle of Mennen spray deodorant. In addition, there was a private arsenal potent enough to stand off a small army: a 6-mm. Remington bolt-action rifle with a 4-power Leupold sight, a .35-caliber Remington pump rifle, a .30-caliber carbine, a sawed-off 12-gauge Sears shotgun, a 9-mm. Luger pistol, a Galesi-Brescia pistol, a .357 magnum Smith & Wesson revolver, and 700 rounds of assorted ammunition.

But the guard saw none of this, and the nice-looking young blond fellow parked his car and continued with his plans for the day. He'd already killed his mother and his wife. Now he was about to kill 13 total strangers and wound 31 more. His name was Charles Joseph Whitman. And in the next hour and a half or so, as the clock chimes above him rang out the quarter-hours, he would forever change the Texas Tower from a notable local landmark to an internationally infamous symbol of terror.

Charles Whitman was a husky young man who stood six feet tall and weighed 198 pounds, but the locker and the contents of the car's trunk were too heavy for him to carry. No matter. As was his habit, he'd thought ahead and come prepared. He dragged the load from the car and wheeled it to the administration building on a mover's dolly that he'd rented earlier that morning. He was sweating heavily; he generally sweated a lot, and on this day, in 98-degree heat, he was overdressed for his labors. He wore light blue nylon coveralls over jeans and a red plaid shirt.

Inside the building, Whitman pushed the dolly to the service elevator that would take him aloft. At 11:35 the door of the passenger elevator opened and zoology professor Antone Jacobsen stepped off with his young son and daughter, nearly stumbling over the footlocker and bundle. The professor observed to himself that the gear had the oily odor of guns.

An elevator attendant, Vera Palmer, thought Whitman was a repairman. She stepped forward and told him, "Your elevator is turned off." She reached inside the service elevator and switched it on for him. "Thank you, ma'am," he said with his customary politeness. "You don't know how happy that makes me." As he rolled the dolly aboard, he kept mindlessly repeating the words. "You don't know how happy that makes me . . . how happy that makes me." Whitman punched the button for the 27th floor and began his ascent.

No one could have guessed what was going on inside Charles Whitman's mind as dawn broke on that sweltering day in Austin. At 5:45 he called his wife Kathy's boss at the telephone company to tell him that she wouldn't be in to work. She had diarrhea and was throwing up, he said. Kathy had been dead more than two hours; as she lay sleeping, her husband had stabbed her four times in the chest with a bayonet. After the phone call, Whitman went about his errands. He had a close schedule to follow. At 7:30 he rented the dolly on which he would load his arsenal. Afterward, he pulled up to the drive-in window of his bank, where he cashed two checks for $250, one drawn on his own account, one on that of his mother, Margaret Whitman. She would not, after all, need the money. Before killing his wife the night before, Whitman had visited his mother at the apartment where she lived alone and, without hesitation, had stabbed her in the chest with the bayonet and shot her in the back of the head.

At 9:00 he went to the Charles Davis Hardware store and bought a .30-caliber carbine, two extra clips, and eight boxes of ammunition. He paid cash for them and told the salesclerk that he was planning a trip to Florida to shoot wild pigs. At 9:30 he stopped at Chuck's Gun Shop and bought four more carbine clips, six additional boxes of ammunition, and one can of Hoppe's No. 9 gun-cleaning solvent.

Charlie Whitman knew Chuck's well. A year earlier he'd visited the shop with his father, Charles A. Whitman, who was in Austin on a visit from the family home in Lake Worth, Florida. On that occasion, young Charlie had ordered the 6-mm. Remington with 4-power scope that he would take to the tower with him. The elder Whitman had explained to the owner at the time that he and his son were planning to go deer hunting together. The father placed an order as well, for a .243-caliber Winchester Sako bolt-action rifle. Charlie Whitman came to the store several times thereafter to make payments on the guns; he once confided to the owner that his father was sending him the money to pay for them.

To the owner's wife, who now waited on him, Charlie Whitman presented an appearance of absolute normality as he casually made his purchases and wrote out a $48.63 check. He even asked her if she was going to call the bank to see whether he had sufficient funds to cover the check—a bluff, since his account was already overdrawn.

After leaving Chuck's Gun Shop, Whitman drove across the street to a Sears, Roebuck and Company store. There he handled a 12-gauge shotgun. Hoisting it to his shoulder, he told the clerk that it felt good, "light compared to the 21-pound gun I carried in the service." He repeated his remark about pig hunting in Florida, bought the gun on credit, and then took all his lethal purchases home.

In the garage, where he kept a lot of his military gear, he began sawing off the butt and the barrel of the shotgun. Postman Chester Arrington spotted Whitman as he delivered some mail to the Whitmans' five-room rented bungalow and paused to chat with him. He was surprised to find Whitman shortening the gun, since he knew this was illegal. Whitman explained that he had to alter the weapon to fit it into his footlocker.

At 10:30, a half-hour before his mother was due to go on duty at her cashier's job at Wyatt's Cafeteria, Whitman called her boss to say that she was ill and would not be in. He was taking no chances of her body being discovered before he could carry out his plan.

So far all had gone smoothly. When he reached the 27th floor of the tower, he had to haul his footlocker and bundle up the stairs to the next floor and down a couple of corridors to the observation deck. In the reception room on the 28th floor he ran into Edna Townsley, a 47-year-old divorcée and the mother of two sons. Her job was to greet people and have them sign the register. Standing only five feet four inches tall, she was considered "a real scrapper" by her friends. Townsley, who should have had the day off, had come in at 8 a.m. to fill in for a coworker and was to be relieved at noon by Vera Palmer, who'd let Whitman onto the elevator.

To Whitman, Townsley was merely an obstacle. He hit her with the stock of his shotgun, splitting her skull to the brain, then turned the weapon and shot her. He was in the process of hiding her bleeding body behind a couch when a young couple, Don Walden and Cheryl Botts, entered the room through the door leading from the observation deck. Unaware of the violence that had taken place in the room while they were outside admiring the view, the couple

Located just beneath the clock faces, the observation deck of the University of Texas clock tower gave Charles Whitman a 360-degree range of targets. He ascended the first 27 floors by elevator, then hauled his gun-laden footlocker up the stairs *(inset).*

Whitman's arsenal included, from left, a 9-mm. pistol; a .357 magnum revolver; a .30-caliber M-1 carbine; a .35-caliber pump-action rifle; a hunting knife; a sawed-off 12-gauge shotgun; and a 6-mm. bolt-action rifle. Strewn among the weapons is some of the sniper's ammunition.

thought little of the fact that the friendly receptionist was gone and that a clean-cut young man was leaning over the couch. As they moved toward the exit, Botts spotted a brownish stain on the carpet beside Townsley's desk in time to warn Walden not to step in it. Neither realized it was blood. Whitman picked up two rifles and turned toward the couple. They smiled at him and said hello, and, as Botts remembered later, Whitman "smiled real big and said, 'Hi, how are you?' " Walden thought it odd that the man should be holding guns and almost asked him if he was planning to shoot pigeons, but decided against it. Walden and Botts turned their backs on Whitman and went downstairs. "The luckiest couple in Austin" is how newspapers described them later.

When they had gone, Whitman shoved Townsley's desk, chair, and wastebasket in front of the glass door to the stairwell. As he was about to go out onto the deck, he was surprised by the sudden appearance of Mike and Mark Gabour, 15 and 18, who were peering at him through the door over the makeshift barricade. Mark shoved the door open, and Whitman wheeled around and fired at the boys with the shotgun. Mike screamed. Sightseers from Texarkana on

their family's first vacation in two years, the brothers were in the company of their parents, M. J. and Mary Francis Gabour, and their aunt and uncle, Marguerite and William Lamport of Austin. Whitman's spray of pellets hit Mike, Mark, their mother, and Mrs. Lamport and sent them tumbling backward down the stairs as Lamport and the elder Gabour were climbing up behind them. Whitman then slammed the door shut. Gabour rolled his younger son over and saw that he'd been shot in the head and was dead. Gabour's sister, Marguerite Lamport, had been killed, too. Critically injured, Mary Francis Gabour and her older son were bleeding profusely. Frantic, Gabour and Lamport dragged the victims to the landing and ran about seeking aid, but they could find none. Workers in offices on the 26th floor, alerted by the shots, the sound of the bodies crashing down the stairs, and cries for help, were anxiously wondering what was going on.

Whitman, meanwhile, stepped out onto the six-foot-wide walkaround into the blinding light and Texas heat. He wedged the dolly against the entrance door to block the way of anyone who might come up after him. He knew the deck

Some 45 minutes after the campus massacre began, a puff of dust kicked up by police bullets slamming into the limestone tower floats near the clock face on the tower's south side. The sniper felled most of his victims in the first quarter-hour of shooting, before police arrived in force and started returning his fire.

well. Ten days previously he'd been here with his teenage brother, John, showing him the view. The boy had come from Lake Worth to spend a few days with their mother. Just under the clock itself, close to the top of the tower, the walkaround was 231 feet above the ground. It was rimmed on all four sides by a four-foot-high limestone parapet with rainspouts that could serve as gunports. It must have struck Charles Whitman as the ideal fortress.

Guns primed, binoculars draped around his neck, Whitman positioned himself under the VI of the clock's gold-edged south face. There was scarcely a cloud in the sky. Looking toward the mall, a large, paved rectangle, he could see scores of his fellow students out in the open. Had Edna Townsley and the Gabours and Lamports not detained him, he might have had another thousand students as targets when classes changed at the half-hour. At 11:48, just after the 17-chime carillon above him had finished ringing the quarter-hour, Whitman put the 6-mm. Remington to his shoulder, peered through the scope, and pulled the trigger. Even a fair shot can consistently hit a six-and-a-half-inch circle from 300 yards using such a rifle, and Whitman was an excellent shot. One after another, bodies began falling over a four-block area.

At first nobody on the ground could figure out what the strange explosions from the tower meant. Then, as people started slumping to the ground, others woke to the danger and ran for cover. On the fourth floor of the tower building, Norma Burger, 23, a Ph.D. candidate, heard the firing, looked out, and saw six bodies sprawled grotesquely on the mall. For a moment she thought it was just a taste-less joke. "I expected the six to get up and walk away laughing," she would recount later. But when she saw the pavement splashed with blood, and more people falling, she knew there was no joke. In the first 15 minutes, relying chiefly on his 6-mm. Remington but switching occasionally to the carbine and the .357 revolver, Whitman picked off most of his victims.

From his high perch on the tower Whitman had an unobstructed view across the South Mall to the intersection of University and 21st streets, some 500 yards away *(right)*. A crack shot, he hit a man near the intersection.

On the mall, Claire Wilson, 18, eight months pregnant, was walking from an anthropology class when a bullet crashed into her abdomen; she survived but later gave birth to a stillborn child whose skull had been crushed by the shot. A horrified classmate, freshman Thomas Eckman, 19, knelt beside her to help and was shot dead himself. Mathematician Robert Boyer, 33, was planning to leave Texas for a teaching job in Liverpool. His pregnant wife and two children were already in England waiting for him. Boyer stepped out onto the mall on the way to lunch and was shot fatally in the back. More fortunate was secretary Charlotte Darehshori, who rushed out to help when the first victims dropped. Suddenly realizing that she was under fire herself, she spent the next hour and a half crouched behind the concrete base of a flagpole.

At the south end of the mall, Austin patrolman Billy Speed, 23, one of the first police officers on the scene, took cover behind a thick, columned stone wall, but a bullet zinged through the six-inch space between the columns and killed him. Still farther south, 500 yards from the tower, electrical repairman Roy Dell Schmidt, 29, walking toward his truck after making a call, was killed by a bullet in the stomach. To the east, 22-year-old Peace Corps trainee Thomas Ashton, who was bound for Iran, was strolling on the roof of the Computation Center when Whitman shot him dead.

Directing his fire westward, the sniper fixed his sights on Guadalupe Street, the main thoroughfare off campus. Known locally as the Drag, Guadalupe was buzzing with lunchtime shoppers and strollers. One of them was Paul Sonntag, 18, a lifeguard at an Austin pool and a grandson of Paul Bolton, longtime friend of then President Lyndon Johnson. Sonntag was accompanying Claudia Rutt, 18, for a polio shot she needed before entering Texas Christian University. Rutt suddenly sank to the ground. Sonntag bent over her, then pitched to the sidewalk himself. Both were dead. A block north, political scientist Harry Walchuk, father of six and a teacher at Michigan's Alpena Community College, browsed in the doorway of a newsstand after working all morning in the university library. A bullet killed him on the spot. A few steps farther up the street, Thomas Karr, 24, a university senior, was walking sleepily toward his apartment after staying up almost all night to study for a 10 a.m. exam. He dropped to the pavement dying. For the injured out in the open there was a triple ordeal to bear until

Crouching behind a flagpole's massive base for an hour and a half, Charlotte Darehshori escaped Whitman's fire. In the background a wounded student lies beside a hedge.

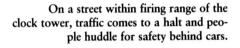

Two people comfort a shooting victim awaiting an ambulance. Less than 15 minutes after Whitman fired his first shot from the tower, ambulances began arriving to ferry the wounded away.

On a street within firing range of the clock tower, traffic comes to a halt and people huddle for safety behind cars.

Among the 15 people Whitman killed were, from left to right, Paul Sonntag, 18; Harry Walchuk, 38; Robert Boyer, 33; and Edna Townsley, 47.

PAUL SONNTAG

rescuers could reach them: the pain from their wounds, the fear of being shot again, and the agony of lying on pavement and cement hot enough to blister skin.

Four minutes after Whitman opened fire, Austin police received a report about "some shootings at the university tower." In seconds, a "0-50" trouble signal went out, directing all units in the vicinity to head for the campus. In a blare of sirens, more than 100 city policemen, reinforced by some 30 highway patrolmen, Texas Rangers, and U.S. Secret Service men from President Johnson's Austin office, converged on the campus. Their numbers were expanded by several local residents wielding everything from deer rifles to revolvers.

Hundreds of rounds of rifle and pistol fire crackled toward the tower. A few of the slugs smashed into the faces on the clock above Whitman; most pinged ineffectually into the parapet in front of him, kicking up puffs of dust. He lowered the white headband he was wearing to keep the dust and flying stone chips out of his eyes. Ducking below the parapet, he began aiming through the narrow drainage slits in the wall. As he'd no doubt foreseen, his position was proving almost impregnable to ground attack while affording him virtually limitless targets—to the north, where he wounded two students on their way to the biology building; to the west, where the Drag was littered with 4 dead, 11 wounded; and particularly to the south, where the mall looked like a no man's land, strewn with bodies that nobody dared to recover.

Unable to get at Whitman from below, police chartered a light airplane, a Champion Citabria two-seater, and sent sharpshooter Lieutenant Marion Lee aloft. Jim Boutwell, manager of a flying school, was at the controls. Lee explained that Boutwell's only protection from the sniper's bullets would be "the fabric side of the airplane and a blue shirt." "Let's go," Boutwell replied. Whitman managed to put two bullets into the Citabria as it pivoted around the tower; to the two men inside, the slugs' impact felt as though sledgehammers were hitting the plane. To make matters worse, heat waves rising from the pavement caused the plane to jig and hop in the air, making it impossible for Lee to draw a bead on the killer. And there was no way to get in close; Whitman's continuing fire forced Boutwell to fly the plane at a safe distance. Nevertheless, the circling Citabria did serve a purpose, drawing Whitman's fire away from the campus below and commanding his full attention long enough for police on foot to enter the tower and dash up to the observation deck.

Among those who responded to reports of the sniper atop the tower were policemen Houston McCoy, Ramiro Martinez, and Jerry Day. Patrolling the university area in his cruiser, McCoy, 26, heard the alarm call come over his radio and unlocked the riot gun in his rack. He drove up and down the Drag several times, catching sight of occasional puffs of gunsmoke coming from the observation deck. He knew he'd need extra ammunition to go up against the well-armed gunman and so, before driving to the tower, he stopped at the Everett Hardware Company to pick up shotgun shells and rifle cartridges for himself and two private citizens. Carrying guns of their own, the civilians had volunteered to help shoot the sniper. McCoy told them to kill him if they could get a clear shot. He parked his car at the base of the tower and looked up. "In my mind I saw a sniper behind every one of those windows," he related later. "I felt there was an army up there. It was just a gut feeling. I got scared as hell." He had plenty of reason to be scared; he was short on protection and short on help. In those days Austin policemen had no bulletproof vests and no portable radios for communicating with one another. Shortly after McCoy arrived he saw Patrolman Billy Speed crumple under one of Whitman's bullets. Afraid or not, McCoy knew that the police had to climb the tower and stop the killer.

Officer Martinez, 29, father of twin five-year-old daughters, was at home getting ready to have lunch when he heard about the sniper. It was a special day, Martinez's wedding anniversary, and he'd just put a pork steak on to cook. As he began his ritual of pressing his uniform and polishing his boots for his 3-o'clock shift, he saw on television that several people had been shot on the University of Texas campus. He telephoned headquarters and was told to go to the scene. Skipping lunch, he hopped into his car and set out for the campus.

HARRY WALCHUK

ROBERT BOYER

EDNA TOWNSLEY

Officer Day heard the police call on his radio and drove directly to the scene of the carnage. He ran around one building, entered another and crossed it, and thus made his way to the tower. Martinez, who'd zigzagged across campus through several buildings, dashed into the lobby and met Day. There they were joined by a civilian, Allen Crum, 40, father of three, floor manager of the University Co-op bookstore. Crum was a retired Air Force tail gunner, but he'd never fired a shot in combat. The three took the elevator to the 26th floor; as they ascended, Martinez said a silent prayer asking God to forgive him for his sins "just in case I didn't come back."

On the 26th floor, where terrified office tenants had blocked their doors with furniture, the armed men ran into M. J. Gabour, who was clutching a pair of white women's shoes. He rushed at them, screaming that his family had been shot. He wanted a rifle so he could shoot the killer himself. As Day constrained the shaken man, Martinez found the stairs and started scrambling up to the 27th floor. Crum insisted on accompanying him. "If he was going up there," Crum said afterward, "he wasn't going alone." Martinez deputized Crum on the spot and handed him a .30-caliber rifle.

Together they went after the sniper. Almost instantly they ran into the dead and wounded of the Gabour and Lamport families lying in a bloody heap on the landing. Mark Gabour and his mother were crying. Mark, who'd been knocked unconscious, had only recently wakened. Fearful that Whitman might come back, the boy had tried to pull himself to safety, but he could only advance slightly because, he said later, "there was too much blood; I could get no friction."

Martinez and Crum found Townsley's desk, chair, and wastebasket blocking their way. They shoved the barriers aside, secured the room, and discovered Townsley behind the couch. She was still alive, but barely. From the windows, they checked the walkaround and could see no one. Martinez slowly pushed away the dolly that Whitman had used to block the glass door onto the deck. The sound of the killer's fire seemed to be coming from the northwest, the opposite side of the tower from where the officers were. Martinez crawled out onto the walkaround and began moving stealthily to the east. Crum followed through the door and turned west. He could hear Whitman coming, crunching underfoot bits of debris that had been blasted out of the tower. Unfamiliar with the rifle he was carrying, Crum accidently discharged it into the southwest corner.

Revolver in hand, Martinez rounded one corner, then more slowly, every muscle tense, turned onto the north side of the walkaround. Fifty feet away from him, in the northwest corner, crouched Whitman, his eyes straining toward the direction of Crum's shot. He had his transistor radio turned on, tuned to a newscast of the shootout. In the meantime, McCoy had arrived and was coming up behind Martinez. Martinez aimed the revolver and began firing. Whitman swung around, half blind from dust and debris sent flying by bullets hitting the limestone, and tried to level his fast-firing carbine on Martinez. Aiming for the white headband Whitman was wearing, McCoy fired his shotgun. Whitman's head jerked back and his headband turned red. McCoy fired again. Whitman's head jumped a second time. Martinez let out a war whoop.

Seeing that the sniper "was still flopping," Martinez slammed his empty revolver to the floor, grabbed McCoy's shotgun, and, as he ran toward Whitman, fired once more at him. At 1:24 p.m., 96 minutes after his first shot from the tower, Charles Joseph Whitman was dead. A dazed Martinez felt all his strength leave him. Trembling, he held the shotgun above the parapet to signal cease-fire. But the shooting continued until Crum grabbed a green towel from Whitman's footlocker and began waving it as an impromptu flag of truce. For a moment, only the radio and the airplane could be heard. Down below, hundreds of excited students poured out of buildings and stampeded toward the tower, nearly knocking over several officers who tried to hold them back. Some were shouting obscenities, others such words as "kill" and "lynch." Up on the tower, McCoy strode over to Whitman's body and knelt down beside it to search for identification. "A puddle of blood was inching toward my boots," McCoy remembered later. "I told him if he got my boots bloody, I'd throw him over the side."

Those who knew Whitman couldn't believe the announcement two hours later that he was the tower sniper. "Oh, no, it just couldn't be Charlie," said one former neighbor in Lake Worth. "He was a nice little boy and made a handsome man." Others spoke of him as "normal," "dependable," "a nice, uncomplicated guy." A former roommate at the University of Texas called him "one of the nicest guys I had met." An incredulous young woman who used to ride to class with Whitman described him as "the nicest person I know at the university. He was always a lot of fun—always joking." An Austin neighbor, whose children played in the Whitmans' yard, said, "All the kids in the neighborhood played there. He loved children and they loved him." In the opinion of a close friend, Whitman was "just a great guy. He was always 'happy Charlie.' He always had something nice to say about everybody, and I never saw him mad at any individual."

The assessments were unanimous: No one could make the link between Happy Charlie and the seeming madman whose rage reached such a bizarre apogee atop the Texas Tower. There appeared to be nothing in his background to foreshadow the bloodbath that he caused. The bare bones of Whitman's biography revealed what passed, superficially at least, for a normal American upbringing. He was born on June 24, 1941, and had the usual childhood illnesses during his early years. His brother Patrick came along four years later, followed by John, the youngest. His mother, Margaret Whitman, a devout Catholic married to a Protestant, regularly took the boys with her to church on Sundays.

The only thing at all outwardly unusual about this early period was that Charlie and his family moved eight times during his first six years. The Whitmans settled in Lake Worth, Florida, in the early summer of 1947, and that autumn Charlie entered the local Catholic grade school. A year later he began taking piano lessons. At the age of 11 he became a Boy Scout, and by the time he was 12, he'd earned the rank of eagle scout, the youngest in the world ever to do so. He had a newspaper route for a couple of years, delivering his papers by bicycle. In 1955 he entered a Catholic high school in West Palm Beach. He did well there and graduated seventh in a class of 72.

Beneath the surface of this typical American life, however, flowed currents of violence. Whitman's father was a plumbing and septic-tank contractor, a scout commissioner, a scoutmaster, and a past president of both the PTA and Chamber of Commerce. He was also a wife beater. "I did on many occasions beat my wife," he readily admitted after the slayings, "but I loved her and I love her to this day. I did and do have an awful temper, but my wife was awful stubborn, and we had some clashes over the more than 25 years of our life together. I have to admit it, because of my temper, I knocked her around."

The Whitman home harbored not only violence but the instruments of violence. Guns hung in almost every room. The senior Whitman described himself as a "fanatic" about guns and a "great hunter," and Charlie followed in his footsteps. They often went hunting together. "My boys know all about guns," the father said. "I believe in that."

Abandoned as a child, the elder Whitman had been reared in an orphanage in Savannah, Georgia. He was a self-made man and proud of it, a man who demanded much of himself—and of his family. He wanted things done well, and with the help of his wife, who ran his office and kept the books, he saw to it that his boys strove to fulfill his ambitions for them. If Charlie was going to play the piano, he'd better excel. Charlie did; by the time he was 12 the boy was an accomplished musician, and a few years later he was good enough to play in his cousin's dance band. But his father objected to the band, so Charlie quit. As a Boy Scout, Charlie had to be the best member of his troop. In response to his father's goading, he earned 21 merit badges in 15 months. "Daddies aren't worth a damn if they don't want their kids to be better than what they are," was the elder Whitman's credo.

In keeping with his philosophy of child rearing, Whitman as a father was a severe disciplinarian. "It's true I was

Policemen Ramiro Martinez *(right)* and Houston McCoy *(far right)* cornered Whitman on the north side of the clock tower and shot him fatally in the head and chest. The dead sniper lay sprawled where he fell *(below)* until an ambulance crew removed the body from the observation platform.

 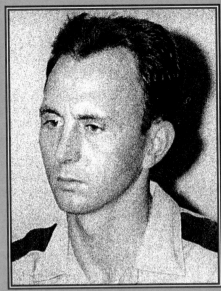

strict," he said in a newspaper interview. "With all three of my sons, it was 'yes, sir' and 'no, sir.' They minded me." To ensure this obedience, the father resorted often to physical punishment. "The way I look at it," he said, "I am not ashamed of anything that I ever did. I am not ashamed of any spankings. I don't think I spanked enough, if you want to know the truth about it. I think they should have been punished more than what they were punished." Despite the punitive treatment, Whitman insisted, his sons "were spoiled rotten—all my three boys were—because they got everything that money could buy. I'm not a rich man by any means, but I made good money in my profession or trade." He claimed that he never hit Charlie with anything but a paddle or his fist.

When Charlie was 18 he came home drunk one night after being out with friends, and his father went berserk. The elder Whitman beat the boy and threw him into the family swimming pool, and Charlie nearly drowned. Young Whitman had endured enough. Telling only his mother, he enlisted in the Marine Corps in July 1959, abandoning his plan of entering Georgia Tech. He was assigned to the U.S. naval base at Guantánamo Bay, Cuba, for an 18-month tour of duty.

In the service Whitman set his sights high, applying for a U.S. Navy and Marine Corps scholarship program with the intention of becoming a commissioned officer. He took a competitive exam, scored high, and then went before a selection committee that voted favorably on him. With other officer candidates he embarked for a preparatory school at Bainbridge, Maryland, where he took refresher courses in physics and mathematics. He then entered the University of Texas to study mechanical engineering. He would switch later to architectural engineering, which suited his artistic talents more. As a student he received his regular active-duty pay, plus allowances for tuition, books, and fees.

To some of his classmates Whitman seemed obsessed with money. He loved to gamble and considered himself a crafty poker player. A friend described him as "always trying to make a fast buck—he liked to plunge." Whitman bragged that he made enough money gambling to put his wife through college. After one game with a couple of shady characters, he owed $200. He paid part of his debt with a check, then canceled the check the next morning, claiming he'd been cheated. The following afternoon the two men went to Whitman's dormitory room and threatened him

with a knife, telling him to have the money the next day or else. Frightened, Whitman reported the episode to the district attorney's office. For several days thereafter he wore a .357-caliber magnum under his sports jacket; only when he heard that the men had been arrested for stealing a car did he set the pistol aside.

On another occasion he gave a bad check to fellow student Robert Ross. They'd played poker all night—Whitman jauntily sporting a ten-gallon hat—and at dawn Ross bet $190. Whitman called and lost. He wrote a check for $190 and tossed it to Ross. The check bounced; the bank would say only that Whitman's account had been closed. Ross weighed 50 pounds less than Whitman, and it was with trepidation that he went to him to demand his money. He found Whitman lying on a dormitory bunk in his underwear throwing a huge hunting knife into a closet door. Whitman grinned. "Look, kid," he said, "my family is loaded. I'll get you the money. Don't worry about it." The check was never made good.

An even seamier side to Whitman came to light after the murders. A merchant on Guadalupe Street remembered Whitman coming to see him three or four years before the tower massacre. "He said he had a nice supply of pornography," the merchant recalled. Whitman then took some pictures out of his pocket and showed them to the man. "He told me there was tremendous profit in them. I said, 'I don't think I am interested.' He treated the whole darn subject as though it were imported sugar cane from South America. He was very technical about it. No sentiment whatever. I asked him what market he had in mind, college kids? 'No,' he said. 'High school and grade school children.' He was like some guy trying to sell an ad in the yellow pages."

This penchant for sidestepping morality when it suited him got Whitman into a brush with the law in 1961, his first year at the university. One night he and two fellow students poached a deer near the LBJ Ranch. The Thanksgiving holiday was approaching, and Whitman wanted to send some venison to his father as a gift. A passerby, noting that Whitman's car had a young buck slung over the trunk, jotted down the license number and reported it to the Texas Game and Fish Commission. Game warden Grover Simpson and three policeman caught the hunters as they were butchering the animal in the shower of Whitman's dormitory room. Although poaching is considered a serious offense in Texas, Simpson found Whitman such a coopera-

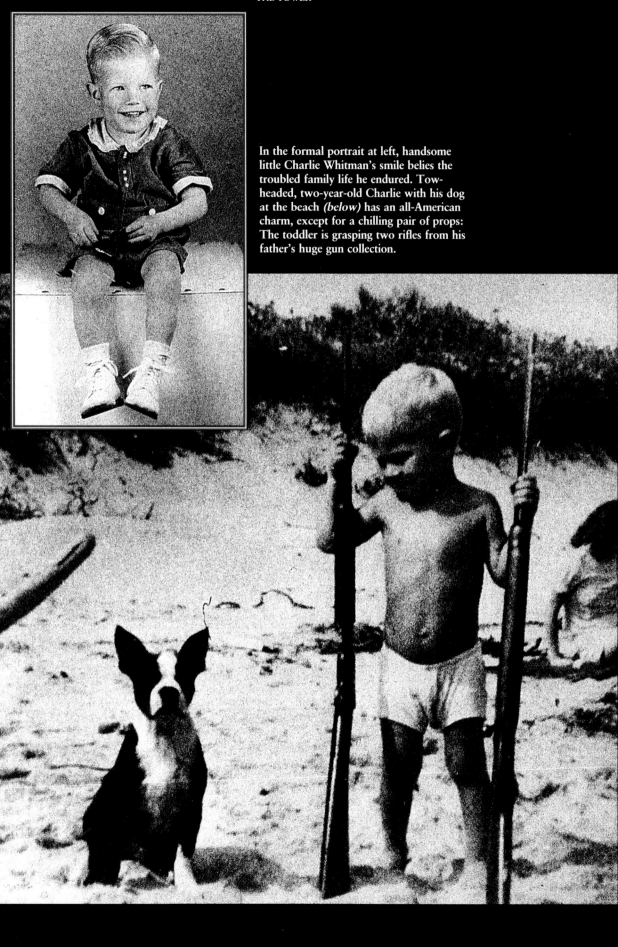

In the formal portrait at left, handsome little Charlie Whitman's smile belies the troubled family life he endured. Towheaded, two-year-old Charlie with his dog at the beach *(below)* has an all-American charm, except for a chilling pair of props: The toddler is grasping two rifles from his father's huge gun collection.

Whitman brothers Patrick, John, and Charlie *(left to right)* gather for Christmas in 1958.

In a family photo that his father released two days after the shootings, Charlie sits at the feet of his first victim—his mother.

Charlie earned the rank of eagle scout when he was only 12. A year later, he poses prayerfully before a church altar.

Whitman's high-school graduation portrait features his familiar—and deceptive—happy-go-lucky smile.

Charles Whitman the Marine grins into the sun in a snapshot taken at Guantánamo Bay, Cuba, where he was stationed for 18 months. During his time in the Corps, his superior shooting ability earned him a sharp-shooter's badge.

tive, "darn nice fellow" that he let him off with a $100 fine.

Indeed, so amiable was Whitman that his friends often found themselves forgiving him for the practical jokes he played, even if some of the pranks were more fiendish than amusing. One night Charlie and a college friend named Jim were involved in an automobile accident. Whitman returned to his dormitory around 5 a.m., bloodied, dirty, and wet, and told a group of young men who'd been up all night playing poker that Jim, whom they all knew, had been killed. "Everyone was speechless," recounted classmate David A. Pratt. "We called Jim's girlfriend on campus even though it was before dawn. Then we sat shaking our heads in disbelief. Suddenly Jim appeared around the corner of the door and said, 'The ghost walks!' Pandemonium broke loose. Charlie lay on the floor and couldn't move, he was so convulsed with laughter."

Whitman was not above playing practical jokes on his fellow student and future wife, Kathy Leissner, during their courtship. Pratt remembered how Whitman would telephone her and tell her to go to her window. "Then he would run out on his sixth floor balcony and, hanging suspended by one arm, would wave at her with the free arm and both legs as she appeared at her window two blocks away."

Perhaps such high jinks made it hard to take Whitman seriously, even though he sometimes made chilling statements. One time as he stood before the window of his dormitory room and stared at the tower, he remarked to Fran-

cis Schuck, Jr., a friend he'd gotten to know in the Marine Corps, "A person could stand off an army from atop of it before they got to him." Another time he said that he'd "like to go up in the tower and shoot people." Schuck never dreamed that Whitman might mean it.

Even so, there was ample evidence that Whitman was capable of violence. Classmates remembered how he'd once collared a Saudi Arabian student who'd sat by mistake in Whitman's seat and threw him out of the classroom. A college friend, John Daigle, recalled how he and Whitman were driving to a target range outside Austin: "He had just bought another pistol to add to his collection of weapons. I was in the back seat with him and Kathy. Two other boys were in front. As we stopped at an intersection in downtown, Charlie suddenly pulled out his revolver and pointed it at a man on the curb, about 20 feet away. He yelled some derogatory remarks; I don't remember what he said. The man turned around and saw him, and the gun, then reached under his sweater for what we assumed was a knife, gun, or maybe as a bluff. But we ducked, the light changed, and we sped away in the car. We were all shook up. I remember saying it was kind of a foolish thing to do. Charlie just thought it was funny. I think Charlie always tried to prove himself a man. And this was, in his mind, the manly thing to do—scare the guy."

Whitman and Kathy, the daughter of a rice farmer and real-estate agent in Needville, Texas, were married on August 17, 1962, the 25th anniversary of his parents' wedding day. Dating and marriage apparently proved distracting to Whitman, who, uncharacteristically, didn't do well during his first year at the university. His grades were uneven at best, ranging, for the autumn semester, from an F in general chemistry and a D in introduction to economics to an A in algebra. In the spring semester he managed three Cs and one B, but no As. During his second year, probably because of a lighter course load, his grades began picking up, but the Marine Corps proved as tough a taskmaster as his father; it found his academic performance unacceptable and yanked him back to active duty.

This must have come as a severe blow to Whitman's pride. From that point on, his Marine Corps career seemed to go downhill. He was sent to Camp Lejeune, North Carolina, to serve out the rest of his five-year enlistment, leaving his wife in Austin to finish her schooling. In late 1963 Whitman reached bottom with the Corps: He found himself facing a court-martial. The charges against him included gambling and usury; he allegedly threatened to kick out another Marine's teeth for failure to pay a $30 debt on which Whitman expected to collect $15 interest. There was also another matter: unauthorized possession of a small, unmilitary pistol.

While he was waiting for the court-martial to begin, the disgruntled Marine started a diary. He wrote that he "seemed to have reached the pit of life's experiences" and that he took comfort in putting his thoughts and feelings down on paper. In big block letters, he labeled the diary *The Daily Record of Charles J. Whitman,* and he wrote in it frequently after his sentence, which involved 90 days of hard labor, 30 days of confinement, and a reduction in rank from corporal to private.

Whitman recognized a definite change in himself: "I don't know if it is for better or worse or if it is real or fantasy but I feel different and I don't know if I am the cause of it all or if other circumstances are adding to it," he confided to his diary. On February 6, 1964, he wrote, "I can't stand the Corps. My love for Kathy and my sense of responsibility to our unborn children is the only thing that keeps me from going berserk. At times it seems as if I am going to explode." Two days later he was in no better shape: "I think so much of Kathy, but when I really start to concentrate on what we have done in the past and what I would like for us to do in the future I seem to explode. Or rather I seem to think I am going to explode, I wonder how long I can go on keeping to myself (I don't associate with very many people here now, and when I do I hardly ever discuss anything serious or my true feelings with them) without going nuts." February 11 found him still unsettled: "I definitely feel as though there is something unusual in my mental state. I don't know if it is my imagination or if my feelings are valid.

Whitman and his 19-year-old bride, Kathy Leissner, link arms after their wedding on August 17, 1962, in her hometown of Needville, Texas. Whitman killed his wife 16 days before their fourth anniversary.

But I notice an unusual uneasiness inside myself. However, I am quieter externally than I have ever been."

Certainly Whitman's buddies did not suspect the depth of his turmoil. According to fellow Marine Larry Phillips, Whitman was well-liked, "a clean-cut guy who would do anything for members of his squad." Phillips spoke from experience. While he and Whitman were serving at Guantánamo Bay, a jeep carrying the two of them and another Marine rolled 25 feet down an embankment, pinning Phillips underneath. Whitman single-handedly lifted the vehicle to free him, then dropped to the ground, unconscious from the effort. Whitman, recalled the friend, "was an excellent soldier" and "an excellent shot and appeared to be more accurate against moving targets during target practice sessions. He was the kind of guy you would want around if you went into combat."

Whitman was honorably discharged from the Marines in December 1964 and returned to the University of Texas to resume his studies. During this period he worked at a variety of odd jobs while receiving up to $380 a month from his father, who also gave him a new car, the black Impala. From September 1964 to April 1965, Whitman worked as a collector for the Standard Finance Company, and then from April to June as a bank teller. Busy as classes and jobs kept him, he still made time to get involved with Scouting, an old love of his, through Kathy's Methodist church. He also sang in the choir. "He probably took to Scouting just where he had left it as a boy," said Albert John Vincik, a realtor and assistant scoutmaster who got to know Whitman well. "It was easy for him because he still was a boy." The ex-Marine took his Scouts camping and on long hikes and nature-trail studies.

But if such devotion seemed exemplary, Whitman was also displaying outward signs of his inner anxieties. Vincik remembered how he would get impatient with the boys and how he chewed his nails nonstop and sweated even when the weather was cold. The young Scouts themselves recalled that their leader had lots of headaches and that he was eating all the time; his weight climbed, and the boys took to calling him Porky. But he taught them marksmanship in the careful, meticulous way of a man who knows and respects firearms. He used to hang a clothespin on a wire fence, start it spinning with .22-caliber slugs, and keep it spinning until the wood had splintered away. One day Whitman brought along a high-powered rifle and showed the boys how it worked. He told them it could kill a man at a distance of a mile.

In conversations with Whitman, Vincik learned that the young man was embarrassed by the fact that his father had begun his business life cleaning cesspools. Whitman told Vincik that his own ambitions were to make money, to achieve, to prove himself. He resented people with government jobs; they didn't work hard enough, he felt. "He said people should have more initiative, get more things done, be recognized, and step up in life," Vincik recalled. Whitman regretted that he didn't have more time to devote to his various ambitions.

It was lack of time that forced him to give up Scouting. Whitman had signed up for 19 credits during the spring semester, and he was determined to do well. "Charlie was like a computer," his close friend Larry Fuess said. "He would install his own values into the machine, then program the things he had to do, and out would come the results." But he paid a heavy price for his compulsiveness. As another friend put it, "Everybody is uptight when they go to school, but Charles was really high strung. He really got uptight about things, courses and tests." One of his instructors in architecture, Barton D. Riley, remembered Whitman's disappointment over receiving a C on an examination. "He hit the table with his fist and, without a word, just walked out," Riley said. "Charlie was used to excelling. He later came back and apologized and always in the future made certain he knew what I was talking about."

None of his friends knew that, while carrying a full academic load in the engineering school, Whitman was under the additional pressure of planning for at least two other possible careers. He was considering going to law school, and he was also preparing to be a real-estate broker. Despite his heavy schedule, he studied for and passed the state licensing exam for real-estate agents. (At the time of his death he was a licensed and bonded agent in Vincik's office, though he never sold anything.)

For help in coping with his self-imposed schedule, Whitman, like many a college student of the '60s, frequently turned to drugs. His friends knew him as a user of Dexedrine, an amphetamine widely consumed by college students in those days to keep them alert through long nights writing papers or cramming for exams. A high-powered drug that can induce insomnia, mood swings, and extreme nervousness, Dexedrine was supposedly available only by prescription (some doctors gave it to patients for weight loss), but underground traffic in amphetamines was common on college campuses at the time. Whitman resorted to this stimulant to stay awake during classes and while studying all night. Often he would go for long periods without sleep; during two weeks of finals for the spring semester he kept himself awake with amphetamines. He told one friend that he ate the pills "like popcorn" and reassured him that "they won't hurt you." But he also complained that Dexedrine gave him terrible headaches; in a letter that he would leave beside the body of his wife, he indicated that he'd "consumed two large bottles of Excedrin in the last three months" for headache pain. Since Whitman evidently didn't see a doctor for refills, he must have been getting the amphetamines through illegal channels. Apparently he had no trouble obtaining them; he kept a regular pharmacy in his black attaché case: amphetamines, tranquilizers to calm him down, and Excedrin for the drug-induced headaches.

Toward the end of the spring semester of 1966, Whitman's parents separated, adding more pressure to his life. He drove to Florida to fetch his mother. He was so afraid that his father would resort to violence against both of them that he summoned a local policeman, who sat in a patrol car at the curb while Margaret Whitman finished packing her belongings. Back in Austin, Charlie assumed the burden of keeping his mother's spirits up. And as the oldest son, he had to be concerned as well about his brother John, who had left home and was living with teenage friends. Shortly after his parents' separation, John was arrested for throwing a rock through a florist's shop window. Given a choice between going back home to live with his father or paying a $25 fine, he chose to pay the fine.

Soon Charlie and his mother were getting regular calls from the elder Whitman. "I'm not ashamed of the fact I spent a thousand dollars a month on the phone bill, begging her to come back," he told a reporter. "I loved my wife dearly, my sons dearly, and I wanted our home to be happy. I kept begging Charlie to come back to me too. I promised Charlie that if he'd only persuade his Mama to come back, I'd swear never to lay a hand on her. But my wife was a fine woman, and she understood my nature, and even when she left me in May—we'd had a clash—she said to me, 'I'm leaving because you've been too good to us all.' She told me that maybe that was where the thing had gone wrong."

Family problems, school problems, drug problems, and overwork were all bearing down: Whitman was nearing a breaking point. He was falling behind in his studies, and he asked Riley, his architecture instructor, for extra time to finish a design project. Riley granted the request, but Whitman was still unable to complete the work. In considerable agitation, he called Riley at 10:30 one Friday night and said that he needed to see him. "He walked into my living room with a bundle of papers and dropped them on the middle of the living room floor," Riley remembered. "He was perspiring. I could see that he was under strain and I asked, 'What's the trouble, Charlie?' He answered he was carrying too much. He blurted out, 'I've got problems.' He said, 'I just despise my father. I hate him. If my father walked through that door, I'd kill him.' " The two talked quietly for a while and Whitman calmed down. Then he began staring at the baby grand piano. "I can't resist it anymore," he said and walked over to the instrument. Whitman crashed into the usually soft and lyrical "Clair de Lune," playing so loudly that he woke Riley's wife. "The music seemed to relax him," Riley said.

The relief that came from his visit to his teacher was short-lived, and Whitman soon reverted to his extreme agitation. He abruptly made up his mind to quit school. He sold his books and his slide rule. "He was giving away everything he could," recalled Larry Fuess. "I walked into Charlie's one morning and he was packing his bags. He said he was going to leave everything—school, his wife, everything—and become a bum. He said he didn't know why, he just had to do it. He kept talking about his parents separating. He had something personal to settle, to let loose. He didn't want his wife to see what it was." Yet as clearly upset as he was, Whitman was also strangely calm, even deliberate. That afternoon he told Kathy he was leaving her. Later they went to the Fuesses' apartment, and Kathy kept asking, "But Charlie, why, why?" He couldn't answer; he only shook his head.

Alarmed by Whitman's behavior, Fuess got Riley on the phone and told him what had happened. A tough ex-Marine who'd fought on Iwo Jima, Riley was upset at his student's apparent intention to throw away both his wife and his college career. Although it was late at night, he called Whitman. "This is ridiculous," Riley snapped. "You are not going to do it." The teacher told Whitman to skip the classes that he taught until he caught up in the other subjects, then return and buckle down. Whitman said,

Some two months before his shooting spree, Whitman *(far right)* looks relaxed as he sits at the dinner table with his wife, Kathy, and friend Larry Fuess.

"Yes, sir." Whitman called Fuess and said, "I'll be there tomorrow." The next day Whitman saw Riley. He grinned. "Thank you, sir," he said. His decision to leave had been made instantly. His decision to stay was just as quick. Then, as if nothing had happened, Whitman went on to recoup his class position and emerge with excellent grades. The episode left Fuess and Riley puzzled.

Whitman was managing to cover up his problems but not to rid himself of them. His wife knew how truly depressed he could get; she'd been afraid to leave him alone on several occasions when his spirits ebbed. She also knew that their marriage was very troubled. There's no doubt that Whitman loved her, but he'd wondered, as early as 1964, whether his dependency on her "is good found in a man" and whether he might be "harmed" by it. At times he also wondered if he would ever become a father; he told a friend that he thought he might be sterile. Perhaps because of his growing dependency or the tensions building inside him or a combination of both, Whitman sometimes got violently angry with Kathy, and on two occasions he beat her. He apparently detested himself for this behavior, which reminded him of his father's treatment of his mother. According to one acquaintance "he was mortally afraid of being like his father," and Kathy confided to a friend that he hated himself when he abused her. He was enough disturbed by the problem to make a list of goals for bettering the marital relationship, titled "Good points to remember with Kathy"— "Don't nag." "Don't try to make your partner over." "Don't criticize." "Give honest appreciation." "Pay little attentions." "Be courteous." "Be gentle." And he tried to follow his own advice, right up until the night he killed her.

Just four months before the killings, Kathy was so worried about her husband's mood swings and erratic behavior that she urged him to go to the Student Health Center and talk to Dr. Maurice Dean Heatly, the part-time campus psychiatrist. Whitman did go, and he spent a couple of hours describing his problems to the doctor. Heatly asked him to come back in a week and to call him in the meantime if he felt a need to talk. Whitman chose to do neither. "After one session, I never saw the Doctor again," he wrote later, "and since then I have been fighting my mental turmoil alone, and seemingly to no avail."

Although he was carrying a work load of 14 credits in the summer session— heavy by anyone's standard—Whitman took a part-time job on a university research project and impressed his boss as being "an unusually good worker." In fact he was at the edge. Only days before going to the tower with his arsenal, Whitman resurrected a poem he'd written in 1964 and scribbled across the top of it that he was having the same feelings that he'd had then:

"To maintain sensibility is the greatest effort required.

"To slip would be so easy. It would be accomplished with little effort.

"Yet, to maintain is necessary in order to benefit from the future.

"Of what benefit?

"Will benefit be derived from the future?

"To burden others with your problems—are they problems—is not right.

"However, to carry them is akin to carrying a fused bomb.

"I wonder if the fuse can be doused.

"If it is doused, what will be gained?

"Will the gain be worth the effort put forth?

"But should one who considers himself strong surrender to enemies he considers so trivial and despicable?"

The fuse was burning. Life had no meaning. And if life had no meaning, what did it matter whom he took with him into death? On July 31, Whitman's last day but one, the temperature climbed to over 100 degrees. At 6:45 p.m., while his wife was at work at the telephone company, Whitman sat down at the typewriter to compose a two-page letter "To Whom It May Concern," writing as if he'd already carried out the murders. "I don't know what compels me to type this letter," he began. "Perhaps it is to leave some vague reason for the actions I have recently performed. I don't really understand myself these days. I am supposed to be an average reasonable and intelligent young man. However, lately (I can't recall when it started) I have been a victim of many unusual and irrational thoughts. These thoughts constantly recur, and it requires a tremendous mental effort to concentrate on useful and progressive tasks.

"I've been to a psychiatrist. I've been having fears and violent impulses. I've had some tremendous headaches in the past."

Whitman then went on to reveal part of his plan: "It was after much thought that I decided to kill my wife, Kathy, tonight after I pick her up from work at the telephone company. I love her dearly, and she has been as fine a wife to me as any man could ever hope to have. I cannot rationally pinpoint any specific reason for doing this. I don't know whether it is selfishness, or if I don't want her to have to face the embrassment my actions would surely cause her. At this time, though, the prominent reason in my mind is that I truly do not consider this world worth living in, and am prepared to die, and I do not want to leave her to suffer alone in it. I intend to kill her as painlessly as possible.

"Similar reasons provoked me to take my mother's life also. I don't think the poor woman has ever enjoyed life as she is entitled to. She is a simple young woman who married a very possessive and dominating man."

But then the arrival of close friends Larry and Elaine Fuess caused him to put his letter aside. When they came in for a chat his typewriter was set out and he said casually, "I was writing to a friend in Washington whom I haven't seen in five years." But the machine was empty, and there was only blank paper beside it. The visitors found Whitman in good spirits—inexplicably good, as Larry Fuess saw it, since Whitman had two tests the next day and was usually very tense before exams. The tests came up in their conversation, and Whitman said matter-of-factly that he hadn't covered the work and didn't intend to take the tests. Fuess would recall later that Whitman "was particularly relieved about something—you know, as if he had solved a problem." Noting that Whitman was no longer biting his nails, he commented on it to him; his friend merely grinned. According to Fuess the habit had bothered Whitman "because he felt it wasn't manly."

Elaine Fuess thought it odd that Whitman spoke of Kathy with much more sentimentality than usual. "You don't sit in front of your best friends and just moon over your wife," she said. "He was unusually tender." Twice Whitman said, "It's a shame that she should have to work all day and then come home to . . ." Neither time did he finish his sentence.

The three friends spent a couple of hours talking. In the course of their conversation, Whitman revealed that earlier in the day he'd signed a $750 contract to buy a piece of land on Canyon Lake some 50 miles northwest of Austin. This puzzled Larry Fuess because he knew that Whitman and Kathy were living on a tight budget. "But he said he had to do it," Fuess said. "Charlie never made a move that was involuntary. He was like that. He'd set up tasks for himself—like taking a heavy schedule in school or getting an A in a course—and then he'd do them. Once he had decided, you couldn't change his mind."

At one point the conversation shifted to a discussion of the war in Vietnam. Fuess remembered that Whitman said "he couldn't understand why boys from the United States had to go over there and die for something they didn't have anything to do with."

After the Fuesses left, Whitman, who had so successfully hidden his despair from his friends, went out to pick up Kathy. She'd worked a split shift, and during the afternoon break her husband had taken her to dinner and a movie. Before leaving the telephone company at 9:30, as a full moon climbed into the sky above Austin, she remarked to a coworker that she hoped she and Charlie wouldn't be stopping off at Dunkin' Donuts, as they'd done occasionally during the last few weeks; doughnuts "are ruining my diet," she said. In truth, she was more worried about Whitman's weight than her own; she'd recently told a friend that ever since her mother-in-law had come to town, Charlie had been putting on pounds, seduced by the sweets Mrs. Whitman kept in her apartment for him.

Kathy retired early. Around 10:30 the telephone rang. Whitman answered; it was his mother, letting him know that she'd gone to a friend's place for ice cream. Whitman told her that it was too stifling in the house for him to study and asked if he could come over and use her air-conditioned apartment. Ever eager to help out her oldest boy, she rushed home and was waiting for him when he arrived. He was carrying a black attaché case—it would turn up in the trunk of his car the next day—with a five-foot length of rubber

Left margin caption:

Whitman typed the first part of a two-page letter *(right)* explaining his motives for murder before he killed his mother and his wife. After those murders, he finished the letter in a shaky scrawl and left it at his house for police to find. He had already posted a note *(below)* on his mother's apartment door to delay the discovery of her body.

Sunday
July 31, 1966
6:45 P.M.

I don't quite understand what it is that compels me to type this letter. Perhaps it is to leave some vague reason for the actions I have recently performed. I don't really understand myself these days. I am supposed to be an average reasonable and intelligent young man. However, lately (I can't recall when it started) I have been a victim of many unusual and irrational thoughts. These thoughts constantly recur, and it requires a tremendous mental effort to concentrate on useful and progressive tasks. In March when my parents made a physical break I noticed a great deal of stress. I consulted a Dr. Cochrum at the University Health Center and asked him to recommend someone that I could consult with about some psychiatric disorders I felt I had. I talked with a Doctor once for about two hours and tried to convey to him my fears that I felt come overwhelming violent impulses. After one session I never saw the Doctor again, and since then I have been fighting my mental turmoil alone, and seemingly to no avail. After my death I wish that an autopsy would be performed on me to see if there is any visible physical disorder. I have had some tremendous headaches in the past and have consumed two large bottles of Excedrin in the past three months.

It was after much thought that I decided to kill my wife, Kathy, tonight after I pick her up from work at the telephone company. I love her dearly, and she has been as fine a wife to me as any man could ever hope to have. I cannot rationally pinpoint any specific reason for doing this. I don't know whether it is selfishness, or if I don't want her to have to face the embrassment my actions would surely cause her. AT this time, though, the prominent reason in my mind is that I truly do not consider this world worth living in, and am prepared to die, and I do not want to leave her to suffer alone in it. I intend to kill her as painlessly as possible.

Similar reasons provoked me to take my mother's life also. I don't think the poor woman has ever enjoyed life as she is entitled to. She was a simple young woman who married a very possessive and dominating man. All my life as a boy until I ran away from home to join the Marine Corps

---

(handwritten left margin note)

Friends interrupted 8-1-66 Mon. 3:00 A.M. Both Dead

(handwritten continuation of letter)

I was a witness to her being beat at least once a month. Then when she took enough my father wanted to fight to keep her below her usual standard of living.

I imagine it appears that I brutally kill both of my loved ones. I was only trying to do a quick thorough job.

m 908158

...autopsy...

Maybe research can prevent further tragedies of this type.

Charles J. Whitman

Give our dog to my in-laws please. Tell them Kathy loved "Schocie" very much.

R. W. Leissner
Needville, Texas

If you can find in yourself to grant my last wish Cremate me after the autopsy.

(handwritten note, lower left — posted on mother's door)

Roy,

I dont have to be to work today, and I was up late last night. I would like to get some rest. Please do not disturb me.

Thank You.

Mrs Whitman

hose inside. Proudly she introduced Whitman to the night watchman as "my Charlie."

Once inside the apartment, Whitman wasted no time; he wanted to finish the deed quickly. Apparently Margaret Whitman tried to run from her son. When police found her body the next afternoon, the fingers of her left hand had been crushed as though a door had been slammed on them, and the diamond had been knocked from her engagement ring. Whitman placed his mother's body on the bed and covered it with sheets. Taking a piece of lined yellow legal paper, he penned a note in neat handwriting and left it beside the bed:

"I have just taken my mother's life," he wrote. "I am very upset over having done it. However I feel that if there is a heaven, she is definitely there now, and if there is no life after, I have relieved her of her suffering here on earth.

"The intense hatred I feel for my father is beyond description. My mother gave that man the 25 best years of her life and because she finally took enough of his beatings, humiliation, degredation, and tribulations that I am sure no one but she and he will ever know—to leave him. He has chosen to treat her like a slut that you would bed down with, accept her favors and then throw a pittance in return. I am truly sorry that this is the only way I could see to relieve her suffering but I think it was best. Let there be no doubt in your mind that I loved the woman with all my heart. If there exists a God, let him understand my actions and judge me accordingly."

Before leaving the apartment, Whitman affixed a note, supposedly from his mother, to the outside of her door, addressed to Roy, the porter. It said that she was resting and didn't want to be disturbed.

Whitman returned to his house and plunged his bayonet into Kathy's chest as she slept. She died instantly. He pulled the sheet up over her naked body.

Now Whitman resumed the letter that the Fuesses' visit had cut short the night before. He used a ballpoint pen instead of his typewriter. At the point where he'd left off, he jotted: "Friends interrupted. 8-1-66. 3 a.m. Both dead." His handwriting had deteriorated into such a scrawl that police would have a hard time deciphering the rest of the note:

"I imagine that it appears that I brutally killed both my loved ones. I was only trying to do a quick, thorough job.

"If my life insurance policy is valid, please see that all the worthless checks I wrote this weekend are made good.

Please pay off my debts. I am 25 years old and have been financially independent.

"Donate the rest anonymously to a mental health foundation. Maybe research can prevent further tragedies of this type.

"Give our dog to my in-laws, please. Tell them Kathy loved 'Schocie' very much.

"If you can find it in yourself to grant my last wish, cremate me after the autopsy."

Whitman then went on to scribble two additional letters, one to his father, the contents of which have never been revealed, and one to his younger brother. "Dear Johnnie," he wrote to the boy he'd taken up on the tower less than two weeks before, "I am terribly sorry to have to let you down. Please try to do better than I have. It won't be hard, John, Mom loved you very much. Your brother, Charlie."

Something now prompted Whitman to go back to his mother's apartment. He didn't have a key and had to be let in. He told the watchman that Mrs. Whitman was sick and needed to have a prescription filled. The man waited in the hall. Whitman emerged, holding up a pill bottle for him to see. What the bottle contained no one is certain, although in the light of subsequent evidence, investigators conjectured that it held Dexedrine. They believed that Whitman inadvertently left the pills behind after the murder and then returned to the apartment to get them.

At some point in the early morning hours, before leaving his house with his guns to drive to the tower, Whitman paused long enough to reread his "Thoughts to Start the Day," a collection of admonitions to himself. On the envelope that contained them, he wrote: "8-1-66. I never could quite make it. These thoughts are too much for me."

And what were they? "Read and think about every day." "Stop procrastinating. Grasp the nettle." "Control your anger. Don't let it prove you the fool." "Smile, it's contagious." "Don't be belligerent." "Stop cursing. Improve your vocabulary." "Approach a pot of gold with exceptional caution. Look it over twice." "Pay that compliment." "Listen more than you speak. Think before you speak." "Control your passion. Don't let it lead you." "Don't let desire make you regret your present actions later." "Remember the lad and the man." "If you want to be better than average, you have to work much harder than the average." "Never forget that when the going gets rough, the rough get going." "Yesterday is not mine to recover." "To-

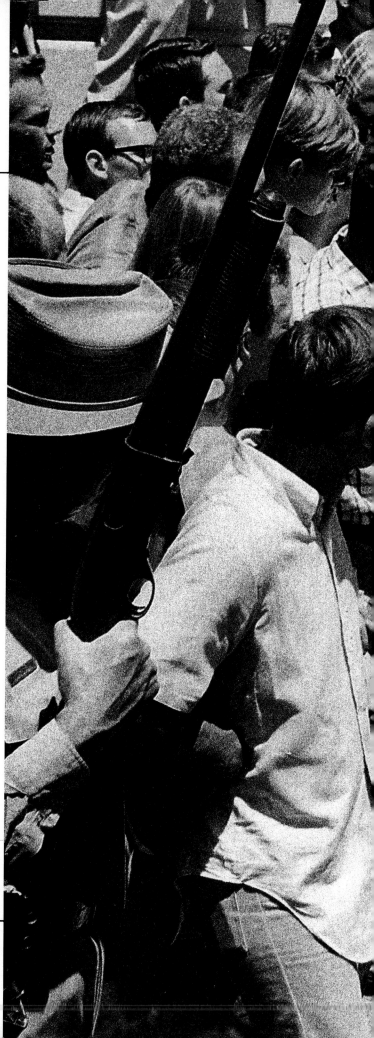

morrow is mine to win or to lose. I'm resolved that I should win the tomorrow before me." For Whitman, there would be no tomorrow.

When the shooting started, Larry Fuess was on campus. As the dead and wounded fell to the ground, he crouched by a building and wondered, as did everyone else, who in God's name was up there. Charlie Whitman sprang to mind, and Fuess was instantly ashamed that he could think such a thing. When the shooting finally stopped, Fuess saw his friend's body being carried from the tower.

News of the shootings spread far and wide. People across the country wanted to know why the massacre had happened, what kind of a person the killer was, and what had driven him over the edge. Many conjectured that Whitman's drug habit was to blame. Found in one of his pockets atop the tower was a metal tube filled with Dexedrine and Excedrin. But whether Whitman actually took Dexedrine before his rampage will never be known. Within hours of his death his body was embalmed on orders of Justice of the Peace Jerry Dellana, the acting coroner. When Dr. Coloman de Chenar, a pathologist and neuropathologist, performed an autopsy on Whitman 24 hours later, the killer's blood, urine, and stomach contents had already been discarded. Using the little blood that still remained in the corpse, de Chenar analyzed it to learn whether Whitman had been drinking before the shootings and found that he had not. But not enough blood was left over to test for the presence of the drug.

The autopsy did, however, turn up something else: a tumor the size of a pecan "in the white matter above the brain stem." There was no evidence, according to the autopsy report, of "malignantly fast growth" and "no correlation to psychosis or permanent pains." In a press conference announcing the findings, de Chenar, who considered the killer "a walking charge of dynamite waiting for a spark," said that "Whitman would have done what he did regardless of the tumor. It did not cause the severe headaches. It did not cause pain because it was not connected to the sensory nerves." Yet when questioned, de Chenar seemed to contradict himself. He conceded that the tumor "could have caused pressure which would have resulted in intense pain and headaches" and that it "could have indirectly caused or contributed to Whitman's actions." This last contention was supported by the 32-man panel of experts that Gov-

ernor John Connally subsequently appointed to conduct a posthumous medical and psychiatric study of Whitman. De Chenar also indicated that while there was no evidence of Whitman's having acted under the influence of Dexedrine, the use of amphetamines could "cause more rapid reaction, more intense readiness to react, reduce the logical control of the acts, speed up the association of ideas and reduce the person's capability to act soberly."

Perhaps the most startling testimony came on the day after the violence, when the balding, bespectacled Dr. Heatly, the part-time campus psychiatrist, stood behind nine microphones and under the glare of six television cameras and told a nationwide audience about Whitman's visit to his office: "He was a large, muscular youth who looked every bit a professional ball player, an energetic, active Marine, which he had once been. There was something about him that suggested and expressed the All-American Boy. He was ruddy complected." Yet, the doctor went on, he "seemed to be oozing with hostility."

Whitman had started the session by telling Heatly that something was happening to him—he did not seem to be himself. He described his father as brutal and confessed that he himself had beaten his wife on two occasions. Recalling his parents' separation, Whitman told how his mother had "summoned" him to the family home to take her to Austin and how his father had called Whitman every couple of days trying to get the son to persuade his mother to return to Florida.

Then the doctor began to read from the memorandum he'd written shortly after Whitman's visit. Whitman "readily admits having overwhelming periods of hostility with a very minimum of provocation," the memo said. "Repeated inquiries attempting to analyze his exact experiences were not too successful with the exception of his vivid reference to 'thinking about going up on the tower with a deer rifle and start shooting people.'" The astonished reporters asked Heatly to repeat the quote, which he did.

Obviously aware of the implications for himself, Heatly said that Whitman's statement about going to the tower and shooting people had not unduly alarmed him at the time; patients often make sweeping statements of general hostility, and the tower had evoked its share of violent fantasies; indeed, as the records showed, three students had jumped to their death from it.

Questioned whether he did not consider Whitman a po-

tential menace to the community after hearing such a statement, Heatly replied: "I think it's possible anyone in this room could be a threat to the community in the next 24 hours as far as possibilities are concerned."

The following day, Texas newspapers reported another murder, this one in the town of Sweetwater. The town marshal had been killed by a 15-year-old boy who'd developed "an urge to kill" after listening to accounts of two events: the Whitman killings and the murders less than a month earlier of eight student nurses in Chicago by a lowlife drifter named Richard Speck (pages 6-29). "I know it sounds crazy," the tall, sandy-haired youth said, "but I couldn't stop myself."

Seven years later the Associated Press sent a story out on its newswire: "Lake Worth, Fla. July 4. John M. Whitman, 24 years old, whose brother killed 16 persons in the University of Texas tower incident, was shot to death after a quarrel in a bar here last night.

"A Lake Worth police sergeant, Bill Openshaw, who knew the family, said that John Whitman went to the bar last night after a day of studying for examinations. 'There were a lot of kids in the bar,' Sergeant Openshaw said. 'An argument broke out. We don't know over what. We don't know whether Whitman was involved or just an innocent bystander.'"

Years later, on the 20th anniversary of the Austin massacre, the elder Whitman, who had remarried and admitted to having beaten his second wife, was asked whether Charlie's intention on August 1, 1966, was to punish him.

"Yes," Whitman replied, "he's punishing not in the way you'd say with a stick or anything like that, he's punishing me in the fact that I had to let the world know that if I did wrong, I'm sorry for it. I did the best a father could do and I saw no wrong in what I was doing. I have tried to rack my brains and asked not only preachers, lawyers, psychiatrists, everybody, 'Where did I go wrong?' The people who know me here—the chief of police in the town where Charlie was raised and all the principals of the schools that he was at—could not give me any answers other than, 'You cannot be responsible. You cannot be to blame for it.'

"Yes, it hurt deeply," the father said. "It always has and there always will be a hurt there. But I don't feel in any way that I was responsible for any of it. I don't feel in any way that Charlie was responsible for his actions, either." ◆

Days of Rage

There comes a day when a man's fury, his hunger for revenge, for righting the real or imagined wrongs done to him, may finally erupt into a deadly rage. Payback Day, one murderer in the grim gallery on the following pages called it — the day to get even, the day to kill, and maybe the day to die.

Most of the killers whose stories are told here were planners for a Payback Day. They drew up lists of enemies, mulled over the time to strike, assembled overkill arsenals, and even picked out a costume for the bloody occasion. One of these careful sorts, a vicious slip of a boy and at 18 the youngest of them, spent his whole adolescence dreaming of murder. Others were less methodical, more spontaneous, and struck like lightning from a clear sky. But they could be just as lethal. In all, the 14 murderers introduced here imposed a terrible toll, together killing a total of 123 people. In seven of the cases, the killer's tally included himself.

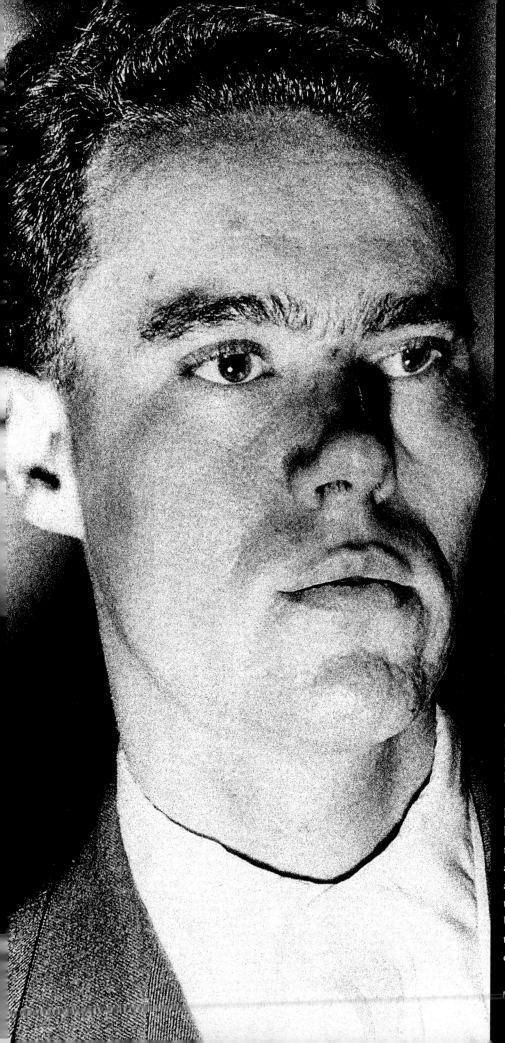

Hometown Boy

In German, *Unruh* means "unrest." In the case of Howard Unruh, the name mean something far worse: "dementia praecox mixed type, with pronounced catatonic and paranoid coloring." In the psychiatric jargon of the day, these phrases meant tha Unruh had withdrawn from reality into a world of delusion and hallucination. The diagnosis was made after Unruh was arrested for shooting 13 people to death during a 12-minute walk through his neighborhood in Camden, New Jersey. The walk was brief but epic, for it established Unruh as the first of America's modern mass murderers.

Looking more like a banker than a murderer, the 28-year-old Unruh was nicely turned out for his lethal stroll that sunny Tuesday morning of September 6, 1949 He wore a brown tropical worsted suit, a white shirt, and a striped bow tie; the dissonant item of the costume was the 9-mm Luger in his hand. He went about his business of shooting people with calculated coolness. "I had been thinking about killing them for some time," he later explained, on his way to spending the rest o his life among the criminally insane.

Convinced that some of his neighbors had been slandering him, Unruh had been keeping a grudge list. Next to an offender' name he recorded the particular misdeed—a snub, a harsh word, an imagined sneer—along with the notation "retal"—for "retaliation." The supposed wrongdoers on Unruh's list made up part of his toll of victims, but not all. He killed others, even children if they happened to be available.

Unruh's dissolution into paranoic schizophrenia was a slow one, doctors con cluded. He'd been a quiet, moody youth, but still in most ways a model boy. He faithfully attended the Lutheran church and studied scripture. When World War II began, Unruh patriotically joined the army. When other soldiers left the barracks to chase girls, he stayed behind to read his Bible—and to care for his rifle, cleaning it, taking it apart, fondling it, reassembling it.

War proved to be the young man's cup of tea. A fearless fighter, he saw a good deal of combat as a tank gunner in Italy and France. A fellow soldier who found a diary Unruh kept was shocked by its contents. The methodical marksman listed the Germans he had killed, by date, hour, and place. If he had the opportunity to view a dead target, he added notes about the body's appearance. Honorably discharged in 1945, Unruh returned home with a collection of souvenir firearms and became a virtual recluse in his parents' house. He seldom spoke, and his principal recreation was target shooting in the basement. Along with shooting, he continued to keep score. Just as he'd tallied his dead Germans, he began tallying insults.

Around the backyard the recluse built a fence with a massive, elaborate gate. During the night of September 5, someone stole the gate. For most people the theft would have been an annoying, even infuriating act of vandalism. For Unruh, it was the trigger to kill.

His mother sensed at breakfast that something had gone awry with him. He stared at her, seething, then picked up a wrench and threatened her. She fled to a neighbor's house. Vaulting the backyard fence and cutting through to a nearby street, Unruh walked several doors to a small shoe shop. School was about to begin, and owner John Pilarchik was repairing children's shoes. He looked up to see Unruh lifting the Luger.

Leaving Pilarchik dead, the gunman entered Clark Hoover's barbershop next door. Seated on a hobbyhorse, six-year-old Orris Smith was getting his back-to-school haircut, as his mother and sister watched. "I've got something for you, Clarkie," Unruh said. When Hoover saw the Luger, he moved to shield the child. Unruh shot the boy in the head, killing him instantly. Then he felled Hoover.

From the barbershop Unruh headed for the corner drugstore owned by the Cohens, hated neighbors who had told him not to walk through their backyard. James Hutton, the Unruh family's insurance agent, was just coming out of the drugstore. He greeted Unruh, whom he'd known since boyhood. Hutton was not on the enemy list, but Unruh shot him dead.

From inside, Maurice Cohen had been watching. He ran upstairs to the family's apartment with Unruh in pursuit. As he passed a closet, Unruh heard a sound and fired twice, then opened the door to find Cohen's wife, Rose. He put a shot into her head, killing her. Minnie Cohen, Maurice's mother, was in the kitchen trying to call police when she was killed. Maurice slipped through a window and was scrambling across a roof when Unruh spotted him and fired. Wounded, Cohen fell to the

sidewalk, and Unruh leaned out a window to shoot him a second time, killing him. Unruh missed 13-year-old Charles Cohen, whose mother had hidden him in a closet.

Back on the street, the killer fatally shot a motorist who had stopped and was bending over James Hutton. A car carrying three strangers was waiting at a traffic light. Reloading, Unruh strolled to the car, leaned in, and killed the driver, her son, and her mother in the backseat. He wounded a trucker, then went into the tailor's shop and killed the tailor's wife, Helga Zegrino, as she knelt and begged, "Oh, my God, don't." Continuing his walk, Unruh saw two-year-old Tommy Hamilton looking out a front window of his house and shot him. The little boy was Unruh's 13th and last victim.

Another half block, and Unruh was back home. Police were already surrounding the house when the telephone rang. The caller, the assistant city editor of the local newspaper, told Unruh, "I'm a friend and I want to know what they are doing to you."

"Well, they haven't done much to me yet, but I'm doing plenty to them," Unruh said.

"How many have you killed?" the editor asked.

"I don't know yet—I haven't counted them, but it looks like a pretty good score."

"Why are you killing people, Howard?"

"I don't know. I can't answer that yet—I'm too busy. I'll have to talk to you later."

The tear gas filling the house flushed Unruh outside, and he saw 50 guns trained on him. He offered no resistance, but he took offense when a policeman questioned his motives. "What's the matter with you?" the officer asked. "Are you a psycho?"

"I'm no psycho," Unruh sniffed. "I have a good mind." ◆

A barbershop hobbyhorse that helped distract youngsters during haircuts stands sentinel over a blood-splattered floor in the wake of Howard Unruh's rampage. Six-year-old Orris Smith, the second of Unruh's 13 victims, was sitting on the horse when Unruh shot him.

Deadly Ambitions

Robert Smith was laughing when the first policeman walked into the Rose-Mar College of Beauty in Mesa, Arizona, on the crisp morning of November 12, 1966. "I shot some people," said the slight, handsome high-school senior, pointing toward the rear of the shop. "They're back there. The gun is in that brown bag."

Four women and a three-year-old girl lay dead or dying in the beauty college's back room. The child had been stabbed as well as shot because, as Smith explained, she "kept jumping around" after he shot her. One other woman and a three-month-old baby were badly wounded. The reason for the carnage: "I wanted to make a name for myself," Smith told the horrified officer. "I wanted people to know who I was."

Smith's big day had been a long time in the making. He'd been mulling the possibilities of murder since he was 13, and in the months preceding the killings he'd focused on a mass murder. Remarkably, however, his dark obsession stayed well hidden beneath a bland exterior.

Smith kept to himself, had few friends, and never dated. He rarely left home except to go to school, and he spent much of his time alone in his room. Nevertheless, he was a good student, and his classmates respected his intelligence and elected him to the student council. Smith's antisocial leanings might have been ascribed in part to his being new at the school. His family had moved to Mesa from Maryland only a year earlier; Robert's father, a retired air force major, worked at an electronics plant in nearby Phoenix.

However unremarkable his exterior life, a horror show played continuously in Smith's head. Doctors would later describe him as schizophrenic. According to a court-appointed psychiatrist, the boy felt that "he was like a god, cut out to be some kind of ruler over other people." The psychiatrist went on to say that the boy was almost wholly without feelings for others, including his own family. Smith had seriously considered killing his father, on one occasion lying in wait for him with a knife.

Smith's homicidal leanings also colored his sexuality; he entertained fantasies in which women were shot or stabbed. Had his parents been aware of such notions, they might not have given him a .22-caliber pistol for target shooting when he turned 18 in August of 1966.

That summer was a bloody one: Richard Speck killed eight nurses on a single night in Chicago *(pages 6-29),* and Charles Whitman murdered 15 people in Austin, Texas *(pages 30-56).* Perhaps spurred by their examples, Smith spent three months plotting his own crime. He wanted to kill at least 40 people and considered going after the teachers at his school before settling on the Rose-Mar, a convenient mile and a half from his home.

The night before the killings, Smith helped his six-year-old sister write a letter to Santa Claus. Then he packed his pistol, 200 feet of nylon cord, rubber gloves, two hunting knives, and extra bullets into a brown paper bag. His equipment had also included plastic sandwich bags with which to suffocate his victims, but after buying the bags, he realized that they were much too small to fit over women's heads.

The .22 was in Smith's hand when he walked through the front door of the Rose-Mar shortly after the beauty college opened. He was so young and small that when he brandished the weapon the five women in the shop thought he must be joking. When he fired a shot into a mirror, they realized he meant business. Laughing frequently and talking as if "he was weak in the head," according to a survivor, Smith herded the women and two children into the back room, where he ordered them to lie down with their heads together, creating an arrangement resembling spokes in a wheel. Still not convinced he was serious, one woman asked, "Are you kidding?" He put his gun to another woman's head as he asked, "Do you think I am?" Another of Smith's prisoners told him that 40 people would arrive at the school shortly. "I'm sorry," he replied, "but I didn't bring enough ammunition for them."

When one of the women began praying, Smith asked angrily what she was doing. "She's praying, if you don't mind," another woman said. "I do," said Smith, and he began firing, shooting each woman in the head. When blood began to flow from Glenda Carter's fatal wound, beautician Bonita Sue Harris could feel it. After Smith shot her in turn, once in the head and once in the arm, Harris pretended to be dead until the police arrived.

After his arrest, Smith admitted he had not expected to find children at the beauty college, but he took their presence in stride. When asked why he shot the baby, he said, "Well, it was going to grow up and become an adult." He declared that he would have killed his sister and mother had they been there. Voicing no regret, Smith said he'd felt exhilarated during the killings.

Guilt for the killings was shouldered by Smith's parents. Finding his son's bed empty that morning, the elder Smith had gone to the police to report Robert missing. If the father had had a premonition of something dreadful, it was quickly borne out. When he arrived at the station at 9:30 a.m., reports of the killings were already on the radio. "I told him we had his boy, and he began to cry and shake," recalled an officer. The father said, "I was afraid of that."

On October 24, 1967, Robert Smith was found guilty of first-degree murder and sentenced to death. Because the U.S. Supreme Court declared a moratorium on the death penalty in 1972, Smith escaped execution. But the other sentences imposed on him—two 99-year terms and four for life—will keep him in jail for good. ◆

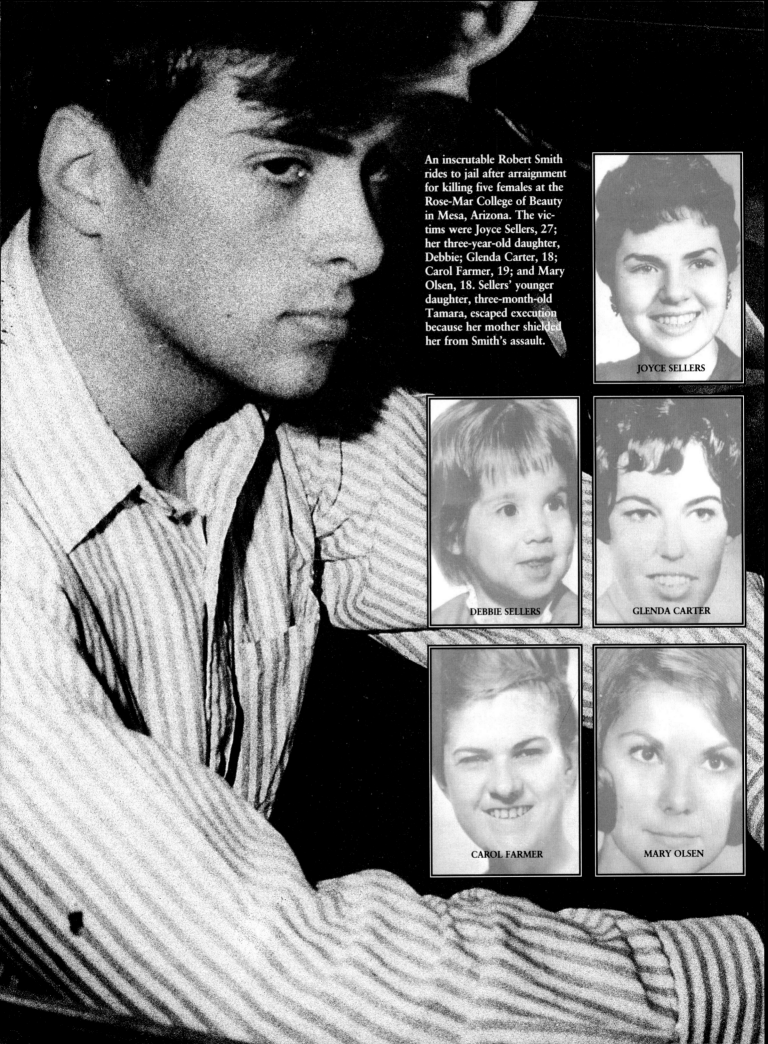

An inscrutable Robert Smith rides to jail after arraignment for killing five females at the Rose-Mar College of Beauty in Mesa, Arizona. The victims were Joyce Sellers, 27; her three-year-old daughter, Debbie; Glenda Carter, 18; Carol Farmer, 19; and Mary Olsen, 18. Sellers' younger daughter, three-month-old Tamara, escaped execution because her mother shielded her from Smith's assault.

JOYCE SELLERS

DEBBIE SELLERS

GLENDA CARTER

CAROL FARMER

MARY OLSEN

Pillar of the Community

The smell of burning leaves was in the air, and the hunters of the tiny Appalachian village of Loganton, Pennsylvania, were thinking about deer season, just a few weeks off. But Leo Held, crack shot and model citizen, had other quarry on his mind. Held left home the morning of Octo-ber 24, 1967, having just seen his children off to school and his wife to work. An hour and a half later, he was being rushed to the hospital with wounds sustained in a shoot-out with police. With grim efficiency, Held had killed six people and wounded another half-dozen coworkers and neighbors.

"Murderer" was certainly not the word that leapt to mind to describe Leo Held. Married and the father of four, the 39-year-old laboratory technician at the Ham-mermill Paper Company had 21 years on the job and was known as a solid citizen — scout leader, school board member, churchgoer, volunteer fireman. Despite those credentials, Held had mayhem in mind on that fatal fall morning when he drove the 18 miles to the mill at Lock Ha-ven. Shortly before 8 a.m. he strode into the mill, a .38 revolver in one hand and a .44 magnum in the other. Moving swiftly and efficiently, apparently picking and choosing his victims, he gunned down three supervisors and two fellow lab tech-nicians. As they fell dead, some 50 other employees ran for cover and cowered in terror behind machinery and desks.

His business at the mill accomplished, Held drove to the Lock Haven airport where his neighbor Geraldine Ramm was a switchboard operator. He shot at her four times, wounding her seriously, then was on

Authorities in Clinton County, Pennsylvania, load the body of Floyd Quiggle into an ambulance. Quiggle's neighbor, Leo Held (inset), killed him because he was angry with Quiggle for burning leaves. Quiggle was one of six victims killed by Held.

the road again heading for Loganton. There he stopped at the house of the Floyd Quiggle family, who were still asleep. Held broke into the house and went upstairs to the master bedroom where he killed Quiggle instantly and wounded his wife in the face and neck. Downstairs again, Held grabbed hunting rifles and ammunition from a gun case. Then, brushing past the Quiggles' four-year-old daughter, he ran across the street to his own house.

Held had hardly gotten past the front door when the police arrived. Moments later he ran out the back door with a pistol and a revolver blazing at his pursuers. An officer returned fire, and Held collapsed, his right thigh shattered. By now both local and state police were on the scene, and they demanded Held's surrender. The prone man snarled "Come and get me," and kept firing. In the end, Held was mortally wounded. He died at the Lock Haven Hospital, too incoherent to answer questions.

However grave their initial shock, Held's neighbors and coworkers were able to piece together some hints of the anger that had simmered behind the murderer's conventional facade. The mental enemies' list that he took to the plant included people whose promotions he envied and supervisors whose authority he resented. Then there had been the Quiggles' burning leaves; Held claimed the family burned the leaves to spite him, knowing he hated the smoke. Geraldine Ramm's offense was dropping out of a carpool because of Held's reckless driving and making no secret of her reason. And even before giving ultimate vent to his rage, Held had allowed occasional glimpses into its depth and madness. He once beat a 71-year-old widow with a tree branch during a quarrel, and in a classic display of paranoia, he believed that his telephone was being tapped.

In the end, Held left no doubt of how completely his fury had consumed him. As he lay dying he murmured to a nurse, "I had one more to go." ◆

Blitzkrieg

It was 7:40 a.m. on Saint Valentine's Day, 1977. Frederick Cowan, a 33-year-old resident of New Rochelle, New York, was on his way to the Neptune Worldwide Moving Company warehouse, where he'd worked for 11 years. Under his military-style khaki shirt he wore a T-shirt emblazoned "White Power." The skull-and-crossbones of a Nazi SS tank division was pinned to his black beret. The trunk of his red 1971 Pontiac GTO was loaded with a .308 rifle, four pistols, a hunting knife, and bandoleers holding hundreds of rounds of ammunition. A sticker on the bumper read, "You'll get my gun when you pry it from my cold, dead fingers."

The bumper sticker was prophetic. At 5:58 p.m. police would find Cowan sprawled in a blood-splattered second-floor office at the warehouse, a pistol still clutched in each hand. He died from a single .45 slug through his temple. It was self-inflicted. Before shooting himself Cowan had shot 10 people. Five died on the spot; a sixth would linger for six weeks.

The shootout stunned many people who knew Cowan—or thought they knew him. Neighbors remembered the ex-GI, a hulking, 250-pound weightlifter, as a quiet young man from a nice family. He lived with his parents, had few friends his own age, and spent much of his spare time with the teenagers of his working-class neighborhood, tossing a football with them, telling them stories about

the army, taking them to stock-car races.

Fred Cowan had been an excellent student at the parochial schools he attended, and he grew up to be a helpful young fellow, the sort who shoveled snow for the neighbor ladies. But there was a dark side to Cowan. "He had a fantasy about being like Hitler," recalled a coworker. "He'd occasionally slap a German tanker's helmet on his head and pretend he was SS."

When police searched Cowan's room after his deadly rampage, they found a trove of Naziana and weapons: photos of Hitler, Nazi flags, several .45-caliber pistols, old muskets, bayonets, machetes. There were also some Nazi books. In one Cowan had written, "There is nothing lower than black and Jewish people unless it's the police who protect them."

At Cowan's neighborhood bar, the Galway, the regulars dismissed him as a crank and tried to avoid him. He talked endlessly of Nazi doctrines, occasionally, with no apparent cause, blurting "Heil Hit-

ler." Once, a drunken Cowan kicked a Labrador puppy in the head, killing it, because it was black. In 1975, two years before his murder spree, Cowan pointed a rifle at a neighbor and threatened to kill her because

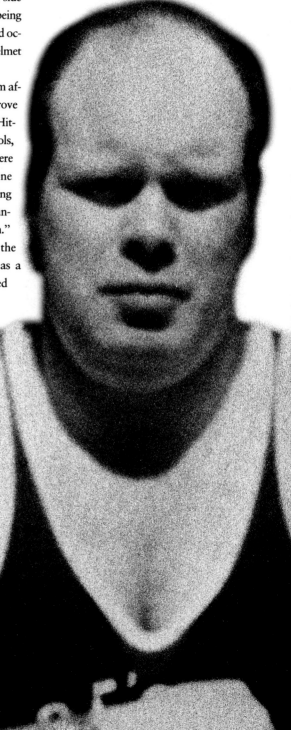

she dated a black man.

Cowan was not much of a romantic. "He said he did not need girls," an acquaintance recalled. He quoted Cowan as saying, "If you want to be a man, get a gun." Once, uncharacteristically, Cowan struck up a conversation with a woman at a bar, only to learn she was Jewish. He was so furious he threw a glass through the screen of the bar's TV set.

In spite of such episodes, the depth of Cowan's rage against Jews and blacks apparently escaped his family and neighbors, who seemed neither to understand it nor to know where it came from. They dismissed his infatuation with Nazism as a hobby he picked up during his army service in Germany. Said a brother after the killings: "We never expected this."

Three of Cowan's victims on February 14 were black, but none was his principal target. What moved him to murder was his long-simmering hatred for his supervisor, traffic manager Norman

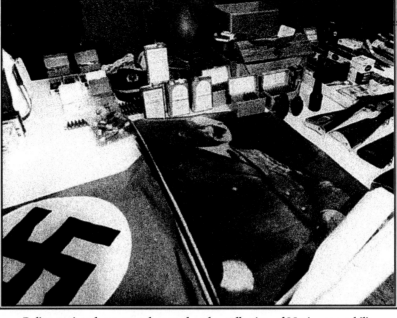

Police retrieved a personal arsenal and a collection of Nazi memorabilia from Frederick Cowan's attic bedroom. Racism underlay Cowan's massacre of six people. He also killed himself.

Bing, a Jew. Bing had recently suspended Cowan for refusing to carry a refrigerator.

Barrelling into the warehouse at 7:45 intent on finding Bing, Cowan encountered Joseph Hicks and Frederick Holmes in the lobby and opened fire with the .308. Next he went after James Green, who had sprinted down a hall. Cowan shot him in the back, killing his third black victim. Moving on to the cafeteria, Cowan shot through the glass doors, spraying the room with bullets and killing Pariyarathu Itty Varghese, a dark-skinned Indian immigrant.

"Where's Norman? I'm going to blow him away," Cowan shouted. Terrified employees ran for cover. Bing, meanwhile, was comparatively safe. He'd happened to glance through a one-way mirror overlooking the entrance just as Cowan entered the warehouse, gun in hand. The supervisor had dashed from his own office into another one, where he hid under the desk.

About 10 minutes after Cowan started shooting, the first police officer arrived. Spotting the shooter, officer Allen McLeod yelled, "Drop that rifle!" Cowan turned and fired, killing McLeod. Three other po-

licemen were wounded as they approached the building. Then Cowan went upstairs, still searching for Bing.

More than 300 lawmen had surrounded the warehouse. Sharpshooters crouched on roofs; helicopters whirred overhead. Via bullhorn, phone, and heating ducts, Cowan's family begged him to surrender. "Pray for Freddie," his mother whispered. "He's gone crazy."

The police were loath to charge the building, fearful that Cowan might be holding hostages. Until around 10 a.m. the gunman kept firing through the windows at nearby houses and businesses, then eased off. At noon Cowan called New Rochelle police headquarters for lunch. "I want potato salad," he told a lieutenant over the phone. "I'm not going to hurt anyone at this point. I get very mean when I'm hungry." He apologized for the "inconvenience" he'd caused.

At 2:23 the police heard a muffled explosion that sounded like a gunshot. Afraid that Cowan had shot a hostage, they decided to sit tight. There was no more firing; still, they waited until dusk to make their move. Then a vanguard of three officers entered the building. Advancing cautiously from room to room, they found 14 scared employees. The last person they came upon was Cowan, dead on the floor of a deserted office with a bullet through his head—the 2:23 explosion.

After bursting so violently into the public eye, Cowan returned to obscurity. He was buried quietly by his family at a location they have steadfastly kept secret. ◆

Proudly exhibiting both his biceps and his tattoos, Frederick Cowan scowls for the camera in a photograph that he sent to a body-building magazine.

PATRICK SHERRILL
JOSEPH HARRIS
THOMAS MCILVANE

Trilogy

Patrick Sherrill, Joseph Harris, and Thomas McIlvane were three murderous peas in a pod—or in a post office. At least in its bare bones, the biography of one was the biography of all: a postal employee fired for poor performance or hanging on to his job by a desperately slender thread; a veteran with a taste for guns; a lonely man nursing a hatred of authority. Oklahoma 1986, New Jersey 1991, Michigan 1991—three places and three times the same terrible scenario was played out in plastic-laminate, government-issue surroundings.

A part-time letter carrier at the post office in Edmond, Oklahoma, Patrick Sherrill had hit bottom on August 20, 1986. The day before, the 44-year-old mailman had been called on the carpet by two supervisors for his poor work. It was not Sherrill's first rebuke. In almost 16 months at Edmond he'd already been suspended twice, once for failing to deliver mail and again for being rude to customers and Macing a dog. Whether he was actually threatened with dismissal is unknown, but Sherrill was alarmed enough to telephone the postal workers' union to ask for a transfer.

Sherrill had nothing and no one to tie him to Edmond. Never married, he'd lived alone after his mother's death in 1978. A pitiable emblem of his solitude was his habit of riding around town alone on a bicycle built for two. But if Sherrill was a sad figure, he could also be an alarming one. He disconcerted his neighbors by peeping through their windows and by scrutinizing

them from a distance through a telescope.

According to a friend from his high-school days in Oklahoma City, Sherrill harbored a dark fear. He confided that his father, who was divorced from his mother, had developed a disabling mental illness in middle age. The boy wondered whether he would be similarly stricken one day.

During a stint in the Marines when he was in his twenties, Sherrill became an excellent marksman. He liked to boast of his service in the Vietnam war, but such tales were pure fabrication. He never went overseas. After his honorable discharge in 1966, Sherrill bounced from job to job, never sticking with any of them for more than nine or 10 months until he was hired by the Edmond post office.

On the morning of August 20, Sherrill dressed in his summer uniform, cooked his breakfast of scrambled eggs, rinsed the dishes, and drove to work. He clocked in at 6:30 a.m. In the mailbag slung over his shoulder were two .45-caliber semiautomatic pistols and about 100 rounds of ammunition. A member of the Oklahoma Air National Guard's marksmanship team, Sherrill had signed one gun out in April and another on August 10 from the guard's armory, supposedly to practice for an upcoming competition. He'd also brought along with him a pair of shooting safety glasses and a set of earplugs.

At approximately seven o'clock that morning Sherrill walked to the office of one of the supervisors who had criticized him the day before. The supervisor had not yet arrived, so Sherrill moved on to target number two. Without uttering a word, the postman drew a .45 from his bag and killed his other critic. He also murdered a mailman at the desk next to the supervisor's.

Murderous postal workers were, left to right, Patrick Sherrill, Joseph Harris, and Thomas McIlvane.

The gunman now stalked through the mazelike work stations in the large one-story building, firing at everyone he encountered. He murdered five people huddling in one cubicle, three in another. After 15 minutes and 14 murders, Sherrill returned to the dead supervisor's desk, seated himself in a chair, and shot himself through the head. He died near his enemy. Six other postal workers, all of them wounded in the chest, survived.

Patrick Sherrill saw to it that he was never fired. Mail clerk Joseph Harris, on the other hand, lost his job at the Ridgewood, New Jersey, post office for threatening his supervisor, then nursed his fury for 18 months before launching his assault. When it came, no one was surprised; Harris had repeatedly shown his bent for violence. "He was always walking around like some karate guy, chopping his hands in the air," one postal worker said. Another recalled how Harris, who worked the night shift for nine years, "would do kung fu stuff in the middle of the night," kicking bags of mail instead of sorting their contents. When Harris was fired in April of 1990, his co-workers feared that their chronically angry

ex-colleague might return to harm them.

The 35-year-old Harris did exactly that. On the night of October 9, 1991, he gathered up an arsenal that included an Uzi assault rifle, a .22-caliber machine gun with a silencer, knives, hand grenades, material for homemade pipe bombs, and a samurai sword and set out to get revenge. But the post office was not his first stop. Shortly before midnight, he broke into the home of his former supervisor. Finding her fiancé watching television, Harris fired one bullet into his head, then went upstairs to the young woman's bedroom. In the course of their violent struggle, Harris fatally stabbed her and slashed her with his sword.

Around 2 a.m. Harris arrived at the Ridgewood post office and shot dead the two mail handlers who'd just come on duty. A driver arriving with a truckload of mail discovered the armed Harris on the loose and rushed away to notify police. The killer holed up in the women's rest room for four hours before surrendering to a police SWAT team. He cut a martial figure—over his black silk Ninja-style hood was a gas mask, and he wore a bulletproof vest and black fatigues.

When the police searched his tiny rented room in the attic of a Victorian house, they found a two-page suicide note. It suggested that the Ridgewood Rambo had a role model in Patrick Sherrill. Harris wrote that his fellow post-office murderer had been "right."

Hardly a month after Harris was arrested and charged with murder, kidnapping, attempted murder, possession of hand grenades, and unlawful possession of two weapons, letter carrier Thomas McIlvane's appeal to be reinstated in his job at a post office in suburban Detroit was denied. Cursing at a supervisor at the Royal Oak station had been the last straw that led to his being fired. Before that he'd made obscene and threatening remarks to clerks, letter carriers, and supervisors alike and had been disciplined for fighting with patrons. People who knew McIlvane were afraid of him. A prizewinning kick boxer with a black belt in karate, he was the kind of man whose threats were usually taken seriously.

It took more than a year for McIlvane's appeal to wend its way through the postal bureaucracy, and during that time McIl-

vane repeatedly warned that there would be hell to pay if the decision went against him. Invoking the ghost of Patrick Sherrill, the 31-year-old ex-Marine said that what he planned would make the massacre at Edmond look variously like "Disneyland," a "tea party," and a "picnic." Supervisors and union officials received threatening calls and visits at home and at work, some of which were reported to police. To one woman he snarled, "You had better not turn your head because you'll be dead! I'm going to get you!" Some workers tried to figure out likely escape routes in the event that McIlvane showed up.

In the wake of the tragedy at the Ridgewood post office, a supervisor McIlvane had dubbed the "snake of snakes" called the post-office security division in Detroit to ask for protection at Royal Oak. The request was turned down. On November 12 the supervisors there were informed that McIlvane had lost his bid for reinstatement. It seemed all too likely that he would retaliate, and another appeal was made to Detroit for help. Again, it was denied.

McIlvane got the bad news via a telephone call on November 13. At 8:45 the next morning he arrived at the post office with a sawed-off Ruger .22-caliber semiautomatic rifle hidden inside his raincoat. He was hunting for supervisors, and he killed four of them; first among them the "snake of snakes." After 10 minutes of terrorizing his former coworkers, McIlvane put a bullet into his own head. He lingered for a day before dying. ◆

WILLIAM BRYAN CRUSE

Bookworm's Revenge

Retired librarian William Bryan Cruse was sure his neighbors in Palm Bay, Florida, gossiped about him, spreading the rumor that he was a homosexual. The clerks at the local supermarkets must have heard the rumor, he reasoned, because when he went shopping they stared at him, slyly eying his crotch. He hated them for it. He despised the neighborhood children, who taunted him and trespassed on his property.

Parents in the community where the 59-year-old Cruse had lived for two years with his wife, a victim of Parkinson's disease, warned their children to keep their distance from him. Some of the kids did in fact intentionally harass the man. But it took no more than a child's merely walking past his bungalow to send Cruse into a rage. Out he would rush, screaming obscenities and making threats. Soon after he moved in, he began shooting a rifle into the air to warn off potential trespassers.

The neighbors' concern escalated in April of 1987 after a complaint to police that Cruse made obscene remarks and sexually suggestive gestures to two little boys. When he was questioned by the police, Cruse didn't deny the boys' accusation. In the course of the conversation, he also volunteered an odd piece of intelligence that seemed to have nothing to do with the subject at hand. The day before, he said, a man at a store had stuck out his tongue at him. "I guess that was his way of saying I was queer," Cruse explained. As far as police knew, there was no evidence that Cruse was a practicing homosexual, either with adults or children. Clearly, however, the man was troubled by his own sexuality, whatever its nature. The notion of being persecuted as a "queer" seemed to be the focus of his paranoid delusions.

A week after the incident with the children, around 6 p.m. on April 23, two boys on the sidewalk across the street went past the Cruse house three times. Cruse saw them and began screaming obscenities. The boys laughed. The librarian then went into his house, grabbed three guns and a bag loaded with ammunition, and rushed back out. A 14-year-old boy—an innocent bystander and not one of the strollers—was tossing a basketball in his driveway across the street. Cruse shot him in the buttocks, then climbed into his white Toyota and drove to a nearby shopping center. Pulling up in front of the Publix supermarket, he opened fire in the parking lot with a Ruger Mini-14, a high-powered .223-caliber rifle. Two Kuwaiti college students died on the spot, gunned down at near point-blank range. A bullet wounded a woman as she sat in her car several yards from the killer, and he walked over to her and shot her fatally in the head.

After failing to get into the Publix—he apparently tried to enter through an automated exit-only door—Cruse got back into his car and headed across the street to another shopping plaza, where he started firing his rifle in front of the Winn-Dixie supermarket. The first policeman to arrive was mortally wounded when Cruse sprayed his car with seven rounds. The second officer on the scene emptied his revolver at the killer without hitting Cruse, who nearly severed the lawman's leg with one shot. As the horribly injured man lay behind his car frantically trying to reload his weapon, Cruse approached and shot him again. The policeman would die en route to a hospital.

Turning from the parking-lot carnage, Cruse blasted his way into the Winn-Dixie. Terrified customers and employees ran out a back door with the gunman in pursuit. He shot and killed a man in the group, then returned to the store. He missed three people who'd hidden in a walk-in freezer, but the ladies' rest room yielded two women. He let one go but kept the other as a hostage. Sporadically firing his gun, Cruse hunkered down in the Winn-Dixie for nearly six hours. He threatened to kill his captive and himself, but the cool-headed 21-year-old hostage managed repeatedly to calm him down. He told her he'd been drinking before he left home and asked how many people he'd killed.

Shortly before one o'clock in the morning Cruse released his hostage, and about an hour later police swarmed into the store and captured him as he tried to flee. The death count stood at six, with another 10 people wounded.

Investigators delving into Cruse's past learned that it had not been untroubled. In his native Kentucky he was remembered as a well-liked, seemingly normal youngster. People who knew him as a middle-aged adult, however, described Cruse as a strange, irritable man who loathed children. In 1980 he was arrested in Lexington for public intoxication. The incident suggested that he might be a chip off the old block, for his father had been arrested in 1950 for going on a drunken spree and shooting up the commonwealth attorney's home after his restaurant was closed down for violating liquor laws and for possession of slot machines.

Cruse persistently claimed not to remember killing or shooting at anyone. At his trial he pleaded not guilty by reason of insanity, and several psychiatrists for the defense testified that he was a paranoid schizophrenic beset by delusions. The jury, however, convicted the defendant of six counts of first-degree murder and recommended the death penalty. In 1992 Cruse was still on death row, and his sentence was under appeal. ◆

Police escort handcuffed former librarian William Bryan Cruse into a Florida courtroom for arraignment on six counts of first-degree murder.

Military Man

Failed military academy cadet Julian Knight had a special dream: killing and dying in combat. He tried to make his fantasy come true on a busy street in Melbourne, Australia, on August 7, 1987. The toll from that Sunday down-under winter evening: 7 dead, 19 wounded. Although Knight's dream included his own glorious death, he lived to make a media spectacle of himself, seeming to relish his role as Australia's premier mass killer. In interviews, he criticized police for their slow response to his attack and corrected authorities and reporters on details of his rampage. Tried and sentenced to 27 years in prison, Knight announced from jail that he planned to write the definitive account of his killing spree, with himself as the hero.

Knight blamed the murders on multiple factors, ranging from not being breast-fed to his ouster from the Royal Military College. He explained that he'd been adopted, that he'd been rejected by a girlfriend, that he'd been beaten up and dismissed as a wimp by his fellow cadets. He said frustration over his car's gearbox blowing up on the day of the murders triggered the massacre. The 19-year-old also blamed the military. "They trained me to kill, and I killed," said Knight, an arms enthusiast who'd spent a half-dozen years in student military programs before entering the academy.

At 9:35 p.m. on August 7, Knight took up his position amid shrubbery on the median of Hoddle Street, a Melbourne thoroughfare. Armed with a Ruger semiautomatic rifle, a Mossberg pump-action shotgun, an M-14 rifle, and 200 rounds of ammunition, he pursued the fantasy that Melbourne was being invaded. It was a game of defensive strategy — harmless, really. But, according to Knight, "Something snapped. I went into automatic pilot mode. I was in an intense state of paranoia." The people on Hoddle Street became the enemy, and Knight dealt with them as he'd been trained to do: "See a target, shoot to kill, don't hurt, shoot to kill."

"He was shooting everything that moved," a policewoman recounted. Aiming at cars, pedestrians, and motorcyclists, Knight fired off his entire cache of ammunition in 38 minutes. His first victim was a driver who got out of her car when bullets shattered one of its windows. Knight shot her six times, then killed two people who tried to help her. Another good Samaritan was cut down when he left a house to rescue a victim, and a single bullet killed a man driving to his job at a brewery.

Kevin Skinner was driving down Hoddle Street with his wife and their infant son when he saw mayhem ahead and sped up, weaving around Knight's downed victims. Then the passenger door seemed to explode, and Skinner turned to see that his wife was dead.

A barrage of bullets knocked Kenneth Shane Stanton off his motorcycle. As Stanton lay screaming in agony, Knight fired repeatedly, stopping only when the cyclist fell silent.

The massacre ended when police captured Knight at 10:15. He later claimed that he'd put a round in his pocket with the intention of killing himself to avoid capture but had lost it and had to surrender. Other than that one possible snafu — there was considerable doubt about the intended suicide — Knight believed his military exercise had been executed admirably. "I performed exactly as my Army superiors would have expected me to perform in a combat situation," he said. "In other circumstances I would have gotten a medal for what I did." ◆

Lovesick

Richard Farley was a tireless letter writer— he had to be, since his beloved rejected his advances and hung up when he telephoned her. So two or three times a week, Farley wrote Laura Black a letter. He often delivered it himself, stuffing it into her mailbox or slipping it under the windshield wiper of her car. On one occasion, when the young woman returned a letter unopened, he wrote on the envelope, "You'd better read this" and tacked it to her front door.

Farley knew for sure that Black was getting his message when she came up to him one day in 1987—he was hanging around the parking lot of her apartment building— and asked if he was planning to kill her. He said no, but Laura Black was not comforted. In a recent letter he'd warned, "This is going to escalate all because you think I'm a joke. It's my option to make your life miserable if that's what you really want." His words frightened her badly, and for good reason—Black knew all too well that Farley was driven by a bizarre passion that nothing seemed to dampen.

For almost four years, Farley had pursued Black relentlessly, and she had just as relentlessly tried to discourage his unwanted attention. The two had met in the spring of 1984 at ESL Inc., a Silicon Valley de-

Richard Farley brings reading material to pass the time during lulls in pretrial proceedings in a California courtroom. His own literary output comprised more than 200 love letters to coworker Laura Black, the object of his unrequited passion.

fense contractor in Sunnyvale, California. The attractive young woman was an electrical engineer at ESL, and the pudgy bachelor, then 35 years old, was a software engineer. A veteran of 11 years in the navy and an avid gun collector, he fell for her the first time he saw her smile and was soon asking her for dates.

To a normal man it would have been clear from the beginning that he would get nowhere with Black. Farley, however, was not normal, and whatever she said and however rudely she behaved, he continued to pressure her. After Black declined to give him her home address and telephone number, Farley began calling her at work and writing his rambling love letters; in time he would write to her more than 200 times. He also gave her a heart-shaped mirror and left other gifts on her desk.

Farley stalked the slender, brown-eyed woman, waiting for her to leave work, shadowing her at company softball games, and materializing on the campus of the University of Santa Clara where she was studying for her master's degree. He watched her comings and goings from a convenience store across the street from her apartment and jotted down the license numbers of her friends. He even joined her aerobics class to be near her. He surreptitiously took photographs of her and used them as spurious documents with which to bolster his fantasies of their life together. He claimed, for instance, to have a snapshot showing her in Vail, Colorado, during a ski holiday with him.

Fleeing Farley, Black moved three times in four years, but he always tracked her down. Once he even tried to rent a unit in her apartment complex. In 1986 she filed a sexual harassment complaint with ESL against him, and the company fired him.

Besides depriving him of a convenient theater for playing out his obsession, Farley's dismissal got him into serious financial trouble. He lost two houses, his car, and even his computer, and he fell $20,000 behind in taxes. His attentions to Black grew more menacing. In 1987 he somehow got hold of a duplicate key to her apartment, which he left on her windshield.

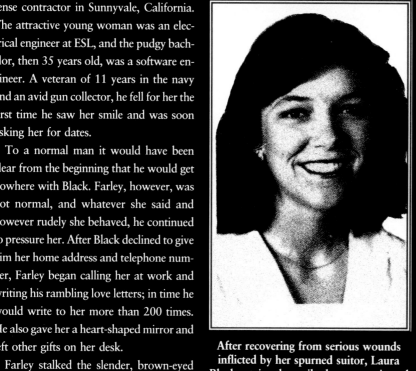

After recovering from serious wounds inflicted by her spurned suitor, Laura Black retains the smile that so captivated Richard Farley in the first place.

Fearing for her safety, Black sought and received a temporary restraining order against Farley in early February of 1988. She wrote to the court, "I have been afraid of what this man might do to me if I filed this action. However, I am now at the end of my rope." Farley was temporarily banned from telephoning Black or getting within 300 yards of her; nor was he free to follow her or watch her, even if he kept his distance. He was scheduled to be at the court hearing on a permanent restraining order on February 17, but events prevented him from appearing. On the afternoon of the 16th, he loaded guns, an eight-inch buck knife, ear protectors, a gas mask, and four gallons of inflammable liquid into a rented motor home and drove to ESL, where he parked outside the building where Laura Black had her office.

For a time Farley sat thinking about what to do next. Then he draped himself with two shotguns, an assault rifle, four pistols, and 1,100 rounds of ammunition, climbed out of the motor home, and gunned down a man walking out of the building. Shooting out the electronic lock of the security doors, he entered and felled another employee, then headed for the

stairs to the second floor, where Black worked. On the way up he killed his third victim. Shooting through doors and chasing terrified workers down the hall, Farley killed four more people on the second floor with a 12-gauge repeating shotgun.

Farley found his beloved in her office. Standing in the doorway, he raised the gun and fired. Black fell to the floor, her left shoulder shattered and one lung collapsed, but she braced her good shoulder against a bookcase and pushed the door shut with her feet. Farley walked away. Laura Black would survive.

Barricading himself in the building for nearly six hours, Farley talked at length by telephone with a police negotiator. "I just wanted her to stop hanging up on me," he said of Black. "All I wanted was to take her out, one time." He claimed he'd originally meant only to damage computer equipment, but when people "popped out around corners," he shot them. As to why he stopped his rampage after shooting 10 people, Farley explained, "Once I had run around and gotten through being upset, it wasn't fun anymore." The police negotiator urged Farley to give himself up, and the gunman did—for a price: a ham-and-turkey sandwich and a large diet soda.

During his 1991 trial Farley insisted that he'd gone to ESL intent on killing himself to make Black feel guilty. He also claimed that on the day of the shootings he fell into a trance in which he envisioned a 10-foot-tall man and police officers the size of ants. He also had, he said, an out-of-body experience in which he saw himself loaded with guns and prowling a hall at ESL. This odd defense proved ineffective, and the defendant was convicted of seven counts of first-degree murder. In 1992 Farley was sentenced to death in the gas chamber. The sentence was appealed.

Even his murderous explosion of rage failed to end Farley's perverse love letters. He wrote to Laura Black several days after his arrest, when she lay in the hospital gravely wounded, her survival still in question: "When I go to the gas chamber," he wrote, "I'll smile for the cameras and you'll know you'll have won in the end." ◆

PATRICK EDWARD PURDY

The Terrorist

When police in Stockton, California, entered the room at the El Rancho Motel that Patrick Edward Purdy called home for the last three weeks of his life, they encountered an army. Outfitted with miniature tanks, jeeps, and weapons, 100 two-inch green plastic toy soldiers stood at the ready — on the floor, the furniture, the curtain rods, in the shower, on the refrigerator. The army's 24-year-old flesh-and-blood general had played a deadly game. On January 17, 1989, he dropped fantasy combat in favor of real murder — murder mostly of children. The killing spree was not, it seems, on the spur of the moment: Four days earlier, Purdy had told his half brother that he would soon be in the news.

Purdy dressed appropriately for the occasion, wearing a camouflage shirt with a flak jacket over it. He had painted his shirt to make his allegiance known. "Libya," "Earthman," and "PLO" appeared on the front. No one would be able to decipher what Earthman meant. The reference to Libya may have applauded that Arab country's alleged terrorist activities, and PLO presumably referred to the militant Palestine Liberation Organization. The back of the shirt proclaimed "Freedom" and "Death to the Great Satin." This last was Purdy's semiliterate, faintly absurd rendering of "Satan," the epithet hurled at the United States by the pro-Iranian terrorist group known as the Hezbollah. The organization's name was carved on Purdy's AK-47 assault rifle, to which he'd fixed a bayonet. He loaded the rifle, along with a Taurus 9-mm. semiautomatic pistol, into his beat-up station wagon and, leaving his

Workers under the direction of the San Joaquin County coroner's office roll the body of Patrick Edward Purdy away from the playground at Cleveland Elementary School in Stockton, California, where Purdy killed five children and himself.

toys behind, drove off to confront the enemy. This would be Purdy's first wartime experience, despite his claims to the contrary. He boasted of serving in Vietnam, but he was only eight years old when the United States pulled out of the Asian conflict in 1973.

Shortly before noon, Purdy pulled up to the back of the Cleveland Elementary School, where he'd been a pupil from 1969 to 1973. His parents had split up when he was a toddler, and he'd lived with his mother and stepfather while attending the school from kindergarten through second grade. His mother and stepfather divorced, and by the time Purdy was 14 he was shuttling back and forth between his parents. He often lived on his own. He was also drinking heavily, perhaps following the example set by his alcoholic mother.

When Purdy was 16, his father died. A high-school teacher remembered Purdy in those days as a friendless loner in an army fatigue jacket. According to the teacher, "you never saw him with other human beings." Purdy gave up on school, dropped out, and became a drifter.

Bunking in seedy motels and skid-row flophouses, the youth supported himself with odd jobs and with small-time drug peddling. He accumulated a criminal record, but his offenses were relatively petty—solicitation of a prostitute, attempted robbery, selling hashish.

It's unclear how and where Purdy acquired his revolutionary notions, but they were in place by April of 1987 when he was arrested for firing a pistol in the woods near Lake Tahoe. When the police took him into custody, Purdy kicked out the window of the patrol car and ranted that it was his duty to help overthrow the suppressors. He also claimed the right to kill anyone who pushed him around. Jailed, Purdy tried to hang himself with his shirt. When that failed, he clawed at his wrists with his fingernails and toenails. Transferred to a mental-health unit because of his suicide attempts, he was judged a danger to himself and to others. Even so, he was released.

Free again, Purdy lived for a time in a Stockton flophouse, then moved on. He crisscrossed the country, going from one job to another. In 1988 he left a notebook behind at one of the countless digs he drifted through, and a nosy clerk later quoted Purdy's assessment of himself: "I'm so dumb, I'm dumber than a sixth grader," the troubled drifter had written, adding a note about his parents in the same blunt vein: "My mother and father were dumb."

Purdy showed up in Stockton for the last time in December of 1988 and made his preparations for his attack on the school. He would leave no explanation as to why he picked this target or why he decided to go to war against children.

The day was sunny and clear, perfect for the mission. In an apparent diversionary tactic, Purdy set his station wagon ablaze with a fire bomb made from a beer bottle, then strode through a back gate and onto a playground nestled in the crook of the L-shaped school building. The midday recess was in progress, and some 400 children, most of them between six and nine years old, were on the playground when Purdy began rapidly and rhythmically spraying them with fire from the AK-47.

According to a teacher who could see the gunman from her classroom window, he did not talk or yell, nor did he seem angry. It was, she said, as if "he was concentrating on what he was doing." As children ran and screamed in terror and teachers tried to herd them inside to safety, the bullets flew with such force that some passed through walls and even through steel girders.

Firing at least 100 rounds, Purdy killed five children and wounded 29 others; a teacher was also hit. About four minutes into the massacre, when the wail of approaching sirens could be heard through the students' cries, Purdy drew his pistol and killed himself with a single shot. ◆

JAMES EDWARD POUGH

Car Trouble

The 1990s did not begin well for 42-year-old James Edward Pough—pronounced "Pew"—of Jacksonville, Florida. His wife of about a year walked out on him in January, and in the same month his red 1988 Pontiac Grand Am was repossessed by the General Motors Acceptance Corporation. Nor did that settle his debt. He still owed $6,394, a daunting amount for a low-paid laborer.

To the casual observer, however, Pough appeared to carry on as usual despite these setbacks. He bought an old Buick to replace the Grand Am and stuck to his work routine, driving off to work at 6:30 a.m. and returning to his run-down duplex apartment around 4:00 p.m. At least he had no shortage of jobs. He was considered one of the best and most reliable workers in his union, and contractors frequently asked for him by name.

A quiet man, Pough kept to himself, but he was not disliked. "He was a nice person. He was a good person," a neighbor across the street insisted. But this was not to say that Pough never gave cause for complaint. He would occasionally stand in his yard late at night firing a gun into the air. Still, his was a tough neighborhood, with no shortage of gunfire, and at least Pough was not aiming at people. Not yet.

June 18, 1990, was a Monday, but

Pough didn't follow his normal routine. Early that morning he called his employer to say that he had something to do and wouldn't be on the job. A less conscientious worker might have just failed to show up, but James Pough was dependable.

At 10:50 a.m. Pough walked into the local GMAC office. At a service counter near the front door customers were paying bills. Pough pointed a .30-caliber Universal semiautomatic rifle at one of them and shot

her dead. Rounding the counter to the large area where dozens of employees worked, Pough stalked the aisles taking aim at people cowering under desks or trying to flee. After shooting eight of them fatally and wounding four, Pough drew a .38-caliber revolver and took his own life.

Police soon learned that Pough's homicidal binge had a prelude in his own neighborhood. On Sunday morning, shortly after midnight, he shot a man and a woman dead. Five minutes later Pough shot and wounded two teenagers he stopped with the excuse of asking for directions. He committed his last known crime of that Sunday about 9 a.m., robbing a convenience-store clerk at gunpoint.

The spree was certainly uncharacteristic, but violence—even killing—was not new to Pough. He'd been arrested in 1971 for killing a man outside a nightclub because the man insulted Pough's girlfriend. In a plea bargain Pough was sentenced to five years' probation for aggravated assault. He seemed to put the trouble behind him and became a good neighbor and excellent worker. But when his deadly potential, dormant for almost two decades, erupted again, Pough amassed a two-day body count of 12, including himself, in committing Florida's worst mass murder to date. ◆

GANG LU

The Knife behind the Smile

At the Sports Column bar, a hangout for University of Iowa students, Gang Lu was one of the regulars—but not one of the crowd. Lu would drink his usual, a pitcher of light beer, standing alone amid the noisy throng. The bartenders called him Sweet Lu because of the smile that never seemed to leave his face, but there was a certain irony in the nickname. Sweetness was not his nature. He was touchy and ego-

tistical, and he had a hair-trigger temper.

His prickliness put people off, and it was aggravated by a communication problem. A native of Beijing, China, Lu spoke English haltingly, even after six years in Iowa City. And he was a loner. He was odd man out in the university's otherwise closely knit physics department, and he declined to join the association of Chinese students at Iowa. He did seem interested in wom-

en, but they were not interested in him.

In 1991 Lu was not only alone but also profoundly angry. That spring he'd achieved what should have been a great milestone: His doctoral dissertation in the rarefied field of space-plasma physics had been accepted. This triumph had been rendered meaningless, however, by what Lu considered a great injustice. He'd hoped that his work would be nominated for a

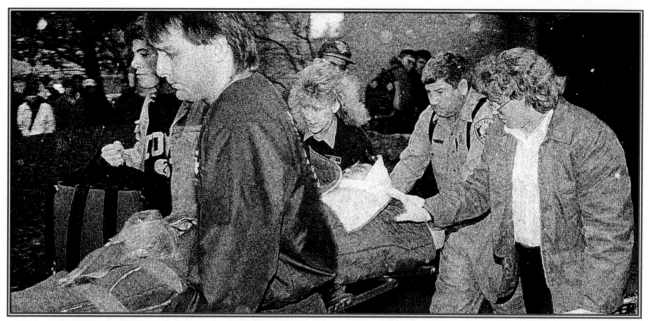

prestigious university award, but he lost out to Linhua Shan, another physicist from China. Convinced that he'd been deliberately slighted by his department, Lu appealed to a series of administrators to review the selection process. By late summer the problem had landed on the desk of Anne Cleary, the associate vice president for academic affairs.

Lu's fury gnawed at him as he waited for Cleary's response. In September he sent an anonymous letter to the *Des Moines Register* asserting his determination "to pursue a fair resolution to this matter at any cost." The cost would be very high.

It was part of the physics department routine to hold seminars at 3:30 p.m. on Friday afternoons. On November 1 Lu walked into the third-floor seminar room carrying his briefcase. He was a few minutes late, and the nine people already there had begun their discussion. Almost immediately Lu left the room for several minutes, then returned, sat down, and drew a .38-caliber revolver from his coat. Without a word, he calmly shot at point-blank range two professors who had been on his dissertation committee. His third target was his successful rival, Linhua Shan. Leaving two people dead and one badly wounded, Lu ran downstairs to the office of the physics department chairman. He killed the chairman with two bullets to the head.

Another enemy dispatched, Lu went

Paramedics and firefighters remove the body of one of Gang Lu's victims from the physics department at the University of Iowa. Lu killed six people in only 12 minutes.

back upstairs to the seminar room. Shan and one professor were dead, but a second professor was still alive, with two colleagues at his side. Ordering them out of the room, Lu finished the professor off with another round and then, for good measure, shot at the other two bodies again before leaving the physics building.

Lu walked through a dusting of snow to the administration building, where he shot Vice President Cleary and her receptionist. Down the hallway from Cleary's office he entered a conference room where he took off his coat, placed it neatly on a chair, and shot himself in the head. Twelve minutes had elapsed since his first shot.

Lu died soon after the police arrived. Cleary died the next day, bringing Lu's tally of kills to six, including himself. The receptionist, a 23-year-old honors student at the university, survived but was paralyzed from the neck down.

Investigation revealed that Lu had planned his mad retribution for months and had organized it as thoroughly as a research project. He'd acquired the murder weapon in July. In September he'd posted his anonymous message to the Des Moines newspaper, and the following month he'd

withdrawn the $20,000 in his bank account and sent it to his sister in Beijing. He'd even prepared a lengthy statement for the news media. Found in his briefcase, the statement detailed his grievances against the university and mentioned every person he'd shot except for the receptionist; it was her misfortune to have been working temporarily for Vice President Cleary.

Lu laid out his skewed sense of justice with frightening clarity: "Private guns make every person equal, no matter what/ who he/she is," he wrote. "They also make it possible for an individual to fight against a conspired/incorporated organization such as Mafia or Dirty University officials." He mentioned his admiration for Clint Eastwood films in which "a single cowboy fights against a group of incorporated bad guys who pick on little guys." Lu, it seemed, saw himself as an underdog hero battling the evil university.

Authorities also recovered Lu's last letter to his sister. In it he announced his own impending death and addressed himself to such practical matters as his own cremation and the care of their elderly parents.

The rage and the cold calculation of Lu's last documents came as no surprise to Xuming Chi, a graduate student who once roomed with Lu for several months. "You would see him smile, but behind the smiling face was a knife," Chi said of the murderer. "I hated that guy. I hated him." ◆

GEORGE HENNARD

High Noon

Six mornings a week, George Hennard stopped at the same convenience store in Belton, Texas, and made the same breakfast purchase: a sausage-and-biscuit sandwich, orange juice, doughnuts, and a newspaper. Ordinarily, clerks at the store would have been glad for the steady business, but in Hennard's case, they'd have been happy to see him take his trade elsewhere. He was scary. He behaved as though he hated the whole world. Once, for no apparent reason, he said to the woman behind the counter, "I want you to tell everybody if they don't quit messing around my house something awful is going to happen."

On October 16, 1991, the day after his 35th birthday, Hennard turned up at the convenience store as usual, but he seemed different. He was calm, even friendly. Seven hours later, at the height of the noontime rush, he rammed his light blue pickup truck through the plate-glass window of Luby's Cafeteria in the town of Killeen, some 19 miles from Belton. He was about to turn the popular eatery into a slaughterhouse, the scene of the worst mass shooting in the history of the United States.

Hennard's crashing entrance into Luby's seemed at first to be a freak accident. His truck hit an elderly man, and patrons rushed to try to help the victim. But then Hennard leaped from the truck with two pistols—a Glock 17 semiautomatic and a Ruger P89—and the horrified diners quickly realized that this wasn't an accident.

The day after George Hennard set a grim record for mass murder in the United States, his pickup truck still stands where he drove it through the front window of Luby's Cafeteria in Killeen, Texas.

As the man felled by the truck struggled to rise, Hennard shot him in the head. Then, moving from one victim to another, the gunman shot most of them in the head or chest, sometimes passing by several people before taking aim at the next unlucky soul. Against the cacophony of screams, Hennard shouted, "Is it worth it? This is payback day!" And: "This is what Belton did to me!" To women he snarled, "Take that, bitch!" or simply, "Bitch!"

The killer seemed intent on thoroughness. He returned to several victims he'd wounded and shot them again. He interrupted his savage spree only to reload. In his only show of mercy, he pointed a pistol at a blood-splattered woman who'd just seen her mother shot dead and said, "You with the baby, get out." The woman and her four-year-old daughter ran to safety. A number of people escaped death via the kitchen door, and when a burly mechanic hurled himself through a rear window, several customers followed him through the jagged opening and thereby survived. One escapee could not forget the look on the killer's face: "He was smiling," the man recalled, "kind of a grin, like a smirk."

Even when police arrived and began firing at him, the gunman directed a few more rounds at the customers before taking aim at the officers. Hit by two police bullets, Hennard retreated to the rest-room corridor. There he put a pistol to his right temple and with his last bullet blew a fatal hole in his head. In the dining room 22 people were dead and 23 others were wounded, one fatally.

The investigation that followed the bloodbath suggested that Hennard conformed to the profile typical of mass murderers: He was a loner and a loser, though a casual glance might have suggested otherwise. He was a handsome, muscular man—the sort who might have appealed to women—and he lived in an upscale house, impeccably kept. And he was hardly a social outcast by birth. His father, who lived in Houston, was a surgeon.

But just beneath the surface, Hennard's apparent assets turned upside down. His good-looking features were often disfigured by a scowl, directed particularly at women. He commonly shouted obscenities at females as they drove down the street, and he'd been seen quarreling violently with one woman in the middle of the street he lived on. His impressive two-story brick house, complete with six columns and a backyard pool, belonged not to him, but to his divorced mother, who'd moved to Nevada in 1989. Hennard took great pains to keep up the place, but he lived in it alone. He seldom saw his father. In his neighborhood, Hennard was reclusive, and his neighbors were glad to leave him alone.

Investigation revealed that Hennard had spent time in February and March of 1991 with his mother in Nevada, where he bought the murder weapons. Early in February he'd received bad news: His appeal to be reinstated in the merchant marine

An uncharacteristic smile softens George Hennard's face in the photograph that was taken in 1987 for his Texas driver's license.

had been denied. From 1981 until 1989 he'd worked as a deck hand, but his license was lifted when he was caught smoking marijuana. His failure to win reinstatement was a bitter blow, for Hennard had considered his years at sea the best of his life. Not that they were placid. A maritime union agent said, "He would come in with a very cold look and be very argumentative, loud, boisterous, sometimes cursing and swearing." Hennard moved from ship to ship, never lasting long on any of them.

Shut out of the merchant marine, Hennard worked in construction, drank heavily, kept his truck spotless—and alarmed the people of Belton, especially the women.

Most of the victims at Luby's were women, and in the wake of his rampage, the depth and extent of Hennard's hatred of women became clear. The most explicit evidence of his antifemale sentiments was a bizarre five-page letter he sent four months before the shootings to two sisters who lived on his street. Noting that he'd found the best and the worst of women in Belton, he assured the young women—whom he'd seen but not met—that they were among the best. As to the others, he wrote, "Please give me the satisfaction of some day laughing in the face of all those mostly white treacherous female vipers." Disturbed by the letter, the young women's mother complained to the Belton police, but no charges were brought against Hennard.

The killer's loathing of women may have been rooted in his relationship with his mother, reportedly a high-strung and domineering person. The two fought frequently, and a seaman who bunked with Hennard in 1982 recalled that he often talked about killing his mother. Moreover, Hennard was given to drawing caricatures of his mother, depicting her as a snake. The viper motif seemed to extend eventually to women in general, and in his paranoia Hennard sometimes complained that he had to hide from women who were harassing him.

It seems evident that murder was on Hennard's mind well in advance of the massacre. Less than a month before it took place, he asked a fellow worker what he should do if he killed someone. The man answered that he should kill himself. Shortly after this conversation, Hennard tried twice to sell his guns. Unfortunately for his future victims, there were no takers. ◆

With a partial listing of the dead over her shoulder, Red Cross volunteer JoAnn Wright staffs telephones to give information about George Hennard's victims, some of whom were her close friends.

My destiny lies
in the bloody death
of racist pigs.

MARK ESSEX

3

Mata

America in the 1960s and early 1970s was a tinderbox, and racism seemed often a flint strike away from igniting a national conflagration. Rooted in the black churches of the South, the civil rights movement that began in the 1950s had touched white America's conscience. But as the turbulent '60s neared their end, a nation free of prejudice was still no more than a distant dream.

African Americans roused to action by the movement were becoming impatient with its gentle tactics and deliberate pace. Strident young voices denounced the nonviolence preached by Dr. Martin Luther King, Jr. Violence, proclaimed the new breed, was a necessary revolutionary tactic for wresting racial justice from a white majority that would never grant it willingly. Then, in the spring of 1968, King was killed by a white bigot. Ironically, his death seemed to prove the radicals' point: Brutality was all the black Americans could expect at the hands of whites, and brutality must be answered in kind. Passive resistance was fading as a tactic. "Black Power" was the new battle cry.

New York escaped the worst of the rioting and burning, but tensions there were palpable nonetheless. Certainly emotions ran high in Harlem, for almost a century the cultural heart of black America. However damaged by poverty and prejudice, Harlem remained a hub of African American art, literature, music, and philosophy. So, in the late 1960s and early 1970s, Harlem was awash with various torrents of black radical and revolutionary thought. The Black Panther Party, the National Committee to Combat Fascism, and the Black Liberation Army all had adherents there.

The New York faction of the Black Panthers—factions were rife among the revolutionaries—put out a monthly newspaper called *Right On* that provided a representative sample of the rhetoric of the day. Along with urging in general terms violence against the "pigs" and "fascists" of the white establishment, the paper provided practical instruction on city guerrilla warfare. It discussed, for example, the making of bombs, the setting of fires, and the use of firearms. *Right On* also ran excerpts from revolutionary writings such as the *Manual of the Urban Guerrilla* by Brazilian communist leader Carlos Marighella. "Shooting and marksmanship," the manual advised, "are the urban guerrilla's water and air."

There was a particular young man who wandered Harlem briefly in those days, moved by the fierce vitality that animated such slogans as Black Power! and Power to the People! He surely read *Right On,* and possibly he peddled it on the street. While not a member of the Panthers, he often agreed with them. He was a short, slight fellow, fine-featured, with a sweet smile and a soft voice. He hadn't been in New York long, and he wouldn't stay long: He was, spiritually and geographically, about equidistant between his gentle origins and his bloody destiny. Unlike most young black men, he'd learned about racism rather late in life; bigotry was comparatively rare in the Kansas town where he'd grown up. But when he did learn, the lesson was even more bitter than usual. By the time he was 21, drinking in the yeasty ferment of Harlem, he had learned how to hate with a wholehearted passion.

The young man's name was Mark James Robert Essex—at least, that was his name for most of his life. His family usually called him Jimmy, and his friends during his brief stint in the U.S. Navy called him Mark. Soon he would take to calling himself Mata. *Mata* is the Swahili word for a hunter's bow—a taut instrument of death. And Mata was the name he preferred when he set out to fulfill his self-appointed mission in life: killing white people.

In 1949, the year Mark Essex was born, Emporia, Kansas, was a quiet town with a population of roughly 15,000 people. Known primarily for its stockyards and slaughterhouses, Emporia was founded in 1857, during a time when the state came to be called Bleeding Kansas because of violent strife over the issue of slavery. Proud of its antislavery stand, Emporia would send a 144-man contingent to fight on the Union side during the Civil War.

Part of the reason that Emporia had very little racial conflict was probably that it had only a small black population: During Essex's boyhood in the 1950s, there were about 500 black residents. Still, local folk prided themselves on a long history of racial harmony. Seldom, claimed the town leaders, had there been serious disagreements between blacks and whites. For Mark Essex, the comparative absence of racism in Emporia was a mixed blessing. A noted sociologist would one day observe that Essex never learned to cope with the harsh reality of intolerance because he was never "vaccinated" against it as a youngster.

The second of five children, Essex grew up in a loving family. His father, Mark senior, was a foreman at a meat-packing plant, and his mother, Nellie, counseled preschoolers in a program for disadvantaged children. The elder Essexes were kindly people, good citizens, and good parents, and young Mark Essex reflected the blessings of a benign upbringing. A former teacher remembered him as a "smiling, friendly boy who was always laughing and joking." He joined the Cub Scouts, played the saxophone in the high-school band, and took pleasure in hunting and fishing near his home. The pastor at the family's church recalled young Essex as a "crack shot on rabbits and squirrels."

Popular in high school, Mark dated both black girls and white, and he once told his mother that he didn't really see much difference between them. His ambition at the time was to be a minister. No more than an average student, Essex probably wouldn't have made a profound theologian. His special aptitude was in technical subjects. He was good with machinery. He loved to tinker.

Throughout his adolescence Mark would remain small and wiry; as an adult he would never stand taller than five feet four inches. In fact, one of his few early brushes with the law was brought about by his short stature. While driving the family car soon after his 16th birthday he was pulled over by police, who assumed he was too young to drive.

After high school Essex drifted for a time. He went to college briefly, but it didn't suit him, and he put in a short stint at the meat-packing plant where his father worked. Concluding that his options were severely limited in Emporia, the youth decided to join the navy and seek vocational training.

It was, on the face of it, a good plan, and the experience started off well. Essex enlisted on January 13, 1969, when he was 19, and within three months he was assigned to the Naval Air Station at Imperial Beach, California, near San Diego. There he was apprenticed as a dental technician. He took to this work and grew friendly with Lieutenant Robert Hatcher, the white dentist who was his supervisor. "He was a good team man," recalled Hatcher, "sort of an all-American boy. In those days he was just the nicest person in the world."

But shadows dimmed this bright portrait. From the time Essex joined the navy, he was struck by the racism he found in the service. At Imperial Beach, he quickly discovered, blacks were second-class citizens, particularly in the enlisted ranks. The navy, he wrote in a letter to his parents, "is not like I thought it would be, not like Emporia. Blacks have trouble getting along here."

When Essex took a job as a bartender at the enlisted men's club, he found that certain rooms were off-limits to blacks. And overt discrimination extended well beyond the club. Whenever Essex passed through the camp's main gate in the used car that he'd bought for his 21st birthday, security guards invariably demanded to see his license, registration, and insurance papers. They often ordered him out of his car while they performed an elaborate search, sometimes even unscrewing the car's door panels. White sailors, meanwhile, drove through the gate unchallenged.

At first, Essex suffered these indignities quietly. But eventually he began talking with other black sailors, who told him that racism was simply a part of life in the navy—a bitter medicine that had to be swallowed. "He was a kid from Kansas," said Fred Allen, a black seaman who had befriended Essex in boot camp, "and it was his first time away from home. He came into the navy expecting to be treated in the same decent way he had always been treated in Emporia, and he found it wasn't like that at all. It wasn't long before he wanted out of the navy, as most of us blacks did."

As Allen noted, Essex wasn't alone. At the time, many blacks were bitter toward the armed forces. A major grievance involved their belief that they were bearing too large a share of the suffering and dying in the Vietnam War—and with little to show for their sacrifices: They fought for America in this strange and distant war, only to return home to the same second-class treatment that America had always dealt them. In the navy, less than one-half of one percent of the officers' corps was black, and morale among the ranks of black enlisted men was so low that there were cases of open rebellion and sabotage. Within a few years the navy would acknowledge the problem and take steps to

correct it. But that would be too late for Mark Essex and for many of his contemporaries.

During his early months in the navy, Essex trusted that he would get along better once he achieved a higher rank. Within a year he won promotion from recruit to seaman, but the harassment from whites continued. It seemed that the situation might come to a head when Essex and a group of his friends were put on report for playing music too loudly. Under normal procedures, they would have faced a routine disciplinary hearing known as a captain's mast. But Essex wanted a more dramatic forum, and he demanded a summary court-martial. That way, he figured, he would at least get a chance to face his accusers.

Before the case could be brought to trial, however, Essex's friend and supervisor, Robert Hatcher, went to his superiors and had the proceedings halted. The dentist convinced the prosecutor that the allegations were false and were racially motivated. The charges were dismissed, but Essex was left without his day in court. Worse yet, he learned that he was to be separated from his friends, who would be quartered in other barracks. He found himself branded a troublemaker and subjected to a whole new round of petty indignities. Bed checks became a nightly matter, and he was assigned more than his share of guard-duty tours. He grew so tense that he began taking sedatives, and a close friend warned him that he "could see an explosion coming."

At the time, no one could have foreseen how devastating the eventual explosion would be, but a mild preliminary tremor occurred when Essex got into a fight with a white petty officer. Though the scuffle was quickly broken up, the episode marked a turning point for Essex. It was the first time he had ever lashed out physically at a white man. He found deep satisfaction in his small act of defiance, but it would cost him. As word of the fight spread through the base, the harassment got more frequent. At last Essex couldn't take it anymore, and on the morning of October 19, 1970, he went absent without leave. Phoning his parents from a bus station, he muttered that he'd reached the end of his rope. "I'm coming home," he said. "I've just got to have some time to think."

Back in Emporia, the AWOL seaman was moody and withdrawn. Whenever he spoke about the navy, his bitterness was overwhelming. "They take everything from you, everything," Essex told his parents. "Your dignity, your pride. What can you do but hate them?"

Apprentice Seaman Mark Essex stands out among his white classmates in their July 1969 graduation picture at the Naval Training Center Dental Technician School.

Despite the young sailor's rancor, his parents persuaded him to return to Imperial Beach after a month's absence to face the consequences of his desertion. Before turning himself in to authorities, Essex sought out Lieutenant Hatcher and poured out his complaints. "I don't want to have anything more to do with the navy," he said. "It wouldn't be fair, not to you or to the patients. The bad atmosphere would affect my work, and I don't want that to happen. The work is the only thing on this base I like."

Essex's trial was largely a formality, since he'd already pleaded guilty to the charge of desertion. Once again Hatcher provided a vigorous defense of his helper's character and praised his job performance, but Essex himself was subdued. As he took the stand in his own defense, his voice quavered. "I had to talk to some black people because I had begun to hate all white people," he informed the military judge. "I was tired of going to white people and telling them my problems and not getting anything done about it."

The disposition of Essex's case amounted to tacit acknowledgment that his complaints were true. The judge noted that "prejudice issues" had influenced the desertion, and he sentenced the sailor to a remarkably lenient punishment: restriction to base for 30 days and forfeiture of $90 of his pay for the next two months. Essex listened to the verdict with an unreadable expression, convinced that it only reaffirmed the judgment he'd confided some time ago to a fellow seaman: "There is no place in this white man's navy," Essex had said, "for a self-respecting black man."

Within weeks, on February 11, 1971, Essex was granted an early discharge. The grounds were "unsuitable character and behavior"—a description that left him stigmatized as a misfit while ignoring the abuse he'd endured.

Once again at loose ends, Essex made his pilgrimage to Harlem, hoping, perhaps, to find there some balm for his lost innocence and injured pride, or some new creed to give shape and direction to his disillusionment. But by and large, the quest failed.

According to Edwin Cooper, then a detective with the Intelligence Division of the New York City Police Department, Essex did make contact with the Black Panthers. "He must have gotten the revolutionary rhetoric hot and heavy," Cooper later surmised. Certainly, during his short stay in New York, Essex had intensive exposure to radical thought and to the philosophy and tactics of guerrilla warfare. But he couldn't quite find his niche in Harlem—perhaps he was too much the product of small-town Kansas to give himself completely to urban radical politics—and he left New York in April of 1971 and headed back to Emporia. The problem was, he no longer fit in there, either. He was so alone with his rage. He loved his family, but he could neither communicate to them his inner turmoil nor dispel the worry he saw in their eyes as they watched him become more and more bitter and withdrawn.

Mark Essex was coming unmoored. His link to his family was breaking down, and he found no comfort in the faith of his childhood. The youth who had wanted to be a minister would soon renounce Christianity as a white man's religion and embrace as his new bible a book called *Black Rage*, written by a pair of University of California psychiatrists, William Grier and Price Cobbs. The authors wrote that history and society had conspired to leave downtrodden blacks no alternative but violence. "As a sapling bent low stores energy for a violent backswing," the book said, "blacks bent double by oppression have stored energy which will be released in the form of rage—black rage, apocalyptic and final."

Such rhetoric resonated with Essex's growing fatalism and harmonized with snippets of stratagems learned during his sojourn in New York: To conserve ammunition, aim each shot carefully. . . . Keep moving; never allow the enemy to concentrate against you. . . . Aim for the head or heart to ensure a kill.

Two months after his discharge from the navy, Mark Essex walked into a department store in Emporia and ordered a .44-caliber magnum Ruger Deerslayer carbine, a lightweight, powerful weapon capable of firing six rounds without being reloaded. For hours at a time in the weeks that followed, he would disappear into the woods near his parents' home and practice his marksmanship. In the navy Essex had received basic instruction in the use of the M-1 rifle and an afternoon's training with a .45-caliber pistol. In New York, he'd learned a lot more about firearms.

In August, Essex left Emporia for good, slipping out of town without telling his parents and driving 800 miles south to New Orleans. No one knows why he headed for Louisiana. Possibly he planned to meet up with a friend from the navy who'd moved there several weeks earlier. In any case, New Orleans was an interesting choice. In some ways, the old city is distinctive when it comes to the African American

experience. Long before the Civil War, a black Creole intelligentsia flourished in New Orleans, and black business people and artisans who called themselves "free people of color" formed a proud and substantial middle class in the city. This is not to say, however, that New Orleans was ever without its share of overt prejudice, and in the early 1970s it was, like many other American cities, racially tense.

By the time Mark Essex got there, many local blacks had come to deeply resent the police department, and the bad feelings had been aggravated by skirmishes between the police and the New Orleans Black Panthers the previous year. Moreover, the city had recently bought a heavily armored police vehicle nicknamed the War Wagon, whose purpose, many blacks felt, was to keep them in their place.

During his months in New Orleans, Essex would move four times, getting a firsthand view of the city's poverty-stricken housing projects. One residence was in the blighted and ironically named Desire project, where more than 10,000 people lived in an area of only 12 square blocks.

Soon after his arrival in the city, Essex enrolled in a federally funded training program that taught vending-machine repair. His instructors remember him as an apt and enthusiastic student who also demonstrated a flair for drawing. One of his sketches showed a muscular black warrior brandishing a large sword.

A neighbor would later recall a memorable encounter. She had been out in her yard hanging clothes to dry when Essex, whom she hadn't met, came out of his apartment and approached her. "You must be my neighbor," he said. "Every morning I hear your prayers, and they fill my soul. I have to stop putting on my clothes until you finish praying, and then I can get dressed and go on to work." Moved, the woman thanked the well-mannered young man. She never saw him again.

Beneath the gentle and apparently normal exterior and the outwardly normal life, Mark Essex was battling repeated bouts of severe depression. He sought relief in a self-taught crash course in African culture and languages. The very word *Africa* became his personal rallying cry, the focus of his muddled views on the need for violent upheaval.

In Essex's troubled, tortured mind, the amateur anthropology and the smattering of revolutionary doctrine and guerrilla training from his stay in New York melded into a dangerous gel. His frustration and confusion gave way to a sense of purpose that was grim yet strangely exultant. He was transforming himself into an efficient, committed urban warrior. He was Mata, the tautly drawn bow. He awaited the release that would propel him toward his fate.

The release was gradual. It began in September 1972, when the New Orleans Police Department announced the formation of a crack unit called the Felony Action Squad. Over the previous eight months the city had seen a wave of 142 homicides, many of them involving wealthy businessmen killed during robberies. The new unit was intended to slow or stop this violence. "The people who perpetrate these crimes are one degree above animals, and we're not going to tolerate them," declared Clarence Giarrusso, the superintendent of police. If threatened, he warned, members of the Felony Action Squad had a standing order to "shoot to kill."

They take everything from you, everything. Your dignity, your pride. What can you do but hate them?

The "shoot to kill" announcement touched off angry protests and demands for Giarrusso's resignation. It appeared to many blacks that the police chief had given his officers license to kill. To Mark Essex it seemed that the nightmare of his navy experience had followed him into civilian life: White men in uniforms were still out to get him.

In November of 1972 tensions in Louisiana escalated when two black students at Southern University in Baton Rouge were shot to death by police during a campus demonstration. These deaths fueled Essex's determination to act. In a letter to his parents, Essex struggled to explain his feelings. "Africa, this is it mom," he wrote. "It's even bigger than you and I, even bigger than God. I have now decided that the white man is my enemy. I will fight to gain my manhood or die trying."

Essex seemed to want badly for his parents to understand. Religion no longer restrained him, society's laws no longer mattered to him, and police no longer frightened him. But he still seemed to want to insulate his beloved family from

the fury that he was about to unleash. On Christmas he called home from New Orleans. "He talked to everyone in the house," Nellie Essex remembered. "He was the same old Jimmy." But of course, by then, Jimmy was gone, and so was Mark; Mata had taken their place. "My destiny," he scrawled on the wall of his apartment, "lies in the bloody death of racist pigs."

In the days following Christmas Essex gave away most of his possessions. Clearly, he didn't expect to need them anymore. On December 31, alone in his apartment, he made preparations: He stashed his Ruger carbine and a .38-caliber revolver in a green duffel bag. Along with the weapons went a large supply of ammunition, a gas mask, wire cutters and pliers, lighter fluid, matches, and a string of firecrackers. He put on a pair of green fatigues and carefully polished his combat boots. When he'd checked his equipment a final time, he hoisted the duffel bag over his shoulder. Across the side he'd printed the word "Warrior."

A few days earlier, Essex had announced his intentions in a letter to a local TV station. "Africa greets you," he declared. "On Dec 31 1972 appt 11 the Downtown New Orleans Police Dept will be attack. . . . Reason—many. But the deaths of two innocent brothers will be avenged. And many others. . . . P.S. Tell Pig Gurusso the felony action squad ain't shit." Essex signed the letter "Mata."

The letter ended up buried under a stack of mail, not to be opened for another week. And that would be far too late.

The Central Lockup of the New Orleans Police Department is a windowless 10-story building of gray concrete, located to the rear of Police Headquarters. A small gatehouse guards the entrance to a short tunnel called the sally port, through which prisoners are escorted on their way to be booked.

Just before 11 p.m. on New Year's Eve, police officers

assigned to the late shift were drifting in to relieve the 3-to-11 watch. It was a cold night, chillier than usual for a New Orleans January, and many of the officers were still feeling the effects of their holiday revels. They shivered in their winter uniforms.

Nineteen-year-old cadet Bruce Weatherford walked toward the gatehouse to report for duty. If the pattern held true, he would sit for eight hours behind a half-inch-thick bulletproof window, raising and lowering the steel-mesh gates at either end of the sally port. It was not a taxing assignment, and Weatherford valued the chance it gave him to study for his classes at the Police Academy.

As he neared the gatehouse that New Year's Eve, Weatherford suddenly heard a sharp explosion. "At first I thought someone was shooting off firecrackers," he later reported. "But then cement started flying off the wall in front of me, and I realized someone was shooting."

Instinctively, Weatherford dived for cover behind a parked car. From the pavement, he turned and saw his friend, 19-year-old Alfred Harrell, inside the gatehouse. Harrell, recently married and the proud father of a nine-month-old boy, saw that Weatherford was in some kind of trouble and pressed the button that raised the front gate to the sally port. Weatherford edged forward, and his friend came running to help him. "I told him to get under cover," Weatherford recalled, "but he started running after me, right across the sally port."

A second volley rang out from a vacant lot across the street. Alfred Harrell spun around and slammed onto the ground, blood gushing from a massive chest wound.

By this time the alarm had spread, and other officers were flooding into the area, shouting that the lockup was under attack. From inside the sally port, Lieutenant Kenneth Dupaquier ran to the fallen officer's side. As Dupaquier knelt down to check for a pulse, Harrell's wedding ring slipped off and fell into the dark slick of blood spreading beneath him. "Al," said the lieutenant, "can you hear me?" Harrell's eyes were wide but unseeing. Gently, Dupaquier picked up the wedding ring and slipped it back onto the cadet's finger.

Mark Essex's war on whites had claimed its first victim, but not the one he'd intended. Alfred Harrell, who died later that night, was a black man, one of the few on the New Orleans police force.

Twenty minutes later, Officers Edwin Hosli and Harold Blappert responded to a burglar alarm that had been tripped at a nearby warehouse. The two men were driving a K-9 unit with a German Shepherd trained to sniff out narcotics and gunpowder. They arrived in front of a building marked Burkhardt Manufacturing at 11:15 p.m. and drove in a slow circuit around the warehouse, looking for signs of forced entry. Hosli, a 27-year-old father of four, was not taking this call too seriously. He'd responded to previous alarms at the warehouse, and all of them had been caused by a security system that tended to malfunction in damp weather. Parking in front of the building, the two men settled in to wait for a maintenance worker from the security company to arrive with keys to the warehouse.

Moments later, a panel truck pulled up and a uniformed worker got out. "You boys planning on a search?" he asked, as the two officers walked over.

"It's probably a false alarm," Hosli responded, "but I think we'll get the dog and have a look."

Hosli turned and walked back toward the car. Blappert followed a few steps behind. As Hosli bent over to open the door, a shot rang out from the doorway of the warehouse. Blappert dropped to the ground, shielded by the car, and scrambled across the front seat to get to the radio. After calling for additional units, he backed out of the car and crawled on his hands and knees to his partner. Hosli lay on his back, blood gurgling from a wound in his abdomen. Blappert was about to drag him back over to the car when two more bullets glanced off the hood and smashed through the windshield. Whoever was shooting had superior firepower, Blappert could see, but he drew his .38-caliber police revolver and began firing toward the warehouse.

Hosli was still alive, but barely. The bullet had ripped through his bowels, spilling fecal matter into his body cavity. When the wounded officer finally reached a hospital, a doctor would liken the damage to pouring drain cleanser into an open wound. It would take Edwin Hosli two months to die.

Within minutes the parking lot outside the warehouse was swarming with more than 30 police officers. Six men lined up with shotguns and opened fire on the front entrance, splintering the door. Deputy Superintendent Louis Sirgo, the department's second-in-command, led a search team into the building. By this time, however, the sniper was gone. Although the police did not yet know the name of their adversary, Essex had left behind plenty of evidence. Inside the warehouse, authorities found a gas-mask canister,

a flashlight, and a brown leather purse with a black owl painted on the side. It contained fifty .38-caliber cartridges. "This is no amateur," declared one officer. "He had enough stuff to take on an army." And there was more evidence of the sniper: Bloody hand prints on a window sill showed that he was nursing a wound as he slipped out a side window.

With one officer dead and another severely wounded, the police launched a massive hunt for the gunman. Teams began a house-to-house search of the neighborhood around the warehouse. It soon became apparent, however, that Essex was making no effort to cover his tracks. In fact, he'd taken the trouble to mark his trail with live rounds

of ammunition. They were arranged in carefully spaced pairs, pointing out the direction the cop killer had taken. "It seemed clear that it was a trap," said one officer. "We were being set up."

The trail led to the 1st New St. Mark Baptist Church, about two blocks away from the warehouse. Outside, one last pair of cartridges pointed to the entrance. Just as the police were about to storm through the doors, a counter-manding order came over the radio. Police Superintendent Giarrusso wanted all officers pulled out of the neighborhood. Reports of police harassment were flooding into headquarters. In the heat of the manhunt, officers had been

The field where Mark Essex crouched to shoot Police Cadet Alfred Harrell shows through the iron grating that seals off the outside of the sally port at New Orleans Police Central Lock-up. The photograph was taken from the spot where Harrell's body fell.

kicking in doors, careless of such niceties as search warrants. Already-strained relations with the community were turning poisonous. To the officers preparing to rush the church, the retreat order could not have been more poorly timed. Many were convinced that they'd been forced to let the gunman slip through their fingers.

It is likely that they'd done precisely that. Apparently, Essex was lying in wait somewhere inside the church, his gun probably trained on the front door. It seemed that Essex spent most of the night in the church. When he finally slipped away, he left the pastor of St. Mark's a note of apology. Perhaps he knew that the church's congregation was black. "I am sorry for breaking the lock on your church door," he wrote. "I had to get right with the Lord." He also promised to send along some money for a new lock.

If Giarrusso erred in withdrawing his forces, it was an understandable mistake. The 47-year-old superintendent had grown up in a tough neighborhood, and he understood the passions that could be ignited when police pushed too hard. A former Golden Gloves boxer and an ex-Marine, Giarrusso had a hard-nosed style that seemed at odds with his sharp intelligence and broad education. He had three college diplomas, marking his studies in law, criminology, and business administration. Though he'd been in the top job less than three years, he had a reputation as a fearless cop's cop. Barely a month after he was appointed, he waded boldly into a shootout with the Black Panthers, exposing himself to fire. "The rightful place for any police chief," he declared at the time, "is leading his men." The episode was criticized by police chiefs in other cities, but it won admiration from the New Orleans rank and file.

To Mark Essex,

Giarrusso was simply the enemy commander, and for now Essex decided to cede the field. Nursing his wounds— apparently not serious ones—the sniper retreated to his apartment and lay low for a few days, surfacing only to buy a few items at a nearby grocery store. Joe Perniciaro, the owner of the grocery, was suspicious of Essex; Perniciaro had been robbed before, and strangers wandering into his neighborhood grocery made him wary. After his customer left, the grocer phoned the police. Perniciaro even handed over the $20 bill that Essex had used to pay for his purchases. Unfortunately, the police lab accidentally burned this piece of evidence while testing it for fingerprints. It would prove a costly mistake, not only for the police but for Joe Perniciaro.

Back in Emporia, on the morning of January 7, Mark Essex's mother attended Sunday services, as was her habit, at the St. James Baptist Church. On this particular morning, Nellie Essex found herself unable to concentrate on the sermon. She fidgeted in her seat, tormented by the inexplicable feeling that Mark was in some kind of terrible danger. Suddenly she jumped to her feet, sobbing, and shouted a plea for the congregation to join her in prayer for Mark. Her son, she wept, "doesn't want to go along with the Lord." And with that, she fainted.

At almost the same moment, hundreds of miles away in New Orleans, Mark Essex burst into Perniciaro's grocery store wearing combat fatigues. The Deerslayer rifle was cradled in his hands. "You!" Essex shouted, pointing to the grocer. "You're the one I want. Come here!"

Joe Perniciaro turned and started to run, but Essex raised his gun and

The 1st New St. Mark Baptist Church was Essex's hiding place after his attack on the Central Lockup. Officers were about to search the church when higher authorities called them off because of rising tensions between police and local residents.

fired. A .44 magnum slug caught the fleeing man in the shoulder, knocking him to the floor. Bleeding badly, he lay still, leading Essex to assume he was dead. The killer darted out of the building.

Four blocks away, Essex stuck the barrel of his gun through the window of a stopped car and ordered the driver to get out. "I don't want to kill you," he told the car's black occupant, "but I'll kill you, too." As the bewildered driver stumbled from the car, Essex jumped in and drove away.

His destination was the Downtown Howard Johnson's Hotel, which faced onto a small park at the center of the city's banking district. The hotel was about five blocks from the much-loved concentration of bars, restaurants, nightclubs, and homes known as the French Quarter. A 17-story building, the Howard Johnson's featured a six-level parking garage immediately above the lobby, and a swimming pool and plaza on the eighth floor. The remaining nine floors (like many hotels, this one accommodated the superstitious by excluding a 13th floor) were given over to guest rooms.

A rectangular structure, it had stairwells running up its narrow north and south sides. A bank of elevators stood about midway between the stairs. On the gravel roof were three concrete outbuildings. The largest, in the middle of the east side of the roof, had two compartments, one housing boilers, the other containing the gear that ran the elevators. The side of this structure visible from the street bore the Howard Johnson's sign. A metal double door and two metal louvered windows were on the side facing the roof. The other outbuildings were two bunkers, one on either end of the roof. These shielded the tops of the stairwells, and each bunker had three compartments. In the middle was a doorway leading up from the stairs, and on either side was a walled-off area, open to the roof, housing ventilation pipes. The Howard Johnson's had already been the site of one disaster: Eighteen months earlier, six people had died when a flash fire swept through the building.

It took Mark Essex only a few minutes to reach the hotel in the light Sunday traffic. Abandoning his stolen car on the

fourth level of the garage, he began working his way up an outside stairwell, searching for an unlocked door.

Hotel maids Hazel Thomas and Carolyn Ardis heard Essex pounding on the door to the eighth floor. "Will you let me in?" Essex shouted through a small window in the door. "There's a guy in there I've got to see."

The women refused, citing hotel regulations against admitting strangers through the security doors. But Essex wouldn't give up easily. "Are you two soul sisters?" he asked. "Then one for two and two for one. Come on now, open up." He lingered for a few minutes but gave up when Thomas and Ardis refused to relent. Only when he bolted up the next flight of stairs did the maids see through the door's window that he had a rifle in his hands. They ran to spread the alarm.

One floor up, Essex tried to talk another member of the housekeeping staff into opening a door. "Let me in, sis," he called. "I got something to do." Again he was turned away. At last, on one of the upper floors, he found a door propped open with a stack of linen. From that moment, Essex roamed freely through the hotel.

Robert Steagall, a 27-year-old doctor, was eating an apple in his room on the 18th floor when he heard a knock at the door. Steagall and his wife, Betty, had been married six months earlier and had come to New Orleans on a delayed honeymoon. Answering the door, Steagall found a hotel maid waiting to make up his room. He asked her to come back later, and the maid moved on down the corridor. Just then, she saw Mark Essex running toward her. "Don't worry," he said as he raced by. "I'm not going to hurt you black people. I want the whites."

Steagall stepped into the hall as Essex ran forward. "What are you doing?" the doctor shouted. Essex raised his rifle and Steagall made a desperate lunge, trying to pull the gunman off his feet. Essex brought the butt of his rifle down hard on the doctor's shoulder, knocking him to the floor. As Steagall struggled to get up, Essex shot him in the chest.

At the sound of gunfire, Betty Steagall ran screaming into the hallway. "Please don't kill my husband," she cried. "Oh, please!" She threw herself down on the floor beside her dead husband. As she cradled him in her arms, Essex aimed again and shot her through the base of the skull. With calm precision, he then stepped into the Steagalls' room, set the curtains on fire, reloaded his rifle, and headed for one of the hotel's interior stairwells.

The gunfire and the smell of smoke prompted several panicky calls to the police and fire departments. Dozens of frantic guests scrambled for exits while others cowered in their rooms, wondering what could be going on. At the switchboard, front-office manager Frank Schneider and bellman Don Roberts decided to have a look around upstairs. Essex, meanwhile, had worked his way down to the 11th floor, setting several fires on the way. "This is a revolution," he told an astonished black hotel maid, Beatrice Greenhouse. "I'm only shooting whites. No blacks."

When the elevator doors opened and Schneider and Roberts stepped out onto the 11th floor, Greenhouse shouted a warning and both men turned to run. Essex coolly raised his gun and squeezed off two shots. The second bullet caught Frank Schneider in the back of the head and tore away half his skull. Roberts kept running and managed to reach the safety of a stairwell.

Essex paused just long enough to set another fire, then moved on down the corridor to a stairwell. On the 10th floor he found the hotel's general manager, Walter Collins, trying to warn guests about the spreading fires. Essex barely broke stride as he shot Collins in the back. Badly wounded, the manager waited until Essex's footsteps had faded, then crawled toward a stairwell. The door to a room opened a crack, and a terrified woman peered out at him. "What can I do?" she asked.

"Call the police," Collins gasped, "and shut the door."

Patrolmen Michael Burl and Robert Childress arrived at the Howard Johnson's shortly before 11 a.m. Though they couldn't quite bring themselves to believe the reports of a crazed gunman roaming the hotel, they boarded an elevator and began a floor-to-floor search. At one stop they ran into a frightened elderly black woman. "When she saw us, she turned around and faced the elevator doors on the other side of the hall like she was afraid of us," Childress said later. "When we told her the place was on fire, she said, 'I know. I seen him. He's shooting white people.' Then the elevator came and she got in and went downstairs. I tell you, I was plenty scared after that."

In an error of judgment, the officers rode the elevator to the 18th floor instead of taking the stairs. Thick smoke was accumulating in the elevator shafts. When the car they were in got stuck, there was little the men could do but take off their jackets and try to seal the cracks under the doors.

While Burl and Childress were settling in to wait for a rescue party, 43-year-old Robert Beamish was stepping through the patio doors of his room on the eighth-floor swimming pool plaza. At just that moment, Essex emerged from behind some bushes and shot Beamish in the stomach. The blast knocked the hotel guest off his feet and into the swimming pool, but he realized that he wasn't badly hurt. Beamish decided to stay in the water until police could rescue him. He would remain in the pool, floating in a widening cloud of his own blood, for almost two hours.

As he crossed the pool plaza, Essex once again encountered hotel employee Beatrice Greenhouse. By now nearly senseless with fear, Greenhouse stammered a request for directions on how to get out of the hotel. Essex obligingly pointed her toward an exit.

Downstairs, the New Orleans Fire Department was confronting extraordinary chaos. Fires smoldered on several floors, and dozens of guests huddled on their balconies, too scared to move. Worse yet, as the firemen fanned out to fight the blazes, they exposed themselves to gunfire—not only sniper's bullets but also a growing volume of wild and undisciplined return fire from police. At the height of the crisis, panic seemed to grip the firefighters. One rescue truck, turning a corner at high speed, flipped onto its side and slammed into a lamp post. A pumper truck, abandoned when a bullet struck the ground nearby, gushed water for six hours before anyone would dare to go near it.

Fireman Tim Ursin was one of the first of his company on the scene. As he carried a hose up a ladder on one side of the building, two patrolmen, Bill Trapagnier and Jack Uhle, followed behind, hoping for a shot at the sniper from above. "I was well behind Ursin, and Jack was behind me," recalled Trapagnier. "I had gone up about 20 steps or so when I saw this guy come out on one of the balconies and lift up a rifle. He aimed at Ursin. I started screaming, but with all the sirens going, Ursin couldn't hear me. Then there was a shot and Ursin was hit good, and the blood just poured down. It was like rain. I started shooting at the guy then, and I kept shooting until my shotgun was empty."

With great difficulty, the two policemen managed to get Ursin to the ground. "It was a mess," Uhle said. "Flesh and bone was hanging out. It looked like someone had slammed him with a pickax." The wounded fireman would live, but he'd lose one of his arms.

Police Superintendent Giarrusso arrived at the hotel shortly after 11 a.m. and found the situation veering out of control. More than a hundred police officers had converged on the Howard Johnson's, and many of them had simply taken out their guns and started blasting away at the upper floors. In order to assess the situation, Giarrusso decided to make a circuit of the hotel, not realizing that this would take him directly into the sniper's line of fire. Only when a police officer shouted at him to get his head down did the superintendent recognize the danger. "It was," he would say, "the dumbest thing I've ever done. I guess that the only

This is a revolution. I'm only shooting whites. No blacks.

thing that saved me was that I wasn't wearing a uniform."

In a move that would draw much criticism in the weeks to come, Giarrusso decided to establish a command post inside the hotel, effectively placing himself squarely in enemy territory. Already he was being swamped with inaccurate and conflicting reports as to the number of snipers and the extent of the damage being done. Even more troubling, the uncoordinated barrage the police were directing at the hotel threatened to do more harm than the sniper fire. One officer, finding a group of eight deputies blasting away in the general direction of the Howard Johnson's, asked what they were shooting at. "The hotel," came the answer.

Giarrusso knew he had to get a grip on the situation fast. "Do you see those idiots across the street?" he snapped to an aide. "They must think they're cowboys. We've got to get them to stop firing their damn weapons unless they've got a target." In fact, the confusion was even worse than he knew at the time. Volunteers—law enforcement officers from jurisdictions outside the city—were descending on the hotel from all directions. Many carried their personal high-powered rifles and shotguns. Some had been issued high-powered weapons in their own jurisdictions, but they didn't know how to use them. "It was unbelievable," said a policeman. "Some of them were actually trying to load the bullets in the wrong places. If they had had to start shooting suddenly, they would have killed each other."

By the end of the day, more than 600 police officers had turned up, coming from as far away as Texas. There were also a few agents from the FBI and the Treasury Department. To Giarrusso's extreme annoyance, there were also several dozen civilian volunteers. One World War II veteran, wearing an ill-fitting Eisenhower jacket, rushed to the hotel cradling an obsolete Springfield rifle. He got as far as the hotel lobby before police turned him away.

Only Mark Essex seemed to be following a plan. As police surrounded the hotel and climbed onto the rooftops of surrounding buildings, Essex moved rapidly from floor to floor, firing through broken windows and setting new fires. By reversing his quilted jacket as he dashed through the building, he managed to confuse witnesses and create the impression that more than one gunman was at work. Firecrackers that he tossed down stairwells convinced listeners that guns were going off all over the hotel.

Not surprisingly, the terrified hotel workers and guests who'd actually seen Essex gave wildly varying descriptions to the police. The gunman's height, build, and race seemed to change with every sighting. "This is great stuff," said Giarrusso, skimming the reports. "He's either a dwarf, a giant, black, or Mexican, or all of them at once."

While Giarrusso was struggling to impose control, police marksmen took up positions. At an office complex across the street, Patrolman Charles Arnold found a prime firing post on the 10th floor—one that offered a clear view of the north face of the hotel. As Arnold pushed open a window, however, a bullet fired from the hotel tore into his jaw, slamming him backward into a desk. Teeth, blood, and pieces of jawbone littered the floor around him. "Good Christ!" shouted a fellow officer. "He blew your face off!" Calmly, the injured man stood up, pressed a handkerchief to his gaping wound, and made his way out of the building to Charity Hospital two blocks away.

Arnold was wise not to wait for an ambulance. The streets on all sides of the hotel were clogged with emergency vehicles, and traffic was gridlocked. Several hundred spectators had gathered, heedless of the danger of being shot from the hotel. Many of these onlookers sat on the hoods of cars, as if watching a fireworks display. A large group of young black men pushed their way forward and began yelling their support for the killer. With each blast of the sniper's rifle, the group raised an approving cry of "Right on!" or "Kill the pigs!" There were even murmurs of joining in on the action once darkness settled on the city.

The onlookers—and virtually everyone in the city as well as people throughout the nation—knew the race and the apparent motives of the sniper by this point. Monitoring police radios, local reporters rushed to the Howard Johnson's just after the shooting started, and television crews began broadcasting live pictures. At first the coverage was local, but the television networks soon began airing the live action as well.

Patrolman Kenneth Solis and his partner, David McCann, were among the officers trying to contain the swelling crowd. On the grassy plaza to the north of the hotel, they noticed a particularly boisterous group of rubberneckers shouting encouragement to the gunman. The plaza lay in the sniper's possible line of fire, but so far he hadn't wounded any spectators. Hoping to move people out of this area, Solis and McCann left their cover and walked directly across Essex's field of vision. "I had just stepped three yards or so onto the plaza when I was hit in the right shoulder,"

Solis would recall. "The bullet felt like a two-by-four. It came out under my rib cage."

Sergeant Emanuel Palmisano saw Solis go down and ran to his aid, only to take a bullet under his left arm. McCann, who tried to carry Solis to safety, saw Palmisano fall and shouted for help. Officers Philip Coleman and Leo Newman heard the cries and drove their patrol car in a weaving track onto the plaza, crouching low in the front seat to avoid a steady barrage of gunfire. Coleman slammed on the brakes and rolled out of the driver's seat, snatching open the rear door so that the wounded officers could be loaded onto the backseat. A bullet caught him in the head. Newman crawled to his partner's side, but Coleman was already dying. Two more rounds struck the car. With the surviving officers pinned down, a nearby news photographer climbed into the patrol car and radioed for help.

Having shot three men in less than five minutes, Essex moved quickly to a new vantage and resumed firing. Just after noon, he ran down a staircase to the fourth level of the parking garage, possibly with the idea of escaping in his stolen car. Through the plate glass of the stairwell door he could see a pair of policemen standing guard. Essex blasted a hole through the glass with his rifle, but the shot missed the officers. Frustrated, he climbed back up to the 16th floor, one of the few levels that was not yet burning. He scanned the street below and spotted a traffic division officer named Paul Persigo, who was trying to clear the sidewalk. Essex aimed and fired, hitting Persigo in the mouth.

An ambulance crew rushed Persigo to the emergency room of Charity Hospital, but nothing could be done to save him. As a nurse bent down to loosen the chin strap of his helmet, the patrolman's head collapsed in a sodden mass of blood and tissue.

By this time, dead and wounded were pouring into Charity's emergency room. Distant gunfire punctuated the screams and groans of the wounded, and stray bullets struck the hospital twice. Hospital workers started nailing thick pieces of plywood over the windows.

Patrolman Arnold was getting treatment for the injuries to his face and jaw when medics brought in the more gravely wounded Solis and Palmisano. While doctors attended to the new arrivals, Arnold's stretcher was pushed into a hallway. "I guess they sort of forgot me," he later said. "I was spitting up a lot of blood into a pan. With the muscle spasms and pain, I couldn't talk, and I was still bleeding

A plain-clothes policeman armed with a rifle dashes to join fellow officers taking cover behind cars parked in Mark Essex's line of fire on the evening of January 7. Civilians milling around on the sidewalk in the background try to observe the action without exposing themselves to fire from the Howard Johnson's.

bad. I started to choke on the blood, and I began to worry that I might bleed to death before they got back to me." Arnold dipped a finger into the pan of blood on his lap and scrawled on the wall, "Help me. I'm bleeding to death." Within minutes he was in surgery.

At the police command center inside the hotel, a number of the city's elected officials, including Mayor Moon Landrieu, held an agitated conference to speculate on what might happen next. The sniper attack, they feared, might signal the start of a more general uprising of blacks. "We wondered whether a revolution was coming," a councilman later recalled. However troubling this notion was, it was the least of Clarence Giarrusso's problems at that moment. Far more pressing was the fact that the gunman or gunmen currently in the hotel seemed to be having no problem standing off the entire New Orleans Police Department.

Shortly after noon, Deputy Superintendent Louis Sirgo arrived at the command center and organized a rescue party to free Officers Burl and Childress, who were believed to be still trapped in an elevator near the 18th floor. Sirgo's concern for the stranded men was typical of him; his support for his troops made him extremely popular with the officers under his command. A blunt, hard-working cop, Sirgo was also deeply committed to civil rights. Months earlier, in a speech to a police honor society, he'd described the mistreatment of blacks as "the greatest sin of American society." Without prompt action, Sirgo had warned, "the problem, like a contagious malady, will destroy us."

The deputy chief picked three veteran officers who he knew would stay cool under fire, and the group started up the south stairwell, stopping on each floor to look for the sniper. What they couldn't have known was that their dangerous mission was unnecessary: Burl and Childress were no longer in the elevator. As smoke filled the cramped car and the lights and ventilator fan failed, the desperate officers had opened the trapdoor in the elevator's ceiling and crawled out. Squeezing between the elevator and the walls of the shaft, they slid down the long, greased elevator cables to safety. Only when they reached the bottom did they learn that a rescue was under way.

It took Sirgo and his rescue party nearly 45 minutes of cautious climbing to reach the 16th floor. They got there at 1:07 p.m. Sirgo heard what he thought was a police whistle from inside the elevator shaft. "Hold on," he shouted. "We're coming up."

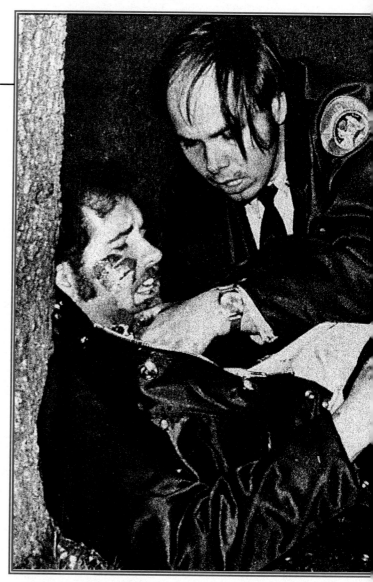

A few yards away, lying in the stairwell's shadows, Mark Essex heard him. Moments earlier, he'd climbed the stairwell trying to reach the hotel's roof. Finding the door to the roof chained shut, he'd turned and started back down the stairs when he heard Sirgo and his men coming up. Essex aimed his rifle and waited. As Sirgo came into view on the 16th-floor landing, the sniper fired at point-blank range.

Sirgo fell backward into the arms of the three officers on the stairs below. Sergeant Bernard Flint, the strongest of the three, tried to clamp his hand over the deputy chief's wound as he carried him down the stairs. Flint's hand sank into a gaping hole, and he felt, to his horror, Sirgo's exposed spine pressing against his palm. He knew that Sirgo had only moments to live.

Somehow the three men managed to carry their superior

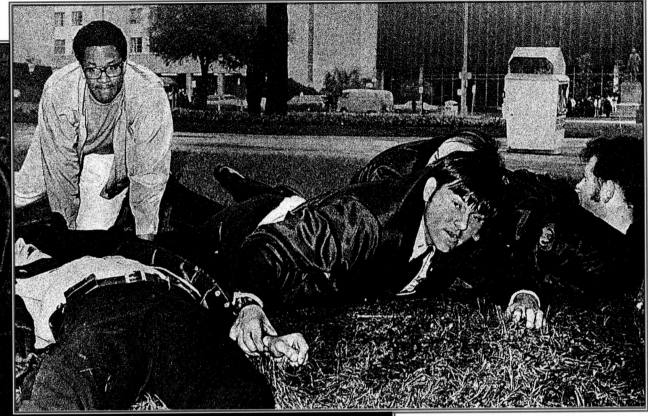

On Duncan Plaza in front of the Howard Johnson's, Officer David McCann tries to stop the bleeding from a gaping wound in partner Kenneth Solis's shoulder *(left)*. Moments later, Officer Leo Newman lies in front of McCann and Solis and feels for partner Philip Coleman's fading pulse *(above),* while an onlooker who crawled over to assist registers shock and helplessness. Responding to McCann's cries for help, Coleman had driven to the rescue, but he was shot in the head the moment he leaped from his car.

down 15 flights of stairs to the ground floor, where an ambulance was waiting. Louis Sirgo, a white man who had championed racial justice, would be pronounced dead on arrival at Charity Hospital.

At his command post, Giarrusso listened grimly to the news of Sirgo's death. He'd lost his second-in-command without moving any closer to capturing or killing the sniper. Though he'd tried so far to shield his men from unnecessary risk, Giarrusso now knew that the crisis wouldn't end until each floor of the hotel had been searched and secured. Reluctantly, he ordered Captain Curtis Gaudet, commander of the night watch, and Frank Haab, a Tactical Squad officer, to launch a room-by-room hunt.

Assembling a squad, Gaudet and Haab began a methodical search of the hotel's rooms. Beginning on the eighth

floor—the first floor of guest rooms—they kicked open doors, put out fires, and flushed out stairwells. Behind each locked door they expected to find the sniper waiting, ready to open fire. Nerves stretched so taut that before the officers even finished with the eighth floor some of them were vomiting from the tension. They took turns kicking in the doors, Haab said, "because we figured that if anyone was in there waiting, the first man through the door was going to get shot. Three men with shotguns were covering, and when the door opened, we would all rush in and check the closets and bathrooms and flip over the bedding. It was like playing roulette." He meant Russian roulette, of course—the game where the loser gets a bullet through the head.

"I came within an eyelash of blowing away a man and a woman," said another officer. "I had my mind made up to shoot because we had heard noises coming from inside, real suspicious ones. I might actually have been pulling the trigger. That's when the woman screamed and I caught myself. If she hadn't screamed, I probably would have killed them." The pair were guests in the hotel.

In time, Haab and Gaudet's team would complete their tour—and the whole nerve-flaying exercise would turn out to have been in vain: Essex was no longer inside the building. After shooting Louis Sirgo, the sniper had made his way to the north stairwell and climbed to the top. It was 1:10 p.m. This time, he found the door to the roof unlocked.

Essex exited into the squat concrete bunker at the north end of the roof. Pivoting in a U-turn to his left, he darted into one of the bunker's two open compartments. Strategically, he was now in an excellent defensive position. His little cubicle was protected on three sides by concrete walls a foot thick. Moreover, by climbing the steel ventilation pipe inside the cubicle, he could get out of sight—and out of the line of fire—of anyone on the roof or at eye level with it. There was only one problem: He had no avenue of retreat. With police covering both stairwells, Essex surely knew that his chances for leaving the hotel alive were nil. But then, he'd probably never expected to escape.

Just after Essex took up his position in the north cubicle, Lieutenant Jake Schnapp, a Tactical Squad commander, led a small team up the south stairwell. The men found the door to the roof securely chained—as Essex had earlier. Officer Larry Arthur kicked the door open, flooding the darkened stairwell with daylight. Momentarily blinded, Arthur nevertheless crouched low and rushed forward through the door. A blast from Essex's rifle knocked him backward into the stairwell. "Free Africa!" Mark Essex yelled from the roof. "Come on up, pigs!"

Arthur was able to leave the roof under his own power, and he would recover from his wounds. But his shooting marked the start of a long standoff. While police marksmen maneuvered into positions that would allow them to shoot into the bunker, Essex continued to fire pretty much at will. He even managed to scatter a TV camera crew on a nearby rooftop. Protected by his shield of concrete, he hurled taunts at his frustrated enemies. "Happy New Year's, pigs!" he shouted. "What's the matter? You afraid, pigs?"

As the afternoon wore on, cold fog and drizzle settled over the city, reducing visibility that was already obscured by smoke. Despite the murky conditions, Giarrusso was afraid to expose his men to fire by sending them onto the roof to flush Essex out. Instead, he ordered them to concentrate a barrage of fire on the cubicle where Essex was hiding. The killer frustrated this strategy by staying so far back in the bunker that the torrent of bullets couldn't reach him. Even tear gas had no effect. A dozen canisters launched from a building across the street dispersed harmlessly in the wet wind that played over the hotel rooftop. "I'm still here, pigs!" Essex yelled.

The siege stretched into the evening. Crowd control remained a problem, and then a local radio announcer made it much worse. Broadcasting what he claimed was a special request from the police, the announcer instructed all citizens with large-caliber rifles to head downtown to help dislodge the sniper. The bogus call for volunteers soon produced "a large number of morons," according to one city councilman, "all of them armed to the teeth." Giarrusso was furious, and as the stalemate wore on, police grew steadily less tolerant of the civilians. When one rifle-toting citizen refused to leave the area without taking a few shots, an angry cop knocked him unconscious. And not all civilians were concerned solely with the welfare of the police. One woman telephoned with an offer of warm blankets. She was afraid the sniper might be getting chilly up on the roof.

But weather was probably the last thing on Essex's mind as thousands of rounds of high-powered rifle fire ate away at the concrete cubicle sheltering him. So far there was no sign that he himself had been hit. Giarrusso entertained several options for getting him out in the open: Suggested assaults involved fire hoses, hand grenades, mortar fire, flamethrowers, and even a crane and wrecking ball. The desperation of these ideas reflected the sniper's relative impregnability. And Essex seemed well aware that he had the edge. "Come on out," he called across the darkened rooftop. "You afraid to fight like a black man?"

In fact, the police department's caution wasn't prompted by Essex alone. As night fell, authorities still believed that the sniper had company. Most officers, Giarrusso included, thought that there were at least two gunmen, and some estimates ran as high as 10. Several lawmen had reported hearing conversations between snipers, and some claimed to have heard two distinct kinds of rifle fire coming from the roof. None of these reports could be confirmed, however, and police could tell the press only that an "unknown force" continued to occupy the hotel.

With the coming of darkness, freezing rain began pelting the rooftop. Police marksmen shivered in windows and doorways, as much from the grinding anxiety as from the chill. In a parking lot near the hotel, a United States Marine Sea Knight armored helicopter touched down to ready for an aerial assault.

Giarrusso had started calling for a helicopter the moment that Essex entered the cubicle, believing that only airborne marksmen could get a clear line of fire. The copter's pilot, Lieutenant Colonel Charles Pitman, was a highly decorated veteran of more than 1,200 combat missions, but the antennas and the three outbuildings on the hotel roof presented challenges he'd never encountered in Vietnam. Wary of these urban obstacles, Pitman nevertheless took his chopper up for a strafing run at Essex. With him were five police sharpshooters armed with automatic weapons. On the first pass, marksmen firing from the chopper poured hundreds of rounds through the opening of the cubicle. The bullets danced wildly off the concrete and the steel pipe, but Essex shinnied to the top of the pipe and escaped harm. Pitman made several more runs, hoping to at least catch the sniper with a ricochet. Essex managed not only to avoid the fusillades but to return fire. Each time the copter turned to leave, he would leap from his perch and shoot at it.

During the course of the siege, the helicopter would make 48 strafing runs over the roof, its sharpshooters often firing blindly through smoke and fog. On one pass, the gunners trained a furious barrage on the door to the north stairwell, unaware that a police assault team was huddled on the other side. "The rounds just poured in on us," said one of the policemen pinned down by the hail of bullets. "Plaster and concrete went flying from the walls and we went tumbling down those stairs. It was amazing no one was killed."

The airborne assaults had failed. In fact, as the first day of the siege ended, Giarrusso and his men had had no success at all in their campaign to dislodge the killer. Essex had killed three police officers that day and badly wounded several more. Small fires continued to fill the hotel's hallways with smoke, and the building's roof and upper stories were pockmarked from thousands of rounds of gunfire. The embarrassing fact was that the sniper had fought the New Orleans police to a standstill, and he'd done it with apparent ease. The police knew it. On the streets below Essex's rooftop stronghold, hundreds of heavily armed officers crouched behind barricades, their faces haggard and tight.

Inside the hotel, Giarrusso assessed the impasse. "Sooner or later I knew that I was going to have to send men up there," he would recall. "Some of the guys were really chomping at the bit." As he reviewed his options, Lieutenant Richard Hunter, who'd spent several hours posted in one of the stairwells, drew him aside. "Chief," said the lieutenant, "I've got 10 men who're ready right now to go and take that roof and get it over with. What do you say?"

Giarrusso pondered the proposal. He knew that his men were tired and frustrated, but he still hoped he could resolve the crisis without putting any more of them in harm's way. "It would be suicide, Richie," he said at last. "There are probably a hundred men without radio communications who'd start blasting as soon as you ran out into the open. No, we're going to take our time. Keep shooting at him. Try to wear him down. But no one goes on that roof."

As Hunter returned to his post, Giarrusso sent one of his black officers up to the roof in a last-ditch effort to persuade Essex to surrender. Carrying a battery-powered bullhorn, the cop climbed to the top of the stairs. "You up there," he blared through the bullhorn toward the scarred cubicle, "I'm a police officer. We don't want to kill you. We'd like to talk to you. What do you say, brother? Why not save yourself? Give up before it's too late."

There was no answer.

"If you don't come down, you're going to be killed," the officer continued. "There's no reason for that. Give it up. Surrender. You can still save yourself. If you're wounded, we can get you medical help."

For a long moment, the rooftop was perfectly still. Then a loud, almost hysterical voice broke the silence. "Power to the people!" Essex screamed.

"Come on down, man," the policeman shouted back. "Don't die. Don't make us kill you."

There was no response. The conversation was over.

Shortly before 9 p.m., the Marine helicopter lifted off for yet another strafing run. Pilot Charles Pitman brought the craft in low over the roof, allowing his gunners to pour their fire directly into Essex's bunker. As he started to pull away, one of the marksmen raised a shout: "No, don't go! He's out there!"

After more than seven hours crouched in the cubicle, Mark Essex apparently decided the time had come for the last, climactic act of defiance and rage. He charged into view, firing his rifle as he ran. He raised his right arm in the clenched fist of the black power salute. "Come and get me!" he screamed. "Come and get me!"

Gunfire poured in from all directions. The helicopter gunners, firing on full automatic, pumped a steady stream of bullets into Mark Essex's small body, while dozens of other marksmen took shots from the surrounding rooftops. "He was looking straight at us, holding the gun at the waist and firing," recalled an astonished Sergeant Antoine Saacks, who was aboard the helicopter. "He took two or three steps before we opened up. I hit him with a whole clip from the thighs to the neck. He was running at full tilt and his momentum carried him another five or ten feet. Then the bullets caught him and held him up, sort of like when you shoot at a pie plate and keep it rolling."

"I hit him in the buttock, and he tumbled forward and dropped his rifle," said Officer Alex Vega, who'd been posted on the roof of a nearby bank. "Then some guys with the big stuff, the .375s and .458 elephant guns, opened up. One of those shells hit his leg. It looked to me like it blew it off."

On one of the buildings across from the hotel, more than 140 policemen were firing wildly, desperate for a shot at the sniper. Detective Gus Krinke later recalled that a number of officers kicked away a protective plywood barrier to give themselves a better view. "There's no telling how many times he must have been hit," said Krinke. "Myself, I had just put in a fresh clip, and when he came out, I zeroed in and emptied it. Guys were screaming, 'Yeah, now we got you, you sonofabitch. Die, you goddamn bastard. Die!' You could feel the release. After all those cops had been killed, now we finally had a chance to do something, to fight back. There was cheering when he went down."

The barrage would continue for nearly four minutes.

Mark Essex lay dead on the roof, one leg almost severed by gunfire, most of his smooth young face blown away. From time to time the wind would lift the remnants of his shredded fatigues, and the rags would flutter, giving the corpse an eerie semblance of life. He'd played out his personal tragedy, but, amazingly, the drama at the hotel would continue for another 19 hours without him.

Police were still convinced that there were more snipers on the loose. "Our greatest ally is time," Giarrusso declared. "We are going to wait."

At least one group of officers counted themselves lucky to be alive to do the waiting. The salvo that had cut Mark

The ventilation pipe that Essex climbed to evade gunfire is visible in the blasted ruin of the rooftop bunker that was the sniper's final refuge. Essex eventually made a suicidal dash from this shelter. His body *(inset)*, ripped by more than 100 police bullets, lay where it fell until dusk the following day.

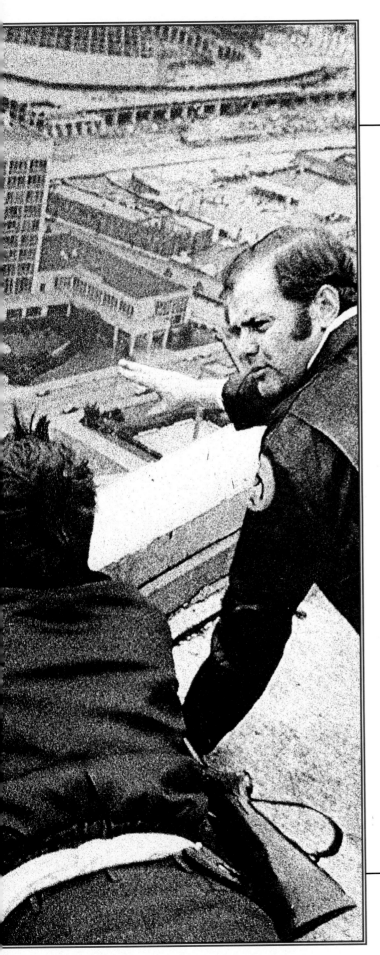

Police riflemen atop the 31-story Bank of New Orleans building discuss strategy as they look down on the roof of the Howard Johnson's. Four helicopters sit in a parking lot behind City Hall; one of the assault choppers had mounted the attack on Mark Essex's rooftop stronghold.

Essex down had also shattered a water pipe on the roof, sending a four-foot wave down the stairwell where Lieutenant Hunter and his men were posted. The flood swept the men down the stairs, depositing one officer in a corridor two flights below the landing where he'd started.

Other policemen began telling of additional sniper sightings. The erroneous reports were understandable. Grief for fallen friends, hours of gut-grinding tension, and the fierce release of gunning down the killer had all taken their toll. Many of the men teetered near hysteria. From the stairs leading to the roof, officers reported hearing voices in both concrete cubicles, and marksmen across the street thought they saw shadows moving across the rooftop. In the darkness, the policemen shouted taunts. "Where does it hurt, Leroy?" they called. "Hurts all over, don't it?"

Shortly before 2 a.m., the scattered reports of sniper activity took on more urgency. At least five officers claimed to have seen a gunman in a white shirt crawl out to a corner of the roof and begin firing. Police in the stairwells confirmed that they could hear the firing of an automatic weapon. More information poured in over the police radio. One caller had the sniper moving across the roof, firing at will.

From the roof of a building to the west of the hotel, an officer radioed to say that he could clearly see the sniper through his binoculars. Giarrusso gave him permission to start shooting, and when he did, spotters from the neighboring buildings began weighing in with damage reports. "You're hitting all around him," claimed one witness. "You're just a hair to the right," said another. Additional spotters confirmed that the sniper was returning fire. "Now he's standing straight up," shouted one officer. "Kill him!"

Although only one officer was authorized to shoot, others joined in, shattering windows on the hotel's upper floors where fellow policemen were positioned. "Next time we're going to shoot back!" cried one officer as he dived for cover.

Hearing that a sniper had taken cover in the cubicle at the north end of the roof, Giarrusso decided to punch a hole through the concrete. Officer Clinton Lauman, an expert marksman, was selected for the job. Using a .375-caliber elephant gun, Lauman fired 30 rounds at the bunker, shaking the whole hotel with each blast. The recoils were so powerful that Lauman emerged from his task with a broken nose and cheekbone. At length, the big gun did punch a hole in the side of the cubicle, and marksmen poured in a thick barrage of fire. "By the time we stopped shooting," said one of the officers, "there was enough brass on the floor to fill a five-gallon can."

Still, the police couldn't be certain that the presumed second sniper was dead. From the lobby, Giarrusso sent up a pair of police dogs. One became so ill from the lingering tear gas that it had to be carried back downstairs.

At 5 a.m. Charles Pitman took the helicopter up for yet another run. As he passed over the southern end of the roof, the heavy vibrations from the whirling blades caused a stairwell door to swing open. From aboard the helicopter, police marksmen saw the barrel of a rifle slip into view. They opened fire on the stairwell.

Once again, the police were firing on their own men. Four officers—Sergeants Robert Buras and Fred O'Sullivan and Tactical Officers Wayne Galjour and Richard Siegel—had been stationed at the top of the stairs. From this position they saw only a blinding light and the muzzle flashes of automatic weapons. They returned fire immediately.

Buras took the brunt of the attack, catching bullets in the chest, shoulder, and forearm. He was saved by a bulletproof vest. Another bullet passed through Sergeant O'Sullivan's ear. Galjour and Siegel suffered minor injuries, and two officers aboard the helicopter were nicked in the exchange.

As the sun came up the following morning, the fear and tension centered in the hotel seemed to be spreading to the entire city. From many corners of New Orleans reports filtered in of armed black gangs roaming the streets, firing at white motorists and pedestrians. Reluctantly, Giarrusso dispatched several units from his exhausted and overtaxed troops to check out the reports. Most were false, and many were ridiculous. When police got word of another sniper a few blocks away from the Howard Johnson's, a squad car rushed to the scene and spotted a black man carrying a long, thin object. Three officers jumped out and trained their shotguns at the suspect, who turned out to be a 70-year-old man toting an umbrella.

At the hotel, police remained convinced that there was at least one more sniper barricaded on the roof. With the crisis entering its 24th hour, Giarrusso concluded that his only reasonable option was a full-scale assault on the roof.

Under the command of Lieutenant Richard Hunter, 16 men took up positions at the top of the north stairwell, ready to storm onto the roof and flush out the three outbuildings. "We thought it was going to be suicide," recalled one of the participants. Just before 2 p.m. the assault team

A U.S. Marines Sea Knight helicopter *(right)* hovers by the east face of the Howard Johnson's on the morning of January 8, looking for more snipers. When the copter survey turned up no new gunmen, a police team ascended to the roof for a definitive check. At that point, authorities still believed that Essex had at least one confederate still hiding atop the hotel. Finding the cubicles on either side of the roof deserted, they gathered along the north wall of the boiler room *(below)*—the last possible hiding place on the roof—and prepared for a final assault.

Police take aim at the entrance to the boiler room *(above)*. Onlookers and a national television audience watched in disbelief as the tense, exhausted officers opened fire. Nine men were wounded by ricochets, three seriously. At left, two policemen help an injured comrade past Mark Essex's body to the stairway.

The boiler room's metal louvered doors were destroyed in the disastrous police attack—to no avail. The last possible hiding place was empty.

burst through the door. Charging forward at a dead run, the men leaped over the body of Mark Essex, which lay a few yards from the north bunker, and made straight for the south cubicle. Almost immediately, they came under fire from police marksmen stationed on the roof of nearby City Hall. "Don't shoot," the men on the hotel roof yelled frantically. "We're cops!"

After sweeping the south cubicle with quick bursts of automatic fire, Hunter's men reached what they believed to be the moment of truth. At the center of the roof stood the largest outbuilding, the concrete rectangle housing the elevator gear and the hotel boilers. There were double doors leading to the side of the cubicle that held the boilers. Here, the team decided, was the only place where the sniper could be hiding. Standing in front of the structure, the officers stood for a moment frozen in confusion over how to open the door. No one had thought to bring keys or an ax. By this time, several more policemen had pushed their way onto the roof to join Hunter's original team, adding to the sense of disarray. "Let's shoot it open!" someone shouted. The officers formed a semicircle, leveling their guns at the heavy metal doors only a few yards away.

"Jesus," gasped a cop, watching the scene from across the street. "They're not going to do what I think they are!"

A shot rang out—one fired, no doubt, by one of the edgy officers on the roof. But its origin was misunderstood. "He's shooting!" came a frantic cry. With this, the men in front of the boiler room cut loose with their automatic weapons, blasting crazily at what they thought was a barricaded sniper. The results were devastating. Fired at close range against the metal door, the bullets ricocheted with deadly force, knocking down cops like dominoes. "Cease firing!" screamed Lieutenant Hunter as a bullet sliced across his hand. "Cease fire!"

In all, nine policemen were injured, three of them seriously. The door, meanwhile, remained securely fastened. As the wounded were carried from the roof, reinforcements arrived, bringing an ax to smash open the door. The boiler room was empty.

The scene would surely have pleased Mark Essex, whose

The walls of Mark Essex's apartment at 2619½ Dryades Street were covered with anti-white slogans, revolutionary rhetoric, and a sampling of his self-taught Swahili vocabulary.

body still lay at the center of the roof. Slowly, shaking their heads in disbelief, the officers filed past to examine what was left of the body. Even in death, the sniper seemed to mock his enemies. His right arm was stretched over his head, the fist still clenched in defiance.

With the solitary gunman dead at their feet, many of the police still could not accept that Mark Essex had inflicted so much damage acting alone. They assumed that his accomplices had somehow escaped. "We blew it," said one policeman, weeping softly in his frustration. "We had them, and then we blew it."

A pair of crime scene technicians arrived to take the body to the morgue. After unceremoniously dumping the remains into a yellow rubber sack, they dragged Essex's corpse to a stairwell. Another officer stepped to the edge of the roof and picked up a small object. After studying it for a moment, he placed it in a cellophane bag. It was Mark Essex's tongue.

It would be about a day before police tracking the sniper's identity learned his name, and it was longer still before they could fully assess the destruction he'd caused. Two policemen died as a result of Essex's New Year's Eve assault on the New Orleans Lockup. Six people died at the Howard Johnson's the day of the shootings there, and a seventh would die of wounds suffered during the hotel massacre. Twelve people were seriously wounded in the course of Essex's two-part spree. But even as a stunned New Orleans buried its dead and tended its wounded, the overwhelming question remained: Why had Essex done it?

"He was a man who was terribly frustrated and decided to fight," said local civil rights activist Larry Jones. "Most blacks deal with frustration in other ways, or, if we are violent, we've been brainwashed to the point where we channel our violence against one another. It was different with Essex. And as I watched the shooting at the hotel that Sunday, I kept thinking, why doesn't that happen more often?" A number of other people concluded—more simply and comfortably—that Essex had just been crazy.

Looking back on the episode months later, Superintendent Giarrusso seemed to think the answer was more complicated than that. "I talked to some black schoolchildren not long after the sniping," he would recall. "And one of them told me, 'You know, I think I could do what the sniper did. But I don't hate enough yet.' That scared the hell out of me. It still does."

To some people, Mark Essex was a murderer—no more, no less. Others believed that his suicidal assault on whites was motivated by a sense of higher purpose, however misguided. Still others viewed him as a martyr, a symbol of the pain endured by all black people. For a time, he was a potent symbol. A few days after the terror at the hotel, police shot a black robbery suspect. As the badly wounded man was being loaded into an ambulance, a woman's voice called out from a sullen crowd of onlookers. "Sniper comin' back," she shouted. "Sniper comin' back to get you all."

Two days after Essex was killed, a small detachment of police visited the dank, two-room apartment where he'd spent his final days. They found what amounted to a shrine to the young man's obsessive hatred. The windows had been blacked out with paint and covered with bedding so that no natural light could penetrate; a single red bulb provided the only illumination. There was little furniture except for a leaky waterbed, and the floor was littered with debris. Investigators would later find a map of New Orleans with thick circles drawn around police headquarters and the Howard Johnson's hotel. In the bathtub there were a few charred pages from the instruction manual for Essex's .44 magnum carbine.

These things escaped attention, however, when the officers first entered the room. Far more striking was the bold red and black lettering that covered every inch of the walls and ceiling. One wall was dominated by the word "Africa" sprayed on in thick black paint. Beneath it Essex had printed: "My destiny lies in the bloody death of racist pigs." Other slogans were scrawled all around. "Revolutionary justice is black justice," read one. "Kill the white man," said another. Dozens of Swahili words dotted the walls and ceiling, along with lists of exotic beasts from African folklore. On one patch of the ceiling, Essex had even taken the trouble to leave a message for his visitors, as though he'd expected them: "Only pigs like you read shit on the ceiling."

Six days after Essex died, his funeral was held at the St. James Baptist Church in Emporia. Two wreaths lay on his coffin, each bearing a satin banner. Like signposts marking the beginning and end of a journey, the messages on the banners seemed to define and sum up the dead man's passage through life. The first banner read "Jimmy," recalling Mark Essex's boyhood nickname. The second one bore a final, weary slogan: "Power to the People," it said. ◆

REVOLUTION

...MAN IN THE THIRD WORLD

AFRICA

CONGO

BLACK

GENET

HATE

NeoBaaho BARAZA

...DOWAMA

BARAMBA

PATA PIG

OSHUMBA

WHITE MA...

ADOMA

YAMBA

ETOMO OCAPA

MAZE

CARA CAPA

BIL.A

SHACAQUA

BABA

DEATH

WHITE DEVIL

BLACK PIG DEVIL

NURU

Revolutionary Justice

CUSAVA CARCOVA

SHOT THE DEVIL LIKE A DOG

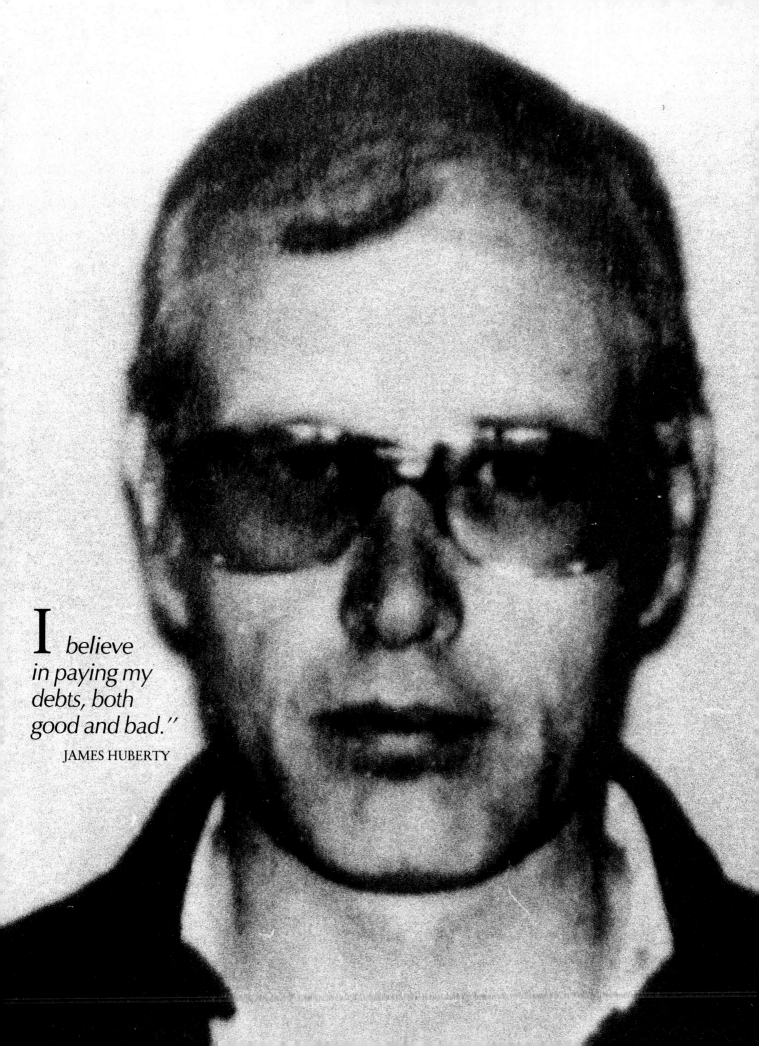

I believe in paying my debts, both good and bad.''

JAMES HUBERTY

4

The Tally

James Oliver Huberty was the sort of man who kept score. He kept a mental tally of everything bad that happened to him—every setback and frustration, every mishap and ill fortune, every annoyance, every tiff, every harsh word and perceived insult, indeed every event and public utterance that rubbed him the wrong way. There were a lot of these bad things in Huberty's life, at least as he saw it—such a great number that there was no way for him to cope with them all. So he kept score, with rising bewilderment and anger. Now and again he made a point of paying off one or more of what he called "my debts." But the debts never ceased to mount, until one day James Oliver Huberty determined to even the score once and for all time. Before that day was over, he had committed what was, at the time, the worst mass murder in American history: 21 men, women, and children slaughtered, another 19 injured. They were all total strangers to Huberty, but that wasn't the point. Getting even was the point—making sure that, finally, the accounts balanced.

Huberty was born on October 11, 1942, in Canton, Ohio, a manufacturing town about 50 miles south of Cleveland. His father, Earl V. Huberty, was a quality inspector at the Timken Roller Bearing Company plant, but he yearned to be a farmer. When Jim was three, scarcely more than a toddler, the boy contracted polio and suffered what his father described as "spastic paralysis." The tyke had to wear leather-and-metal braces on his legs, and when he eventually shed them he was left with an odd, rolling gait. A teacher would remember that the other kids made cruel fun of the awkward way he walked. The laughter and mimicry were the first of the debts.

When Jim was seven his already difficult world began to come apart. Father Earl, living a dream, bought a 155-acre farm near Mount Eaton, about 20 miles from Canton. Earl bought the place not so much to work it, but as an investment and a nice place to live while continuing at the factory. However, his wife, Icle (pronounced "eye-sell"), refused to

live "out in the middle of nowhere"; she wouldn't even go look at the farm. Icle felt a powerful call herself, and it wasn't from the land but from the heavens. Abandoning her husband and children, she headed west as a Pentecostal missionary to Indian reservations. When her son's awful story climaxed 34 years later, Icle Huberty, then 70, was a street preacher in Tucson, Arizona, dropping to her knees on sidewalks to exhort passersby to come to Jesus.

Earl moved his two children—Jim and an older sister, Ruth—to the farm and sent for his mother to keep house. The boy was devastated. His father recalled, "I found him out by the chicken house and he was sobbing. He missed his mother." Decades after she left, Earl was still passing judgment on his wife: "You shouldn't leave your family," he was wont to say. "You shouldn't leave your children."

Mount Eaton was in an area settled by Amish and Mennonite farmers, and those strict, clannish folk did not take readily to the new neighbors. At school the other kids were very aware that Jim came from a broken home, and they often harassed him. "They grabbed his cap and threw it out the school bus window a lot," his father remembered. Jim was a lonely child, a dog named Shep his chief companion, and a sullen anger began to grow within him.

Then he discovered guns, and a lifelong obsession took root. A family acquaintance remembered him as "a queer little boy who practiced incessantly with a target pistol." Guns equal power and control; for an unhappy child who felt abandoned, who was shunned and ridiculed at school, perhaps they represented a sense of authority that he could experience from no other source.

Small-town high schools often are consumed with sports, but Huberty, by now a tall, skinny youth, was largely uninterested in athletics. Once he tried out for basketball at Waynesdale High, but for reasons no one could remember it didn't work out. He played a little chess—a game of tactical one-to-one combat—and his passion for weapons grew stronger. He flunked one course in school: something called "Civil Service," designed to teach students the practical

necessities of life, such as how to balance a checkbook. Years later, the teacher would remark, "I can't believe I failed him and I don't remember him." That last comment just about summed up the boy's high-school career. Jim finished unmemorably, 51st in a class of 77; he was one of only two graduates who failed to have a picture taken for the class of 1960 yearbook.

But he was getting to be very good with guns. Young Jim Huberty was now an amateur gunsmith, loading his own ammunition and making small improvements in sights and trigger mechanisms. In adulthood he would experiment with hot loading, using a greater quantity or higher quality of powder to push a weapon beyond its designed muzzle velocity. Once his grandmother found a mess she took for dust, swept it up, and tossed it in the furnace. The stuff was gunpowder, and she was singed when it flashed up.

A fascination with firearms seemed to run in the family. A paternal great-uncle of Huberty's had invented the Lewis machine gun used by the Allies in World War I, and a prototype of the weapon, with the firing mechanism blocked, was among the family mementos. Naturally, Jim had to investigate. When he was 16 he took the gun apart, removed the blocks, loaded it, and fired a burst out the farmhouse window. "It scared the heck out of my mother, and I gave him the dickens," his father would recall. Earl Huberty buried the bullets and returned the gun to a non-operational state.

Jim Huberty attended Malone College, a small Quaker school in Canton, where he studied sociology, but then he changed his mind about a career and went through the Pittsburgh Institute of Mortuary Science in Pennsylvania. "He saw that mortuaries made a lot of money, and he wanted to make a lot of money," said his father. In early 1965 Jim Huberty married Etna Markland, whom he'd met at Malone College. The pastor who married them, the Reverend David Lombardi of Trinity Gospel Temple in Canton, had immediate reservations about the bridegroom. "He had real inner conflicts," said Lombardi. "By the time he was dating Etna he was atheistic and blamed God for taking his mother away from him." Huberty made his position very clear to the minister: Any God that required a mother

Class pictures from yearbooks at Waynesdale High School in Apple Creek, Ohio, show a young James Huberty who managed to remain inconspicuous despite his height. He didn't play sports or take part in any extracurricular activities. The nearest he came to socializing with his schoolmates was an occasional game of chess, a pastime suited to his introverted nature.

to leave her children was not one that he wanted to serve. Lombardi regarded Huberty as "halfway intelligent, but when you dealt with him you always felt a little uneasy about the way he harbored something inside. He was pent up; he was a loner and he had kind of an explosive personality."

Nevertheless, the couple started out well enough, with Jim landing a job at a funeral home in Canton. Unfortunately, that did not last very long. Don Williams, director of the mortuary, remembered that Huberty was good at embalming but bad for business. Huberty was comfortable in the rear embalming room, but awkward out front in a parlor filled with grief-stricken relatives and friends. In Williams's opinion, Huberty simply did not like people or crowds. "I told him he was in the wrong business," the

mortuary director said. After two years in the funeral trade Huberty left to become a welder, and Williams thought he knew why his former employee was better off in that line of work. "He could just pull that mask down and be by himself," Williams said.

In 1969 Huberty hired on at a public utility plant in Canton managed by the engineering firm of Babcock & Wilcox. By this time he and Etna had bought a handsome and roomy old house in the town of Massillon, 10 miles west of Canton, and the future seemed secure. By all accounts Huberty was an excellent worker, quiet, reliable, able to run a steady welding bead, safe behind his mask. He willingly took overtime, pulled down $25,000 to $30,000 a year, and became modestly prosperous. Still, the main thing people noticed about him was his reclusiveness. He was clearly a loner, thinking his solitary thoughts, doing for himself.

But there was something else they noticed: his flaring temper. Sometimes his coworkers at the factory called him

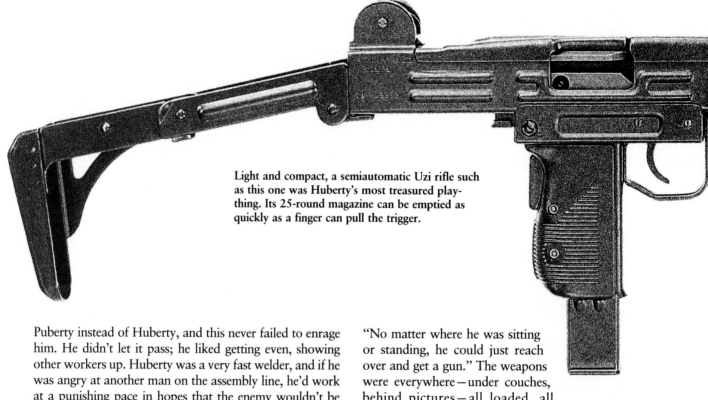

Light and compact, a semiautomatic Uzi rifle such as this one was Huberty's most treasured plaything. Its 25-round magazine can be emptied as quickly as a finger can pull the trigger.

Puberty instead of Huberty, and this never failed to enrage him. He didn't let it pass; he liked getting even, showing other workers up. Huberty was a very fast welder, and if he was angry at another man on the assembly line, he'd work at a punishing pace in hopes that the enemy wouldn't be able to keep up. Some of the men made friendly overtures, but Huberty struck them as an exceptionally sour individual with a conspiratorial view of the world. He ranted about Communism, warned of nuclear war with the Soviets, and spewed out a litany of complaints about the government. He carped about President Carter, and then, being a nonpartisan grumbler, he griped about President Reagan.

About the only one at B&W to strike up anything approaching friendship with Huberty was James Aslanes. Aslanes shared Huberty's passion for guns, although not to the same obsessive degree. Aslanes recalled that Huberty would talk for hours about various types of pistols, rifles, and automatic weapons, and the damage that certain caliber bullets could inflict on the human body. Automatic weapons were a special fetish. If word got out that a worker had one, Huberty was sure to track down the man and offer to buy it. Gradually his home filled with small arms: shotguns, revolvers, semiautomatic pistols, and semiautomatic rifles with kits to make them fully automatic.

"There were guns throughout his house," Aslanes said.

"No matter where he was sitting or standing, he could just reach over and get a gun." The weapons were everywhere—under couches, behind pictures—all loaded, all ready to fire, no safeties on. According to an acquaintance who ran a tavern in Massillon, Huberty would sit just inside the half-opened front door of his home, a loaded shotgun on his lap, as if inviting an intruder to step through.

Earl Huberty was lonely after both his children left home and eventually he remarried. Jim Huberty was bitterly opposed to the match, refused to acknowledge the new wife, and gradually grew more distant from his father. Huberty's first child, a daughter named Zelia, was born in 1972, soon after he became a welder. Another daughter, Cassandra, came along two years later. But Huberty took the youngsters to see Grandfather Earl only twice—which was fine with the neighbors in Mount Eaton. They remembered that when Jim Huberty came to visit his father before their last falling-out, he often arrived firing a pistol into the air from his car window. Hostility came easily to him.

So did a strange kind of calculated carelessness: Huberty could be frighteningly reckless around firearms for an experienced marksman and gunsmith. His pride and joy was a semiautomatic version of the Israeli-made Uzi assault

"Shot it right there," neighbor Vaughn Mohler related. "Huberty said, 'There, I took care of it.'"

weapon. One day, he invited Jim Aslanes to fire it at a rolled-up rug in the basement. Aslanes was aghast at the idea of blasting away at a rug, indoors, in town. He declined—and then saw that the rug was already riddled with bullet holes, and that bullets had gone clear through it and had chipped the concrete basement wall. "It was little things like that showed me there was something wrong with him," Aslanes said later.

Aslanes's discomfort intensified when he and his two sons went shooting with Huberty out in the country. Again, the Uzi was the favored weapon—and Aslanes was appalled when Huberty started firing at rocks from which the slugs could easily ricochet back at the shooters. "I made up my mind never to go shooting with him again," Aslanes said.

Neighbors were uneasy about Huberty, and not just because of the guns they heard going off inside and outside his house. People knew him as a peculiar, short-tempered man, prickly about privacy. He kept his blinds drawn and his doors triple locked, and there were No Trespassing and Beware the Dog signs all around. "He was weird," said Betty Matecheck, who lived down the street. "I can remember him losing his temper and screaming like a madman. You had to be here to understand how strange he was."

Take the dogs, for instance. Huberty kept German shepherds and liked them much better than he liked people. So much better, according to neighborhood kids, that he gave them birthday parties with baked cakes and fried their canned dog food to make it tastier. The dogs were allowed to roam free through the neighborhood, getting into garbage, annoying people, scaring children, occasionally biting. Neighbors frequently called the police, a move guaranteed to send Huberty into a howling rage.

As much as he loved his dogs, however, Huberty did not allow them to interfere with his keeping score. One day one of his German shepherds jumped up on an acquaintance's car and scratched the paint. To the man's utter astonishment, Huberty dragged the animal out back and killed it.

Moreover, Huberty's affection for his own dogs definitely did not extend to dogs in general. Once a poodle defecated in his yard. Neighbor Cindy Straight remembered seeing Huberty, gun in hand, run out of his house and across the street in pursuit of the dog. He was about to shoot it when her father came out and urged him not to. "My dad convinced him not to shoot, and then he told my dad never to set foot on his property or he'd kill him," Straight said. "We didn't talk much to them after that."

So many things to be angry about. So many scores. So many debts piling up.

The Hubertys suffered a major setback in the winter of 1971 when the kitchen ductwork in their Massillon house caught fire just after Etna Huberty drove off to pick up Jim at work in Canton. When they returned, the house was gone; only the foundation remained. Huberty kept quantities of gunpowder in the basement. When fire hit the stuff it exploded. Firefighters found window frames and drapery hardware blown clear across the street. Huberty's cherished gun collection, including the old Lewis machine gun, had melted into ruin.

But Jim and Etna rebounded quickly, buying a handsome, three-story brick house that stood on an adjoining lot. Where their old house had been, the Hubertys built a six-unit apartment building that they managed themselves.

Probably, Etna Huberty did most of the managing, since that was the pattern of the Huberty marriage. Realizing early in the relationship that her husband was, at best, a very fragile personality, Etna became his handler and liaison with the world. She managed the house, the children, and the bills. She packed Huberty's lunches, got him ready for work, and often drove him to his job in the morning and picked him up in the evening. Contact with people made Huberty nervous, and when he was nervous bad things happened, so his wife shielded him.

His temper was sudden and ferocious, and he slapped the

children around and punched Etna when he got upset. "Generally, it was just one hit," she said philosophically. Yet on one occasion he went for her with such violence that he "messed up my jaw," as she put it, and he often pointed guns at her. In a fit of rage he also once held a butcher knife to the throat of his younger daughter, Cassandra.

Almost anything could touch off one of these explosions, but Etna did what she could to avoid riling Huberty. For instance, the sight of bills in the mail drove him wild, so, according to neighborhood gossip, Etna would hide them in one of the doghouses until she could pay them when her husband wasn't around.

It sometimes seemed that Huberty was a headstrong dog dragging Etna around as she held on to his leash, but she had her own ways of dealing with him—ways that were often both ingenious and manipulative. For example, she claimed she could tell his future in playing cards. He believed her, and when she made recommendations about business deals and other matters based on her supposed readings, he usually went along. Once a visitor watched Etna make an elaborate show of laying the cards out on a table twice, wearing an expression of great alarm. Huberty watched over her shoulder, becoming more anxious by the minute. He asked her several times what she saw. She finally told him he was going to die violently before the age of 43.

There was nothing in Etna's bag of tricks, however, that could curb her husband's obsession with guns. He rebuilt his weapons collection, kept thousands of rounds of ammunition, and was always experimenting with high-powered loads in his basement firing range. Once, shouting to his wife to "run someplace," Huberty fired a shot in the basement that ricocheted up through the dining room floor and into the ceiling as Etna fled the room.

Odd as Huberty was, there's no question that his wife was a stabilizing influence. Even so, Etna Huberty had some eccentric moments of her own. One September day in 1981 she was charged with four counts of aggravated menacing for pointing a fully loaded 9-mm. Browning semiautomatic

pistol at four women whose kids, she said, were picking fights with her daughters. Etna pleaded guilty to a reduced charge of disorderly conduct and paid a fine of $200 plus court costs. The pistol was returned within the month, eventually to make its own history.

Over the years, Jim Huberty's rage and isolation increased. His friendship with Jim Aslanes faded. Then he began to hear voices. He told Etna that God and Jesus Christ were consulting him about the government and President Carter. Huberty reported other, less illustrious contacts as well. He told an acquaintance that he'd killed one of his dogs for speaking to him. The dog spoke through his eyes in ways that Huberty could understand, he said. In 1976 Etna started urging her husband to seek mental help. He refused, insisting that she was the crazy one.

In his madness, Huberty found it increasingly difficult to steer an even course from day to day. Even the smallest things fueled his anger. One summer day in 1982, eight-year-old Cassandra, nicknamed Bobbi, and Zelia, 10, fell into a backyard scuffle with two neighbor children, Angie and Katherine Goodnough. As the Goodnough girls told it, the fight was over Bobbi's habit of kicking people when she was irritated. The Goodnough girls wrestled her to the ground, and Zelia ran off to tell Daddy.

Jim Huberty waited two weeks to begin his revenge, arranging the retaliation around a backyard party for the kids. With a handful of neighborhood youngsters assembled, he disappeared into his house, and Bobbi, in an obviously rehearsed move, stepped up to Angie and punched her full force in the eye. Art Goodnough, Angie's father, went over to ask why Huberty had set the kids up to fight. Linda Goodnough, the girls' mother, remembered Huberty's answer.

One of these days when you least expect it, I'm going to get you alone!

"I believe in paying my debts," he said, "both good and bad."

A couple of months later, Katherine Goodnough was walking down the street when Bobbi jumped from behind a bush and walloped the child with a karate chop as Huberty looked on. The Goodnoughs rushed out to stop the squalling fight that ensued, and Huberty called the police. Massillon cops knew him well; he called them often, with one complaint or another. The officers dutifully responded, but when they refused to arrest anyone Huberty was enraged.

Linda Goodnough remembers the rest of it. "As soon as we got home, the phone rang. I said, 'Oh God, Art, that must be him.' When Art picked up the phone, Huberty said, 'One of these days when you least expect it, I'm going to get you alone!'"

Huberty never made good on that threat. However, the idea of evening up scores was beginning to rule his life. When the Canton Insulation Company's work on his house didn't meet his expectations, he and Etna picketed the office. To get him to quit, the company wrote off the remaining $1,900 of his bill. Some kids teased his daughters; he got into a yelling match with the youngsters that grew so loud the police took him in for disorderly conduct. He put his daughters into karate class to better equip them to do their part in the cause of vengeance.

What the press called the "Rust Belt Recession," the decline of older midwestern industrial areas, caught up with Ohio and the Hubertys in late 1982. The public utility managed by Babcock & Wilcox shut down. Jim Huberty's job was terminated after 13 years on November 15, and at that point, his life began its final spiraling disintegration.

Etna foresaw the coming storm and tried to prepare: She put their properties on the market at once. Huberty, meanwhile, was in a murderous mood. Etna was sure he was having a nervous breakdown. A fellow laid-off Babcock & Wilcox worker, Terry Kelly, remembered Huberty saying that if he couldn't make a living for his family anymore, he was going to kill himself and "take everyone with him." To Huberty, it seemed that the plant closing was evidence of the massive conspiracy operating against working people—against him.

Selling the apartment house proved to be a nightmarish tangle of threats and lawsuits. Huberty expected to sell the building for $144,000 but eventually had to settle for $115,000. When a deal for the higher figure fell through, he sued his real-estate broker and threatened to burn the place down. The whole mess was further proof to Huberty of the forces working against him. His curses against "the rich" increased.

There was a brief respite in May, six months after the layoff, when Huberty landed a welder's job with Union Metal Manufacturing Company in Canton. But five weeks later that plant abruptly closed as well. Huberty sank into ever deeper despair and his vain protests against the injustices of the universe grew louder.

On August 17, 1983, Huberty's car was rear-ended. He sued the other driver, of course, but the matter didn't end there. Ever since childhood Huberty had suffered neck pains, and the accident made them worse. His hands shook on occasion now as well, and he sometimes had trouble holding glasses and bottles. This infirmity was crushing for a welder, who has to have a steady hand. Huberty was becoming unemployable in the only field he knew—not that it much mattered, since the jobs were vanishing.

The strange voices came more often, and the doomsday dialogues led Huberty's mind toward suicide. In front of Etna one day he raised a little silvered pistol to his head. "I grabbed his arm," she recalled. "I pried his fingers off the gun. I left the room to hide the gun. When I came back he was sitting on the sofa crying." Within a year Etna would say she regretted stopping him that day.

Putting the house up for sale tolled another dirge for Jim Huberty's wounded spirit. He'd loved the place, and he and Etna had remodeled it room by room, working side by side for months. However, their emotional attachment to the house may have given them inflated notions of its value. Huberty again felt betrayed when it failed to attract much attention in a market depressed by layoffs and plant closings. Reluctantly, they let it go for $12,000 in cash and the buyer's assumption of their $48,000 mortgage. Etna complained bitterly that they'd lost $69,000 on the transaction.

Ohio had failed them utterly. The wrongs to set right were reaching monumental proportions.

The decision to move to Mexico sprang from Huberty's conviction that the United States was going to the dogs. Exactly what he hoped to achieve below the border is not entirely clear, but evidently he thought it would be cheaper to live in Mexico, and he expected to get better interest rates from Mexican banks. He confided cryptically to one person before leaving Ohio that he was going to Mexico to make a lot of money, adding, "We're going to show them who's boss."

Near the end of October 1983, the Hubertys headed

APPLICATION FOR EMPLOYMENT

Referred By

Qualified applicants are considered for all positions without regard to race, color, religion, sex, national origin, age, marital or veteran status, or the presence of a non-job related medical condition or handicap.

PERSONAL INFORMATION

Social Security Number: 291-40-0055
Application Date: MARCH 22, 1984

Last Name: HUBERTY
First Name: JAMES
Middle Initial: Oliver
Telephone Number: 428-3293

Present Address No. and Street: 230 Cottonwood Rd.
City: SAN YSIDRO
State: CALIF.

Permanent Address No. and Street: 230 Cottonwood Rd
City: SAN YSIDRO
State: CALIF.

If you are not a citizen of the United States, please indicate your authorization to be employed.

Military Service Status: 1-4
Draft Classification Status:

EMPLOYMENT DESIRED

Position(s) applied for: MERCHANT PATROLLER or ARMORED CAR GUARD

Date You Can Start: ANYTIME
Salary Desired: STANDARD

Are you currently employed? NO
If so, may we contact your present employer?

If you have applied to this company before, please indicate where and when. NO

If you have relatives employed by this company, please give names. NO

If you have ever worked for this company before, please indicate when and position held. NO

Do you seek full or part-time employment? BOTH
Shift or hours preferred: DAYS

Do you have special skills, experience or qualifications related to the position(s) applied for? HIGH RANK YELLOW BELT KARATE

Do you have any physical limitations which would hinder your performance in the position applied for? NO

SPECIAL QUESTIONS

DO NOT ANSWER ANY OF THE QUESTIONS IN THIS FRAMED AREA UNLESS THE EMPLOYER HAS CHECKED A BOX PRECEDING A QUESTION, THEREBY INDICATING THAT THE INFORMATION IS REQUIRED FOR A BONA FIDE OCCUPATIONAL QUALIFICATION, OR DICTATED BY NATIONAL SECURITY LAWS OR IS NEEDED FOR OTHER LEGALLY PERMISSIBLE REASONS.

☐ Height _____ feet _____ inches
☐ Weight _____ lbs.
☐ _____

☐ Citizen of U.S. _____ Yes _____ No

PREVIOUS EMPLOYMENT

Please Explain Any Gap In Employment History Below

Please List Most Recent Employment First	Name and Location	Position	Salary	Reason For Leaving
1 From MAY 83 To July 83	UNION METAL MANF. MAPLE AVE. CANTON O.	WELDER	9.30	LAID OFF.
2 From 6-30-69 To NOV 15 82	BABCOCK & WILCOX RAFFRD. CANTON OHIO	WELDER FITTER	9.30	PLANT CLOSED.
3 From 67 To 69	MACOMBER INC. LOUISVILLE OHIO	WELDER	3.50	ADVANCEMENT
4 From To				

AICO FORM NO. 55-114

PLEASE TURN OVER

PRINTED IN USA

Rudy Bernstein, owner of the Bernstein Security Service of Chula Vista, scribbled a concise and unequivocal rejection on Huberty's job application. Then, so there could be no mistaking his intent, he rewrote it with a darker pen. Bernstein recalls that Huberty gave him "a big line of bull" during an interview.

south with their car and van, Jim's huge gun collection, a thousand rounds of ammunition, and his 1982 Honda motorcycle. They left most of their furniture and other possessions in storage in Ohio.

The family landed in Tijuana, a border town just across the line from San Ysidro, the southernmost suburb of San Diego. Every day Etna drove Bobbi and Zelia back into the United States to a school in San Ysidro. She and the girls at first took to the new scene—the friendly neighbors, vivid colors, and exotic food. But Huberty hated it. The people looked odd to him. He spoke no Spanish and his paranoia probably injected insults into every incomprehensible word that was being said around him. "He felt lost, rejected, hopeless," Etna said later.

The Mexican experiment lasted scarcely three months before the Hubertys retreated back to the United States. Another defeat. Another disappointment. They crossed over to San Ysidro and took a two-bedroom flat in the Cottonwood Apartments on Cottonwood Road. Huberty was morose, silent, cold. They were the only Anglo-Americans in the complex, a fact that aggravated and focused Huberty's dislike for Hispanics.

A Mexican-American woman whose apartment was near the Hubertys' encountered them one day as she took out her trash. They were sitting by Huberty's motorcycle, and she nodded and said "Hi." They stared at her. She wondered if they hadn't heard. "Hi," she repeated. "The man just kind of looked at me with a cold stare," she remembered.

Etna Huberty shared her husband's distaste for Hispanics to some degree, but she wasn't as obvious about it. Besides, she was a far more sympathetic figure than he was. She was clearly a beleaguered woman, worn out by the strain of trying to keep her husband from plunging over the edge. The people at Cottonwood tended to like her and the girls. It was Huberty who scared them. The neighbors were jolted awake in the night by the sound of gunfire from the balcony of the Huberty apartment. One man remembered Huberty standing there and firing a long black gun from the hip—a Rambo stance—into a clump of trees. Once, Huberty thought he saw someone trying to steal his motorcycle and blasted away with a pistol. He didn't hit anyone.

In his new and alien environment, Huberty began remembering Ohio as a paradise lost. "In his mind," Etna said, "everything in Ohio was done right, and he could not adjust to the way things were done in California." His memory seemed to dim about being jobless in Ohio. After all, he was jobless in California, too. Still in pain from the auto accident—and increasingly deranged—he was much too shaky to run a welder's bead. Then he saw a newspaper ad offering security guard training in a federally funded program. Huberty was eligible on the basis of low income and unemployment. Things began to look up a little.

The course lasted several weeks, and Huberty's grades placed him near the top of his 27-member class. A fellow student remembered that he qualified as an expert shot the first time out on the pistol range. On April 12, 1984, after a routine FBI check revealed no criminal record, the California Bureau of Collections and Investigative Services issued a security guard registration card valid for two years. Soon after, the San Ysidro police gave Huberty a firearms permit allowing him to carry an exposed .38-caliber or .357 magnum pistol on duty.

Six days after completing the course, Huberty presented himself at Bernstein Security Service of Chula Vista, a community near San Ysidro, and interviewed for a job. He made a vividly negative impression on owner Rudy Bernstein, who scrawled "NO" across the application in letters four inches high. Huberty had a "bad attitude," Bernstein said later. "He told me how well he handled himself and how he would only work for top security firms. He gave me a big line of bull." But Huberty connected with another Chula Vista security outfit and went to work as a guard in a condominium complex on the 8 p.m. to 2 a.m. shift.

With some money coming in, Etna Huberty had the family's furniture shipped out from Ohio. But her husband was deteriorating fast. The voices became more insistent: God and Jesus and everybody else were talking to him, Etna would later tell a police interviewer. Huberty believed the U.S. government was wholly crooked, she said, and that "a trilateral commission is taking over everything." The voices, a confused chorus of paranoia, told Huberty that young women went into the armed forces and got raped at Camp David. Apparently the voices did not know that Camp David was a presidential retreat, not a regular military post.

Military matters seemed much on Huberty's troubled mind. He ordered a pair of camouflage pants from a magazine, and though they were cheap and thin, he loved to wear them. Playing soldier seemed to please him. Huberty had tried to enlist during the Vietnam War and was turned down for what his father claimed were physical reasons.

Now, the war filled his feverish thoughts. He told Etna that he believed he was a war criminal. In the grip of this delusion, he approached a police car one day and told the officers that he was a wanted war criminal. They checked with the Border Patrol and the FBI, found no record of him, and sent him home. Etna patiently explained to him that he could not be a war criminal because he hadn't been in the war. Still, he couldn't shake the notion.

Still obsessed with the military, Huberty decided to share his firearms expertise with the Department of Defense. His knowledge of automatic weapons gave him ideas for modifications such as a device to increase a gun's rate of fire. He sketched out his ideas and sent the drawings to the Pentagon. The Pentagon never wrote back. He was outraged at being ignored and at the military's failure to appreciate his valuable contributions.

Huberty was still hanging on to the job as a guard, and his pay enabled the family to move from the hated Cottonwood Apartments to a $475-a-month, two-bedroom apartment on Averil Road near San Ysidro Boulevard. From the rear the Hubertys could look down on a McDonald's restaurant about a block away.

Old patterns followed the family to their new home. As before, the neighbors liked Etna and the girls but were repelled by Huberty. "He didn't like kids," one neighbor said, "He was always yelling at kids." He didn't even seem to like his own kids much. Karl and Wanda Haseley were the neighbors who knew the Hubertys best, and from time to time they saw the Huberty sisters with welts on their faces. The girls confessed that their father had hit them. Other times, Bobbi and Zelia sat outside for hours while their parents screeched at each other inside their apartment. The

whole apartment complex heard the quarrels; it was impossible not to hear. Infuriated by a new orthodontic expense for Zelia, Huberty stormed into the girls' room waving his Uzi and

The view from the rear of the Hubertys' apartment in Averil Villas included the McDonald's on San Ysidro Boulevard, and the family often ate there. The site would become Huberty's killing ground.

shouted, "Why spend money on the girl's teeth, she'll be dead anyway!" The child was, in fact, having a recurrent nightmare that she was in a casket.

As bad as things were, they were about to get worse: Huberty lost his job. His superiors at the security company concluded that he was too nervous for the work, and they fired him. It was July 10, 1984. The walls were closing in; the score was running up.

Voices babbled in Huberty's head. They said that the CIA was following him and that the military controlled the security company and had ordered him fired. It had to do with the ideas that the Pentagon was stealing from him.

Hope blossomed briefly and for the last time on Sunday, July 15. For the first time, Huberty acknowledged that he might have a mental problem. On Tuesday, the 17th, Etna noticed him by the phone and asked what he was doing. Calling a mental clinic, he said. He'd requested an appointment. They would get back to him.

But hours passed without a return call from the clinic. In one of those bizarre turns of fate, the person at the clinic had misheard his name and recorded it in the log as "Shouberty." Further, Huberty's polite, composed demeanor had conveyed no sense of urgency, so his call was listed as a "non-crisis" inquiry, to be handled within 48 hours.

Irritated, Huberty thundered off on his motorcycle. Etna

began calling clinics in the yellow pages; if she found the one he'd contacted, she intended to say that her husband had guns and might kill. In fact, she did reach the right clinic, but because his name had been recorded incorrectly, she was told that no one named Huberty had made an inquiry. During her desperate session at the telephone, she told the person who answered at one clinic about her fears. But she didn't follow the advice she was given: Call the police.

An hour or so later Huberty returned in a surprisingly good mood. Etna had made pizza, and he ate with gusto, took a nap, and then quietly awaited the phone call that would never come. Late in the afternoon the whole family went for a bike ride, and the girls then went off to baby-sit. There was a favorite movie on TV that night, and Jim and Etna watched it. He fixed a snack for them, toasted raisin muffins. Things might be turning around, Etna prayed.

On Wednesday morning, July 18, the Hubertys were due in traffic court over a minor infraction. The judge let Huberty off with a warning, since he was a newcomer to the state. It was nearly noon when Jim and Etna got out of court. They stopped for lunch at a downtown McDonald's, then went to the zoo and strolled around.

In the course of their walk, Etna recalled, he told her that his life was over. He rambled, as he so often did, about the good ideas he'd sent to the Pentagon. And he referred to the mental health clinic's failure to get back to him. "Well," he said, "society had their chance."

Back home, Etna went to the kitchen to fix lunch for the kids. Presently she went upstairs to lie down. Huberty walked in. He was wearing his favorite camouflage pants and a maroon velour shirt with short sleeves. "I want to kiss you good-bye," he said. She kissed him and asked whether he did not want to stay at home—she would be putting dinner on soon. No, he said, he was going hunting.

Zelia was Huberty's favorite child. She saw her father leave and remembered that he said, "Good-bye. I won't be back." He was carrying something wrapped in a blue-and-white-checked blanket. Zelia saw the barrel of a gun poking from the bundle.

In view from the street in front of the apartment house, down the hill and left on San Ysidro Boulevard, between the post office on the far side and Yum Yum Donuts on the near side, stood the local McDonald's. It was a pleasant place, much favored by families and children. Built in 1973, it had an area out front with oversize comic figures for the children to play on and around. A row of neatly tended shrubs separated the play area from the street.

The hour was a little before 4 p.m., and business was picking up, with perhaps 30 people in the restaurant. It was time for coffee breaks, for a snack on returning from shopping, for a late lunch, for kids to show up for refreshments. The manager, 22-year-old Neva Caine, made a trim figure in her neat uniform—blue slacks and shirt, short blue vest, and brown shoes. A petite, pretty woman, she'd come from a McDonald's in Phoenix, knew her business, and was soon promoted to manager. A month earlier, she'd married Andy Caine, a young chiropractor. A glowing newlywed, she made a happy atmosphere for all those around her.

Things were going smoothly that afternoon. Caine's crew was composed mostly of youngsters, whose overlapping, part-time short shifts made for complex scheduling. But the young workers were conscientious, and it all worked out. Two assistant managers, Kenny Villegas and Poco Lopez, both 22, were in a booth working on restaurant records. Luz Perez, 16, was at the number 4 cash register taking food orders, while Albert Leos and Alex Vasquez, both 17, manned the grill. John Arnold, 16, had finished his stint at the grill and was sweeping up. Everybody willingly did a little of everything, and Neva Caine proudly surveyed a bustling, well-ordered domain.

Customer Gus Verslius had just come in for his daily coffee break. Verslius was 62. For 38 years he'd driven a delivery truck in the neighborhood, and he was about to retire. This was his last day on the job; a retirement party was planned after work. He told the kids at McDonald's that he and his wife would soon fly to Spain on the trip of their dreams.

Ronald and Blythe Herrera, 33 and 31, were driving home to Orange, California, from a Mexican vacation. Their 11-year-old son, Matao, was with them, as was his best friend, Keith Thomas, also 11. The Herreras had been driving a good while; Ron Herrera decided that it was time to stop for a bite, and he turned the car into the McDonald's parking lot.

At about the same time, three pals, each 11 years old, were deciding that ice cream and a Coke at McDonald's was just what they needed. Joshua Coleman, Omar Hernandez, and David Flores were out of school for the summer, and, gloriously, their time was their own.

A rare smile lights James Huberty's usually glowering face in this 1983 studio portrait. To Etna Huberty (inset), her husband's moments of normalcy proved that he could function "as long as he didn't really get flustered." She made it her job to shield him from life's pressures.

Neva Caine *(below)* and Victor Rivera *(opposite)* made the fatal mistake of confronting Huberty early in his rampage. Caine was shot once, Rivera 14 times.

Jackie Wright Reyes, 18, two months pregnant, had organized a shopping expedition. With her were Carlos, her eight-month-old son; a friend, Elena Colmenero, 18; Reyes's niece, Aurora Pena, 11; and a couple of other friends, sisters Imelda and Claudia Perez, 15 and 9. The shoppers browsed through a nearby K-Mart, felt like a snack, and headed for McDonald's on the way home.

Another fast-food patron that afternoon was businessman Hugo Velasquez, the national vice president and regional manager for Banamex, the Mexican banking giant. Velasquez, 46, had only recently been promoted to the important post and had not yet moved his family from the southeastern city of Cordoba to the bank's regional headquarters in Tijuana. He'd spent the day getting acquainted with Banamex's U.S. affiliate in San Ysidro and was taking a break before returning to work.

Miguel Victoria, 74, and his wife, Alicia Aida Victoria, 70, were devoted family folk. They'd lost a son in an airport mishap, and they made it a point to stay close to their widowed daughter-in-law and their two grandchildren in Chula Vista. The Victorias lived in Tijuana, but every week they took their laundry to a launderette in San Diego and then went to see the grandchildren. Before heading back across the border, they regularly stopped in at McDonald's for a bag of takeout hamburgers as treats for their two sons still living at home.

All these lives, and many others, were about to intersect with the rage of James Oliver Huberty.

Huberty put the bundle wrapped in the blue-and-white-checkered blanket into his battered black Mercury Marquis sedan. He drove down the hill and across San Ysidro Boulevard into the McDonald's parking lot, where he pulled up near the west door. He emptied the blanket, carefully locked the car, and walked into the restaurant. In a soft holster on his belt he carried a 9-mm. Browning semiautomatic pistol with a 14-round clip—the same gun that had been returned to Etna after she paid her fine for disorderly conduct back in Massillon. Huberty's favorite weapon, the 9-mm. Israeli-made Uzi, was slung over his left shoulder; the Uzi's clip held 25 rounds. In one hand he carried a Winchester 12-gauge pump-action shotgun that held five shells. He also had a cloth bag filled with ammunition.

Assistant manager Kenny Villegas, sitting diagonally across the room from the entrance, spotted the heavily armed man as soon as he entered. Villegas assumed that a robbery was in progress and took a careful look so he'd be able to describe the thief later. The man he studied appeared to be about 40 years old. He was balding, a little over six feet tall, weighed about 190 pounds, and was strongly but trimly built.

Sweeping the floor near the entrance Huberty used, John Arnold looked up to see the muzzle of the shotgun pointed at his face. Twenty-year-old Guillermo Flores, another assistant manager, shouted from the serving counter, "Hey, John, that guy's gonna shoot you!"

"He was pointing that gun right at me," Arnold later recalled. "He pulled the trigger, but nothing happened. Then he brought it down and started messing with it." Arnold walked off, thinking that this must be some kind of a joke. Flores called to Neva Caine, who was sitting near Villegas, and she quickly stood up.

A shotgun blast hit the ceiling. Chips and chunks of insulation showered down. Neva Caine was out of the booth and striding angrily. She reached the counter area and turned toward Huberty as he raised the Uzi.

"Look out, Neva, look out!" Flores screamed. Huberty had the gun on her at point-blank range. He shot once. Neva Caine, the newlywed manager, dropped with a bullet hole beside her left eye. She died within minutes.

The shotgun blast had riveted everyone's attention, and the sight of Neva Caine dying made it clear that this was not a joke. John Arnold ducked as Huberty fired the Winchester at him. A cone of heavy buckshot brushed Arnold's left side as he dived under a nearby table.

Suddenly, Huberty was shout-

NEVA CAINE

ing. Everyone remembered what he said a little differently, but all agreed on the sense of it:

"Don't anybody move or you'll die!"

"Everybody on the ground!"

"Lay down or I'll kill you!"

"I'll kill you like I kill lots of 'em!"

Simple animal instinct told them all to obey. There was a frantic, clattering rush as people hit the floor, scrambling under tables, behind counters, anywhere that offered cover. Kenny Villegas heard a roaring shout: "You dirty swine, Vietnam assholes," Huberty screamed. "I've killed a thousand and I'll kill a thousand more!"

VICTOR RIVERA

Methodically, Huberty started paying off his lifetime of debts. He shot steadily, sometimes picking off targets with shotgun blasts, sometimes firing the Uzi. He moved a little for tactical advantage now and again but generally held his position in the center of the restaurant. From time to time he squatted and sprayed fire under the tables, as someone might flush away dirt with a hose. It dawned on the terrified people that the gunman meant to kill them all. There was no help, no appeal, nothing they could do to stay this mad executioner. As Guadalupe del Rio, a young woman from Tijuana, would say later, "minutes seemed like hours and hours like days, and I thought that no one even knew we were there."

Maria Rivera, 23, had just found a table near the door when she heard the first shotgun blast; she was holding her 16-month-old baby, Mireya, and her husband, Victor, was at the counter getting food. Their seven-year-old daughter, Maria Diana, was outside on the playground. When she heard the shooting, the child rushed through the door in alarm to her mother, who scooped her up. Clutching her two children in her arms, Maria saw Victor, 25, turn to face the gunman and beg him not to shoot anymore. But Huberty turned the Uzi on him, and Victor fell with a scream of pain. He kept crying out. Huberty stood over him, shouted, "Shut up!" and fired again and again. Maria knew that her husband was dead; the coroner would later find 14 wounds in his body. She collapsed on the floor, the children still in her arms.

Mario Yepes, a 40-year-old professor from Tijuana, was eating with his wife and daughter at a table outside when the shooting started. He herded his family against the brick front wall, where they lay unhurt throughout the carnage.

Guadalupe del Rio had come across the border from Tijuana for a late lunch with two friends, Arisdelsi Vargas Vuelas and Gloria Ramirez Soto. They were about to leave McDonald's when Huberty strode in. At the first blast Vargas and Ramirez pushed del Rio down. The women slid under the table—del Rio and Ramirez with their heads pressed against the wall and their legs drawn up to their chests, Vargas as close as she could get behind them. There were fewer people on their side of the restaurant, and they prayed that they would be overlooked. Huberty found them and lashed them with fire. Ramirez was unhurt. Del Rio was hit several times but not seriously wounded. But a single 9-mm. slug tore out the back of Vargas's head and destroyed her brain. She would die the next day, the only person of those Huberty killed who lived long enough to reach a hospital.

Shopper Jackie Wright Reyes, her baby, Carlos, in her arms, was at the counter with the rest of her group. They'd just gotten their order when Huberty fired into the ceiling. Aurora Pena, Reyes's niece, later remembered that they all dropped to the floor; Reyes tucked Carlos against her and shielded him and Aurora with her body. Huberty looked down at them and started firing. He killed Jackie's friend Elena Colmenero with a shotgun blast to the chest; he fatally shot nine-year-old Claudia Perez in the cheek, chest, belly, thigh, hip, armpit, and head. Imelda Perez was lucky; she was only hit in the hand. Aurora Pena would survive a bullet wound in her left leg.

Both girls remained conscious. Aurora, lying up against Jackie Reyes, could feel her aunt's body jerking and bucking when Huberty turned his weapons on her. He shot the young woman in the head, neck, shoulders, breast,

Huberty killed Jackie Reyes *(below, left)* as she shielded her infant son and her young niece. Blythe Herrera and her son Matao were fatally hit after the gunman barked an order for everybody in the restaurant to hit the floor.

JACKIE REYES

MATAO HERRERA   BLYTHE HERRERA

back, buttocks, left arm, and both legs—48 wounds by the coroner's count. Beside his dead mother's body, baby Carlos sat up and started wailing at the top of his lungs. Huberty shouted at the shrieking child in the red jumpsuit—then took careful aim and killed the infant with a 9-mm. slug through the center of the back.

The homeward-bound Herreras, with their son, Matao, and friend Keith Thomas, were eating in a booth when Huberty entered. Blythe Herrera and Matao went under one booth, Ron Herrera and Keith under another. Ron lay there, the boy between him and the wall, and after a while he saw that Keith had been wounded. Then a bullet struck him in the left arm. He made no outcry. A few minutes later he was hit in the stomach, a bit later in the hip, later in the shoulder, last—a ricochet, he thought—in the back of his head. He never lost consciousness. He and Keith survived; Blythe and Matao were dead, both with numerous wounds to the head.

Counter clerk Luz Perez ducked to the floor when she saw Neva Caine fall. She scrambled frantically on hands and knees toward the stairs leading to the basement. Four young employees were ahead of her. Then she saw a woman holding a little boy in her arms and crawling toward her. Guillermina Hernandez had grabbed her infant son, Manuel junior, and fled the instant she heard the first shotgun blast. Perez directed the mother to come with her to the basement. There they ran into a storeroom and bolted the door. Above them the firing went on and on.

Not long after Huberty began his assault, Lydia Flores turned into the McDonald's parking lot. Her two-year-old daughter was with her. Flores circled the building and stopped at the drive-in order window. When no one responded, she pulled ahead to the food pickup window. No one was at that position either. Then she saw the shattered windows and heard the sound of gunfire. "I looked inside and there he was, just shooting," Flores reported later. "He turned and looked at me." Huberty raised the Uzi. Flores slammed the car into reverse and stomped on the accelerator, hurtling backward until her car crashed into a fence.

She snatched out her child, scaled the fence, and hid in some bushes until the shooting finally ended.

Maria Emelda Diaz was in the restaurant with her sister and her two-year-old son. Acting on utterly human impulse, the two women bolted out the nearest door at the first shotgun blast. Then, as more shooting erupted inside the restaurant, Maria Diaz remembered her little boy. She crawled back and peered in. There he sat, obediently waiting at the table and whimpering. Frantic, she waved, trying to catch his eye. At last he saw her. She gestured furiously, and he slid off the chair and toddled for the door. She snatched it open, grabbed him, and all three fled to safety.

Guillermo Flores, the assistant manager who'd tried to warn Neva Caine, found himself cowering behind the grill with the two cooks, Alex Vasquez and Albert Leos. Three young women from the counter squeezed in with them, Paulina Aguino, 22, Margarita Padilla, 18, and Elsa Borboa, 19. The women were weeping. Guillermo managed to grab a phone on the wall and punch 0 for operator as he slid to the floor. He told the operator that someone was shooting up the restaurant. She said to dial 911. He said he'd be killed if he stood up to dial 911. She said dialing 911 was the way it was done. Those were her instructions. Dial 911. He pleaded with her to connect him with the police. At last she said she would.

About this time, the three 11-year-olds coming for afternoon ice cream and sodas rode their bikes into the west parking lot. Joshua Coleman later remembered that someone yelled something unintelligible from across the street. Puzzled, the boys hesitated, looking around. Before they could register anything, Joshua recalled, they heard the roar of a shotgun from inside McDonald's and were thrown violently down in a tangle of bodies and bikes. Joshua knew immediately that he was hurt badly. He looked at his friends, Omar Hernandez and David Flores. They were covered with blood. Joshua saw it pooling on the ground. He saw them retching and thought they were dying. He himself was bloody and in great pain, but he lay very still and quiet, hoping that whoever had shot him would think he was dead. Eventually, the police got to him. He survived with wounds in his stomach, buttocks, hands, and arms. Both Omar and David died of massive injuries to the head and body before police could reach them. Later, Etna Huberty would recall how young Omar Hernandez had taught her how to operate a Laundromat washing machine a few weeks before the shooting.

Now the Victorias were arriving, the oldest victims that bloody day—Miguel and Alicia, come for those hamburgers to take home to Tijuana. They parked and walked to the west door. Huberty met them with shotgun blasts. The buckshot caught Alicia in the face and threw her down. It ripped into the old man as well, and he, looking in horror at his wife, screamed, "Goddammit, you killed her!" Then he tottered and fell. He pulled himself to a sitting position and wiped the blood from his wife's face, wiping and cleaning and cursing the maniac who'd murdered her.

Oscar Mondragon, 27, of Tijuana, was in the restaurant with a friend, Maria Rusbelina Sevilla, when Huberty entered. The two slid to the floor, but Mondragon could see the end of the Victorias' ordeal. The old man kept wiping his wife's ruined face while his own blood ran down his chin as he shouted curses at the gunman inside. Mondragon saw Huberty walk to the door. He heard him yell angrily at the old man—then saw him shoot him from only inches away. Victoria crumpled beside his dead wife. When next Huberty paused to reload his weapons, Mondragon pulled Sevilla to her feet and they dashed out into the parking lot.

Huberty was using a lot of ammunition, and he'd reloaded a number of times from the supply of 9-mm. and 12-gauge ammo in his shoulder bag. Whenever he occupied himself with the task, those still alive on the floor gauged their chances of escape. But most were too far from a door, too close to the gunman, too badly wounded, or too fearful of drawing more fire. So they just froze and waited—for death or deliverance.

Poco Lopez, the young assistant manager going over paperwork with his colleague Kenny Villegas, had been playing a radio softly in the booth while they worked. Both young men were now under the table and had been wounded, but not seriously. Villegas could see Huberty's feet as the killer moved around, and he watched in terror as Huberty walked over, firing as he came, and took the radio. The gunman carried the radio over to the order counter and fiddled with the dial. A number of people thought he was searching for news reports of his exploit. He tried several stations, then left it on one. Some of his victims, lying as motionless as possible but occasionally sneaking a peek, saw Huberty shuffle into a grotesque little dance to the radio music as he walked around shooting.

Every now and then Huberty would let out an angry shout. Once he yelled that he, referring to himself, did not deserve to live—but that he was taking care of the matter. Still, the dominant impression he made on his terrified audience was one of calm. Between the outbursts Huberty acted as if he were just doing a job, following a routine— nothing very different, really, from paying some bills and balancing the checkbook.

The wall clock in McDonald's had ticked off only 10 minutes since the first shotgun blast when a Mexican couple, Astolfo Felix, 31, and his wife, Maricela, 23, started inside with their four-month-old daughter, Karlita. Felix

MIGUEL VICTORIA   ALICIA VICTORIA

Alicia Victoria was hit by a shotgun blast as she and her husband, Miguel, approached the entrance to the McDonald's. Victoria cradled his dying wife outside the doors until Huberty killed him with a second volley.

Omar Hernandez, 11, lies dead, his small body still tangled in the bicycle he was riding when Huberty shot him. His head rests on a T-shirt belonging to Reserve Police Officer Juan Echavarria. Echavarria was using the shirt to try to stanch the flow of blood from Hernandez's face when gunfire drove him away from the dying boy.

noticed that the windows were shattered but heard no shots. He assumed the figure approaching from the inside was coming to fix the windows. The man inside hollered something, but Felix and his wife spoke no English. Then the figure raised a shotgun and fired. The pellets struck Felix's wife and baby and hit him in the belly. She staggered back against him. He took the bleeding baby from her, and they ran to the parking lot of the nearby post office.

Meanwhile Jose de Jesus Amaya Velasco, 37, a teacher, had parked in the post-office lot. His wife, Lucia Marias Velasco, waited in the car. He was inside for three minutes and returned to find his wife standing by the car. She said that someone was robbing the McDonald's. Velasco heard several shots. He ran into the post office and yelled for someone to call the police. Suddenly bullets were hitting the post office, shattering glass. Patrons flattened themselves on the floor behind the masonry walls. Velasco ran outside to find the Felixes staggering toward his wife.

Lucia Marias Velasco took the shrieking, bloody child as Maricela Felix started to collapse against the car. Velasco put his wife and Felix's child in the car, then helped Felix carry Maricela into the post office. He told Felix that the Velascos would care for the child, then dashed outside to his car and roared away. In a nearby shopping center he found a police car, which took Mrs. Velasco and the infant to a hospital. All three Felixes survived.

By now the San Diego police radio network was alive with the 245 call—assault with a deadly weapon. Assistant manager Guillermo Flores inside McDonald's had finally been connected to a police operator. But the first officer to arrive, Miguel Rosario, knew only that he was answering a 245. Pulling into the parking lot of a bank adjacent to the post office, Rosario saw people pointing at McDonald's. Jumping from his car, he saw Huberty in a doorway of the restaurant holding a gun and looking straight at him. Huberty cut loose with the Uzi, and bullets hammered into the police car as Rosario scrambled around to the trunk for his rifle and bulletproof vest. People were huddled behind cars in the lot. Rosario hollered for them to go into the bank as he shrugged into his vest and started making his way toward McDonald's.

Meanwhile, Officer Arthur Velasquez was racing in from the opposite side. He could hear shooting ahead. He yelled for motorists on San Ysidro to make U-turns and keep out of the line of fire. He entered the far door of the Yum Yum

Surrounded by harried SWAT team officers, 11-year-old Joshua Coleman lies dazed while a paramedic tends his wounds. For more than an hour Coleman talked and sang to himself while the shooting continued. He survived his injuries.

Donut shop beside McDonald's and went out the shop's back door toward the restaurant lot. A burst of fire seemed aimed at him, and he dived for shelter at the foot of a two-foot retaining wall separating the Yum Yum parking lot from McDonald's.

Across the way, where Rosario was, more patrol cars rolled up. Rosario told the officers to cover him while he ran for a concrete-block wall enclosing the restaurant's Dumpster. Huberty pegged some shots at the zigzagging Rosario, and the covering cops fired back. Huberty ducked back into the restaurant. Rosario was in good position now, but the restaurant was too dark for him to get a firm fix on the killer. And the policeman was not about to fire any snap shots; his rifle was a military M-16 using high-velocity .223-caliber ammunition—powerful enough to penetrate the restaurant's walls and possibly hit somebody other than the gunman. "I was in excellent position to take him down if he had exited," Rosario said, "but I had made up my mind not to shoot him inside."

Stalking around the restaurant, Huberty was not in the least cowed by the cops closing in on him. A man was moaning, so Huberty finished him off. By now Gus Verslius, the friendly truckdriver stopping for coffee on his retirement day, was dead, his chest riddled with half a dozen gunshot wounds. Hugo Velasquez, the rising international banker, was dead too. A single bullet in the chest had brought him to this improbable end in a little fast-food restaurant in an American border town.

On some impulse, Huberty vaulted the counter to check the kitchen and found Guillermo Flores on the floor talking to police. With Flores were Alex Vasquez and Albert Leos, the grill men, and the three crying young women who worked the counter. Vasquez remembered that Huberty looked quite surprised. "Oh," he observed calmly, "there's more." And then, in a flash of rage, "You're trying to hide from me, you bastards!"

He raised the Uzi. One of the women screamed in Spanish: "Don't kill me! Don't kill me!" Huberty opened fire. The three men leaped up to flee. Flores was ahead, Vasquez behind and pushing him. Flores jumped down a set of steps that led to an emergency exit and a moment later was outside. Vasquez scooted down another stairway to an exit and escaped. Albert Leos tried to run, but one of the women grabbed him and pulled him down and he was caught in the fire. Wounded but still alive, he crawled to the shelter of a

table, but Maggie Padilla, Paulina Aguino, and Elsa Borboa were dead. Huberty had taken pains to shoot all three of them in the head, among other places.

Luz Perez was with the others in the storeroom, listening to the firing overhead that was slaughtering her coworkers at the counter. She heard the emergency door alarm go off as Flores and Vasquez got away. Then Perez heard a tapping on the door. She and the others froze. The knocking came again, faint and feeble. Steeling herself, she opened the door a crack. There was Albert Leos, bleeding from arm and leg wounds. Perez pulled him inside and relocked the door. He lay draped across her legs in the tiny storeroom.

At some point, Etna and Zelia Huberty drove past in the van. Bobbi was baby-sitting at the Haseleys'. Etna and Zelia had gone grocery shopping, but as Etna later told police, Zelia had become oddly ill with an apparent vision that involved a lot of police and ambulances around a McDonald's restaurant. They were on their way to a friend's house when they passed the restaurant, and Etna recognized the black Mercury Marquis in the lot. At the friend's house, she learned of the shooting from TV and heard that the gunman was wearing camouflage pants. Heart sinking, Etna asked her friend to call the police.

Meanwhile, at San Diego police headquarters, Officer Catherine Nance was rounding up the Special Weapons and Tactics team. But it was well after 4 p.m., the rush hour was on, and the SWAT team members were scattered all over the city. Almost an hour passed before the team was in place, relieving the harried cops who'd first responded and were surrounding the restaurant.

Among the SWAT team officers was Charles Foster, 27, a crack shot assigned to the role of sniper. He was armed with his personal rifle, a .308-caliber bolt-action Steyr-Mannlicher with a five-shot magazine and a Bushnell telescopic sight, four to 12 power variable—a kind of scope akin to a zoom lens in a camera. The team leader, Sergeant John L. Madigan, positioned Foster on the post-office roof overlooking McDonald's. If Foster could get a clear shot, he was authorized to kill Huberty.

Inside the restaurant, Huberty continued to shoot at police. A fire truck appeared, and he stitched it with bullet holes. He'd poured himself several soft drinks from various machines, draining the cups and throwing them at bodies. For a while, he walked around pelting people dead and alive with food. The floors were wet and slick with blood. Its

rich, sickening odor filled the restaurant. Huberty left bloody tracks as he walked around firing at whatever caught his eye. He shot out the windows and blasted away at lights, tables, machines. He probably didn't realize what a good idea it was to smash the windows: The shards of glass hanging in the frames reflected glittering light to the police outside, making it hard for them to see him.

Like Officer Rosario, the SWAT team cops were being very, very careful. Some people trapped in the restaurant might still be alive and at risk from indiscriminate fire. Worse, a shot that missed or merely wounded the gunman might so infuriate him that he would kill more of his hostages. The police couldn't have known it at the time, but they might as well have taken their best shots, even at an elusive target. Huberty needed no additional fuel for his unquenchable fury; he was killing anyone who moved or appeared alive.

Eleven-year-old Aurora Pena, lying beside her dead aunt, Jackie Reyes, Reyes's dead baby, and the two dead friends,

The shooting over, paramedics wheel a casualty out of the restaurant past a frantic crowd waiting for news of the dead and wounded. Rescue workers inside were sickened by the carnage. "In all my days in this type of work," SWAT team officer Emmitt Henderson wrote in his report on the massacre, "this incident is one that will take some time to wear off."

noticed a lull in the firing. She opened her eyes to see if the gunman had gone. He was standing only six feet away and happened to be looking at her. With a surprised exclamation, Huberty hurled a bag of french fries at her and then opened fire. The girl was hit in the right arm, the chest, and the neck, but she was still alive. She lay motionless and silent despite the terrible pain. And this time she kept her eyes shut.

On the phone, the police operator was gently and expertly questioning Etna about her husband. It seemed a relief for her to describe his disappointments and furies and generally insane ways, and she told the police everything she could think of about his arsenal. She didn't know exactly what weapons he had with him, so she went through the whole list of handguns, shotguns, and rifles. She made a special point of explaining that Huberty had close to 1,000 rounds of armor-piercing ammunition.

Etna told the police all about Huberty's skill with small arms. He was ambidextrous, she disclosed. "If he's shot in one hand, that doesn't mean a thing. He can shoot as well with his left as with his right. In fact, maybe better."

By now it was about 5:10, and a team of some 60 SWAT officers was encircling the McDonald's restaurant. The area had been cordoned off for several blocks, and people had been evacuated from nearby buildings. News-media helicopters were hovering low overhead, and they were making such a racket that the SWAT team had to suspend opera-

tions briefly because its members couldn't hear one another.

As for Jim Huberty, it was undeniably his moment. After all those years of failure, of not getting along, of being ignored, there was no question that now he had everyone's undivided attention. But he couldn't savor his sudden celebrity over Poco Lopez's portable radio anymore. For some reason, Huberty had shot the little set off the counter, and it was emitting no more than a loud buzz.

The police saw the gunman inside moving continually. On the roof of the post office, sharpshooter Foster kept his eye glued to his telescopic sight. It was adjusted to six power for greater definition in the difficult, dancing light, and Foster occasionally glimpsed the flitting shadow through the glare of the glass shards. Huberty apparently could see out with no trouble; he noticed another officer in a window below Foster. Several rounds cracked against the frame of the window where the officer was crouching.

There was a brief period of confusion over whether the SWAT team commanders had actually authorized their officers to kill the gunman. But it didn't matter. Foster waited and waited, but had no clear shot. He lay there on the roof, watching through his scope. He could make out bodies on the floor. The gunman came in and out of the cross hairs.

The time was now 5:17. Huberty moved from the counter toward the double doors by the drive-up window on the post-office side of McDonald's. "He was about in the middle of the service area, out in front of the counter," Foster later reported. "There was no other movement inside the restaurant. I could see the dark shirt, the camouflage pants, and the weapon in the hands of the suspect.

"At this point, I had a clear and unobstructed view of the suspect from the neck down. There were no obstructions through the broken glass door between my line of fire and the suspect. I fired one round, and the suspect fell backwards to the floor."

The high-velocity, soft-nosed .308 slug smashed into Huberty's chest, severed his aorta,

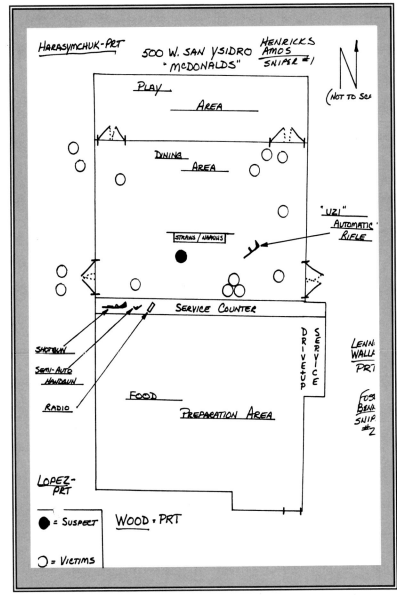

Police investigators drew this sketch with circles showing the positions of bodies in the McDonald's dining area and just outside the restaurant's front doors. Several bodies may have been removed before the diagram was made: 18 people died in this area. There are only 15 circles.

For a time, the dead were simply left where they had fallen *(background)*, as rescue workers hurried to aid the wounded. Guillermina Hernandez *(left)* was freed from the basement storeroom hideout she shared with five other survivors. Twelve-year-old Keith Thomas *(right)*, who was shot in the dining room, escaped with relatively minor injuries.

Two restaurant employees who survived Huberty's assault cling to each other as the full horror of the killings sinks in. They hid in the basement throughout the ordeal, listening to muffled screams and shots.

ripped out a portion of his spine, and mushroomed out his back, leaving an exit hole more than an inch square. It was a killing shot. His chest heaved, then relaxed.

James Oliver Huberty was dead. Yet police still weren't sure it was all over. So much firepower had been expended—close to 150 shots—that police wondered if there was more than one gunman. The SWAT team approached the silent, shot-up building with extreme caution.

Foster, watching through his scope, reported that the suspect was motionless. Sergeant R. O. Brown led a team of officers into the restaurant. "I saw a man in a red shirt and camouflage pants lying in the middle of the floor," Brown reported. "I also saw a weapon which appeared to be an Uzi or 9-mm. automatic at his feet. I trained my gun on the suspect even though he appeared to be dead. I then saw a girl move beneath the serving counter. When she looked up at me I asked her if the man I had my gun on was the suspect. She said yes."

Officer W. T. Michalek moved in and handcuffed the dead Huberty's wrists. Police were taking no chances.

Etna, still on the phone to the police, heard on TV that the gunman had been shot.

"Oh, God," she said.

"What's the matter?" the officer asked.

"It's on the news."

"Okay."

"Oh, God, he's been shot."

"You still there?"

"Yeah, I'm here."

"Okay."

"Oh, God."

"Okay. You still there?"

"Yeah, I'm here."

"You okay?"

"I feel sick."

"Yeah, that's understandable. Can you stick with me for another couple minutes?"

"Oh, God, it's that semiautomatic weapon. It's that Uzi. He's got that Uzi. Oh, God."

"Stay on the line with me, okay?"

"Oh, God. Oh, God."

"You okay?"

"I think so."

"Okay."

"Oh, God."

And later, sadly, "He's been shot and they've got him. He's not dangerous anymore."

The officer didn't specifically say that Huberty was dead. Etna learned that a little later, at the police station.

It took the shocked survivors in the restaurant some time to convince themselves that the killer was dead. The San Diego Police Department SWAT uniform is military camouflage blouse and pants, and the survivors cautiously opened their eyes to see men dressed as the murderer was dressed. Many assumed that more terrorists had arrived to complete the killing and froze into death postures again.

A medic team led by Dr. Tom A. Neuman, 38, went in seconds after the lead SWAT officers declared the restaurant secure. Neuman had arrived in a Life Flight helicopter from the University of California-San Diego Medical Center; the Life Flight and several other choppers were standing by to ferry the wounded to hospitals.

Walking into the carnage was a singular experience, even for medical personnel hardened to catastrophe. "It was like they had just stopped in time," Neuman said. "All these bodies were lying around. Heads were slumped on the table. The old man walking out the door was lying on the floor, donuts beside him. The two kids were dead by their bikes. The infant was dead in the arms of the people. There were two burned hamburgers on the grill."

Neuman's medics went swiftly from body to body, seeking out the living, evaluating those most in need of immediate care. Twenty of the victims already were dead, many having bled to death in the hour elapsed since they were shot. Medics and police wrapped the bodies in yellow plastic sheets and laid them outside, making vivid splashes of color on the macadam. There was still a flicker of life in Arisdelsi Vargas Vuelas, but she was found to be brain dead on arrival at the hospital. Another 19 wounded were hospitalized, and all of these would survive.

Maria Flores Delgado knew that her son, David Flores, often rode his black-and-gold bicycle to McDonald's in the afternoon with his pals, Omar Hernandez and Joshua Coleman. She hurried to the restaurant when she heard of the shootings and waited with the thousand or so spectators behind barricades. "The police wouldn't let me near, but I could see the bicycles and Omar," she said. "They sent me to the police station, and as I turned to leave I saw David's body on the ground, face up. I knew right then he was dead because no one was helping him. They help the wounded first." She was just the first of a chain of grieving family members and friends about to face incalculable loss.

Twenty-one dead in a mad spasm of violence in a setting so prosaic as to be an American cliché. It stunned the nation. There was nothing like it on record, no such mass slaughter perpetrated in an hour by a single hand.

The very randomness of the act was, perhaps, the most troubling thing. Why would one man kill a bunch of strangers? Seeking to explain it, the National Institutes of Health asked the San Diego coroner to examine Huberty's brain for any abnormality—a tumor, a scar, any tangible clue to madness. But the coroner found Huberty's brain to be normal, healthy, without any perceivable defects. Rage and vengeance have no substance, no form.

Because most of the victims were Hispanic, theories abounded that Huberty's motives were purely racial. San Diego Police Chief William Kolendar disposed of that notion. "He didn't like anybody," Kolendar said.

The day after the massacre, reporters in Ohio visited Earl Huberty, the careworn 73-year-old father whose son had lived and died so badly. The old man had taken up painting in his retirement, and he gestured toward a canvas he'd just finished. "I painted this for my church," Earl Huberty said. "There are 12 sheep there, see, by the river Jordan, tended by their shepherd. And there's one apart, by itself. It's the lost sheep. . . ." He began to cry. "Yesterday was the worst day of my life," he said. "I feel so sorry for those people." ◆

Flags at McDonald's restaurants throughout the San Diego area flew at half mast the day after the massacre. McDonald's made a gift of $1 million to a survivors' fund, razed the San Ysidro restaurant, and donated the land it had stood on to the city.

F*eminists have always
had a talent for enraging me.*

MARC LÉPINE

5

Small Game

He seemed to be following a script, said some survivors of his rampage. Every word and movement were precise, as though he'd carefully rehearsed them. On December 6, 1989, the day Marc Lépine went out to commit the worst mass murder in Canadian history, he was in complete command. He had, after all, been preparing for a long time.

No one will ever know exactly when he began his countdown to carnage. His choice of targets — women — had certainly been in the making for years. And he'd spent months on the tactical planning itself. He'd carefully reconnoitered his chosen killing ground, the engineering school of the University of Montreal. People later remembered seeing him at the university's cafeteria, in the student co-op, in and around the administrative offices. He looked like a student — in his twenties, casually dressed, his curly black hair contained under a baseball cap, his acne hiding under a patchy beard. He was slender, five feet 10 inches tall, and altogether nondescript.

A key step in his painstaking preparation for the slaughter had come on November 21, 1989, the day that Lépine walked into a store called Checkmate Sports on St. Hubert Street in central Montreal. He was a regular visitor there, drawn to the store's well-stocked gun section. Among the handguns, shotguns, and rifles, he browsed with a fond and knowledgeable eye. Lépine knew and loved guns. For years gun magazines and books on military subjects had been his favorite reading matter. But this visit was not to inspect the store's offerings or to savor the feelings of competence and power that weapons stirred in him. He'd come to buy. Back in September he'd filled out gun-permit forms and been granted a firearms acquisition certificate by the Quebec provincial police. There had been no reason to deny it, since the applicant had no criminal record and was not a mental patient. The certificate entitled him to buy a nonrestricted firearm — a hunting rifle, for instance.

Lépine's choice was a gun called a Mini-14, a .223-caliber rifle made by Sturm, Ruger & Company of Southport, Connecticut. The Ruger Mini-14 had many virtues as a killing instrument. It was a semiautomatic weapon, built to shoot each time the trigger was pulled, with no manual action to slow the rate of fire. It weighed only six and a half pounds. It used high-performance ammunition — a brass cartridge nearly two inches long that contained a large charge of gunpowder and would propel a slug from the muzzle at a speed up to 3,330 feet per second — more than twice the muzzle velocity of an ordinary .22 rifle. The gun was accurate at distances of hundreds of yards and had a reputation for "knockdown power." Its designers intended it for use against game such as deer and coyotes, but the efficient Mini-14 had also found a market among police SWAT teams, prison guards, and military units.

As a clerk looked on, Lépine put the gun's brown walnut stock to his shoulder, leveled the blue steel barrel, and slowly squeezed the trigger, listening to the snick as the firing pin entered the empty chamber.

"What are you going after?" the clerk asked.

"Just small game," Lépine said.

The Mini-14's magazine held only five rounds. Lépine asked for a higher-capacity magazine, a curved, so-called banana clip that would permit the firing of 30 rounds before reloading. Then he selected five boxes of ammunition — 100 rounds in all. The total bill came to $765.03. Lépine paid cash. On his way out of the store he passed under a large banner that bade a cheerful farewell to customers. "Good luck and good shooting," it said.

Marc Lépine was not, in fact, a man who believed in luck. He was methodical, logical, a planner. He was also a person who relied entirely on himself. Since 1987 he'd been living in a five-room apartment on the second story of a town house at 2175 de Bordeaux Street in a French-speaking, working-class section of Montreal. A high-school acquaintance named Erik Cossette had shared the house with him for a year or so, splitting the $285 monthly rent. Then Cossette went backpacking in South America, and a cousin of Lépine's, Michel Thiery, moved in. The cous-

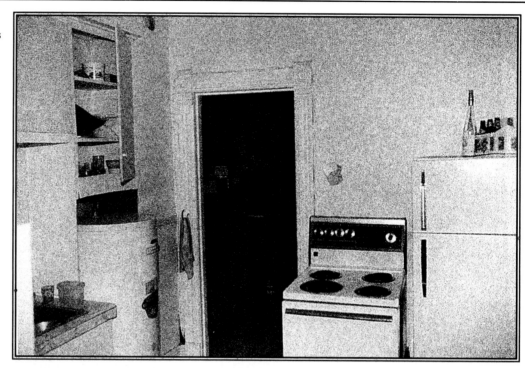

Marc Lépine's modest apartment on Montreal's de Bordeaux Street included a small kitchen *(right)* and an outdoor stairway leading from the front door to the street *(opposite)*.

ins saw little of each other. Lépine was essentially a loner.

Out of a job, immersed in his thoughts, he spent much of his time in his 8-by-10 bedroom. His single window offered a view of a dingy alley and drooping telephone wires. On a desk in front of the window were an Apple computer and bits and pieces of electronic gear; Lépine had been an electronics hobbyist since childhood. Books and magazines were everywhere, stacked floor-to-ceiling. Piles of videocassettes added to the clutter; many of them were war movies, taped from the television set in the sitting room. Along one wall was a sofa bed. Above it hung a poster of a war scene, drab against the turquoise paint that Lépine and his mother had applied to the room when he moved in.

People in the neighborhood viewed Lépine as shy and reclusive and a bit strange. From one window of her apartment, a neighbor had a view of his dining room; on a bookshelf there she saw what looked like a human skull. Even more disturbing were the noises she heard through a connecting wall. For weeks, she said, there were sounds suggesting that someone was blowing his nose, followed by the sound of a man "laughing like crazy." Only one voice was audible. "It seemed strange," she said, "to hear only one person laughing."

Lépine seemed a little eccentric, to be sure, and sometimes his manner was agitated and abrupt. Still, he didn't attract much attention. He paid his rent on time, and there was no sign of drinking or drug use in his apartment. On a few occasions he played music so loud that neighbors called the police, but these episodes were merely irritating, not crazed or dangerous. "He lived normally, like other boys," a middle-aged neighbor said. In truth, Marc Lépine did not live very normally. And although he was only 25 years old, he was tired of living at all.

By December 6, Lépine was ready to die, and he dressed for the occasion. The focal point for his ensemble was a blue sweater with black stripes, featuring on the back the jaunty image of a skull wearing glasses. The sweater was worn over a blue corduroy shirt that was tucked into jeans. He put on a pair of new work boots and threaded his belt through the loop of a sheath that held a hunting knife with a six-inch blade. As though coming out of hiding, he'd already shaved off his beard.

A cold rain fell, and the afternoon gloom deepened. Lépine took up a ballpoint pen and composed a letter in French, filling three pages with his handwriting.

"Excuse the mistakes. I had 15 minutes to write this," he

began. "Please note that if I kill myself today 12/06/89 it is not for economic reasons (because I waited until I used up all my financial means, even refusing jobs) but for political reasons. Because I decided to send *Ad Patres* the feminists who have always ruined my life. For seven years my life has brought me no joy, and, being utterly weary of the world, I have decided to stop those shrews dead in their tracks." *Ad Patres:* gathered to the fathers—in short, dead. Thus Lépine reduced his deadly plan to a succinct snippet of Latin.

When he'd finished writing, he put on a short gray parka and a white baseball cap. He folded the letter and put it into a jacket pocket and gathered up several boxes of ammunition for the Mini-14. The 30-shot magazine for the rifle was loaded and in place. He slipped the gun into a green plastic garbage bag, then headed downstairs to the small car that he'd rented the previous day.

It was after 3 p.m. and traffic was beginning to thicken. Lépine started the engine, switched on the windshield wipers, and eased out into the street, heading for the École Polytechnique. The biggest engineering school in Canada, the école was part of the University of Montreal, located 3¾ miles away on the north slope of Mont Royal, the high hill in the center of Montreal that gave the city its name. Marc Lépine was going into battle. Women were the enemy— women who didn't know their place, women who dared intrude on such rightfully male domains as engineering.

Someone had to do it, Lépine reasoned. Society had grown foolish and muddle-witted on the subject of sexual equality. One of the last paragraphs of the letter in his pocket said: "The other day, I heard they were honoring the Canadian men and women who fought at the front during the world wars. How can you explain then that women were not authorized to go to the front??? Are we going to hear about Caesar's female legions and female galley slaves who, of course, will occupy 50 percent of total forces in history, despite the fact that they never existed. A real *Casus Belli.*" A real cause for war indeed. Lépine, who seemed to feel that Latin added tone and weight to his complaints, ended his letter with a botched citation from Julius Caesar, misquoting a phrase used so often that it has become *the* cliché for a fateful decision that allows no turning back: When Caesar, as proconsul of Gaul, crossed the Rubicon River with his army in 49 BC and marched toward Rome to seize control of the republic, he said, *"Iacta alea est"*— "The die is cast."

"Alea Jacta Est," wrote Lépine. He was calm as he approached his own Rubicon. In the past few weeks, Lépine's customary edginess had abated. The bouts of misery and frustration that had plagued him for so long had given way to the peace of a true warrior, as he no doubt saw himself— the peace of a man prepared to die.

He was also a man prepared to kill. Lépine's day at the École Polytechnique was summed up by a coroner's report this way: "It was an aggressive armed assault by one individual. The events proceeded in several places inside the school. Fifteen persons were killed and 14 others were injured, some very critically."

The roots of those "events," as the coroner antiseptically put it, reached to the deepest levels of Marc Lépine's life—deeper than his own life, really. The beginning might be traced to a night in 1962 when a 26-year-old nurse named Monique Lépine met a 30-year-old Algerian-born businessman named Rachid Liass Gharbi in a Montreal restaurant. She was a devout Roman Catholic and had briefly studied to become a nun. He was a Muslim, swarthy and handsome, with a talent for fast talk and a taste for fine clothes and fancy cars. A year after they met, they married—over her parents' objections. About a year after the marriage, on October 26, 1964, their first child was born. He received a Roman Catholic christening as Gamil Rodrigue Gharbi. By the time he reached his teens, he would so hate the name that he'd insist on being called Marc Lépine and would answer to nothing else.

The family was enlarged by the birth of a daughter, Nadia, in 1966. By then, Rachid Gharbi was prospering as a salesman for a $2 billion financial enterprise called Investors Overseas Services. Founded by Bernie Cornfeld, a hard-charging American financial operator, I.O.S. sold mutual funds outside the United States—and beyond the reach of securities laws that Cornfeld considered unnecessarily restrictive. At its freewheeling peak the company had 15,000 salesmen at work in 110 countries around the world, and Gharbi was one of the best—a clever man who spoke several languages and had great gifts of persuasion. In pursuit of customers he moved with his wife and children to Puerto Rico, then Costa Rica, and finally back to Montreal in 1969. There he bought a triplex on Prieur Street, furnished it lavishly, and also rented a 30-room weekend retreat in Ste. Adèle, a mountain village 42 miles north of Montreal.

In this undated family snapshot, a smiling Lépine wears the beard that he would shave off shortly before going on his bloody rampage.

Members of his wife's family often vacationed at Ste. Adèle.

Gharbi was a millionaire for a time. But in 1970 careless management and dubious dealings brought Cornfeld's financial empire tumbling down. Cornfeld went to jail, and the shareholders in Investors Overseas Services—among them Rachid Gharbi, whose wealth consisted mostly of I.O.S. stock—were left with almost nothing.

By then, however—well before the big houses and big cars vanished—the Gharbi family had begun to descend into a domestic hell that reporters Greg Weston and Jack Aubry of the *Ottawa Citizen* would later detail. Gharbi was a man of reckless sexual appetites. According to a friend he kept several mistresses and fathered a number of illegitimate children. He was blatant in his sexuality, making a crude play for almost any woman who caught his eye. His wife later recalled that she dreaded going to parties with him. "I feared those outings," she said, "because of the advances he made to women and his habit of rubbing himself against the women he danced with."

Gharbi was increasingly violent toward Monique. "He would speak of love and other things," she remembered, "and out of nowhere I'd get blows to my face. He was a very brutal man who did not seem to have any control of his emotions." He expected her to work for him as a secretary, although she had no training in that field, and he forced her to type his business correspondence far into the night. If she made the slightest mistake he would hit her in the back of the head. One night he threw a glass of liquor in her face after she came home late from an evening with friends. On another occasion, at their weekend place, he tossed his dinner out into the snow in a rage and then beat her. Underlying these volcanic outbursts was a stark, uncompromising view of the roles of the sexes. "He believed women are not men's equals," his wife recalled, "that women are servants to men."

The children often saw their father beat their mother, and they were beaten themselves. When they were still very small, Gharbi would hit them if they disturbed his sleep by singing in the morning or if they failed to greet him properly. Little Gamil bore the brunt of the punishment; his father often hit him so hard across the face that the marks stayed visible for days. Nor was his mother allowed to comfort the children after they had been beaten. Her husband, she said, "would stop me from taking them in my arms and consoling them."

Gharbi abused his family psychologically as well as physically. He seemed to particularly enjoy humiliating them in front of others. When friends were invited to play bridge, he forced Gamil and Nadia to stand at rigid attention against a wall for hours at a time. His wife would endure similarly stern control. "He would ignore her," a friend later said. "When the four of us were talking, she wasn't a participant. She was just there physically. He would cut her off. It was all him. She'd no rights to anything."

After a beating one evening in the winter of 1970, Monique tried to break free. Telling her husband that the marriage was at an end, she fled with the children to the weekend place. He soon came after her and vented his rage by heaving her against a stone wall. When her sister's husband tried to intercede, Gharbi struck him as well.

Yet the savagery was followed by soft talk. Gharbi promised his wife that things would improve, and he played on her Roman Catholic belief in the sanctity of marriage vows. He worked on her emotions for two months, and in the end, he persuaded her to give him another chance. The reconciliation lasted for more than a year, despite Gharbi's early relapse into physical abuse. Finally, in the summer of 1971, Monique and the children moved away for good. Legally separated from Gharbi, Monique filed for divorce in 1974. The final divorce decree was granted in 1978. In the course of the divorce proceedings, Gharbi sought custody of the children and denied being overly harsh. "It is certain that from time to time during life that someone receives a slap or something else," he said. "But to hit in the sense to hurt? No." The judge failed to appreciate this fine distinction and granted custody to Monique.

Gamil was seven years old and his sister five when Rachid Gharbi went out of their lives. The boy was already withdrawn and prone to bleak moods—traits that would only intensify as he grew older. He hated his father and loved his mother, but he saw that his father had power and his mother was helpless. It's possible to theorize that Marc Lépine's murderous rage was rooted in this bitter situation. No matter how much he loathed his father, Gamil began to identify with him: better to be the abuser than the victim. The boy began to adopt Rachid Gharbi's contempt for women.

Materially, the family's situation did not change greatly after Gharbi left, at least not at first. Monique got support payments of $100 a month after leaving the Prieur Street apartment, and in 1972 she was awarded ownership of the

triplex. But Gharbi retaliated for the loss of his home by cutting off support payments, and the triplex was repossessed in 1973. Monique Lépine and the children moved to a rented apartment on a busy street in the city.

During this period, young Gamil occasionally visited an uncle who lived on a farm. This man was a former paratrooper, and he taught the boy how to use a gun.

As time passed, Gamil saw less and less of his mother. In 1973, restless and in need of money, Monique Lépine resumed her old career as a nurse and began to take courses that would enable her to get ahead in her profession. The children were left with relatives and friends; she usually saw them only on weekends.

Monique Lépine's hard work paid off professionally. She was appointed director of nursing at a Montreal hospital, St. Jude de Laval, where she headed a staff of 160. But the time spent away from her family took its toll. Not long before she got the nursing director's job at St. Jude's, she placed herself and the two children in a psychiatric program at another Montreal hospital. They remained in the pro-

Marc Lépine spent the happiest time of his life in this house in the Montreal suburb of Pierrefonds, where he lived with his mother and sister from 1976 to 1982.

gram for a year. "It seems we had difficulties expressing our need to love and be loved," she told the divorce court. She did not say so, but part of the problem might have been that her young son, already very troubled over gender issues, had suffered a new setback on that front: He felt himself abandoned by a successful woman, a woman who seemed to put her career before him. Rachid Gharbi would have put such a woman in her place. Like father, like son: Gamil felt keenly that his mother had transgressed the natural order of things. Such transgressions should not be allowed. Such transgressions should be put right.

With some financial help from her father, Monique Lépine bought a house in the middle-class suburb of Pierrefonds in 1976, when Gamil was 12. The neighborhood was pleasant and the house new, an attractive stone home with white shutters and a yard that backed up to woods and a river. In these quiet surroundings Gamil found a friend, a schoolmate who lived close by, Jean Belanger. The friendship was Belanger's do-   ing. "So," he remem-

bered years later, "here was this new guy on the bus, and I'm the talkative type, and he obviously wasn't. So I sat next to him." For six years Jean and Gamil were almost inseparable, riding bikes together, playing in the woods, shooting pigeons with their pellet guns. "He could shoot one while it was flying," Belanger recalled. "He didn't miss a lot."

Gamil was closemouthed about his family, but one day when he was 13 he told Jean that he hated his father so much that he intended to change his last name to Lépine. As a first name his initial choice was Jean, but his friend persuaded him that two Jeans would be confusing. He then plucked the name Marc out of the air. The change would not become legal until he was 18, but as far as he was concerned, Gamil Gharbi did not exist. He signed all his school papers Marc Lépine.

In Lépine's opinion, the University of Montreal's École Polytechnique *(below)* admitted female engineering students at the expense of male applicants. He applied for admission in 1986 but was rejected.

At home, the shift of identity was not so easy. In becoming Marc Lépine, he gave a weapon to his younger sister, Nadia. "She used to taunt him all the time," said Belanger. "She used to call him Gamil, Gamil, Gamil, and he would get really pissed off." Nadia and her brother were opposites in many ways, especially as they grew older. She preferred the company of the wilder kids, while he was rather priggish. He disapproved of every form of wildness—drinking, drugs, even rock concerts.

Deeply wary of the opposite sex, Lépine was uneasy when, at the age of 15, Belanger began dating a vivacious girl named Gina Cousineau. But the friendship of the two boys remained intact. "He was extremely shy," Cousineau later said of Lépine. "After about a month with me, though, he was fine. He said I was not just a typical girl. I was more like one of the guys." Belanger urged his friend to date. "I always tried to get Marc to get himself a girlfriend, to find out what girls were all about, but he had a lot of problems with that." Lépine refused to attend school dances and turned down invitations to parties. When he wasn't with Belanger and Cousineau, he stayed home. His mother paid him to take care of the house.

Lépine's favorite activity was fiddling with electronic gear—taking apart old radios, rigging up switches to control lights or telephones, designing all sorts of gadgetry. Belanger and Cousineau often joined him in this hobby, but Lépine was the most intense of the trio. "His ideal," Belanger remembered, "was to become an electronics engineer or a computer engineer. He was interested in both." Although his schoolwork was poor in English and mediocre in French, he excelled in science. "He was so good," said Belanger, "that he never took any homework home. He didn't feel the need to. The guy was a brain."

Despite his intelligence, Lépine remained socially backward, and his mother worried about the absence of a father figure in his life. When he was 14 she sought to remedy the situation with the help of the Big Brothers Association. As a suitable older companion, the group suggested a man named Ralph—tall, affable, and in his forties. For about three years Ralph regularly spent time with Lépine and Belanger on weekends. He was an enthusiastic participant in their electronics hobby, and he taught them about photography, introduced them to motorcycles, and took them to movies. Then he vanished. Belanger asked Lépine what had happened. At first Lépine was evasive; finally he said that

Ralph was homosexual and had been jailed for assaulting another boy. Belanger didn't know whether to believe him.

Whatever the truth about Ralph, Marc Lépine, now 17, had come to a turning point. One day he walked into the Montreal recruiting office for the Canadian armed services and tried to enlist. Just what happened there has never been made clear, but according to military records he was "interviewed, assessed, and determined to be unsuitable."

meant by "asocial," but his reference to Lortie and an arsenal was plain enough. More than five years earlier, on May 8, 1984, a 25-year-old army supply clerk, Corporal Denis Lortie, had stolen two submachine guns and a pistol from the Ontario military base where he was stationed. He drove a rented car to Quebec City, slipped into a side entrance of the building where the provincial assembly met, and headed for the legislative chamber. As it happened, the assembly was not in session, but the corridors offered some human targets. Spraying bullets around, Lortie killed three government employees and wounded 13 other people before surrendering to the police. He received a sentence of life in prison for his assault on officialdom. At the time of the Lortie murders, many Canadians feared that the wide publicity would inspire others to emulate him. Their fears may have been justified: The memory of Lortie's deed was firmly fixed in Lépine's mind.

By the time he was rejected by the military, Lépine had started to lose the fragile mental balance that he'd maintained through his teenage years. In 1982 his life tipped sharply downward when his mother decided to move the family to an apartment nearer her work at St. Jude de Laval Hospital. Thereafter Lépine saw much less of Jean Belanger, his only friend. Lépine grew more reclusive than ever, passing the hours in his bedroom with books, his beloved gadgetry, and a computer. In furtherance of his ambition to someday be an engineer, he entered a local junior college, taking an all-science program. Sometimes his studies went well, but he failed several courses.

In 1983, after finishing at the junior college, Lépine enrolled in a three-year program in vocational training. He did well, but in his final term he abruptly stopped going to classes, without telling anyone why. The reason may have been another rejection. At about this time—in January of 1986, when he was 21—he applied to the École Polytechnique, the engineering school of the University of Montreal. His application was turned down.

Lépine soon left home, moved into a one-bedroom apartment by himself, and went to work at his mother's hospital. For $10 an hour he pushed food carts around, washed dishes and floors, and, for a while, served meals in the cafeteria. His acne was now so severe that other employees didn't want him handling their food, and he was relieved of his cafeteria duty and consigned to cleanup duty in the kitchen. His behavior became steadily more erratic and frenetic. He

That rejection was mentioned in the handwritten letter that Lépine carried in his parka pocket on the afternoon in 1989 when he drove to the École Polytechnique. "I had already tried in my youth to enlist in the Military Forces as a student officer," the letter said, "which would possibly have allowed me to enter the arsenal and precede Lortie in a rampage. They refused me because asocial." Writing in haste, Lépine omitted words and did not explain what he

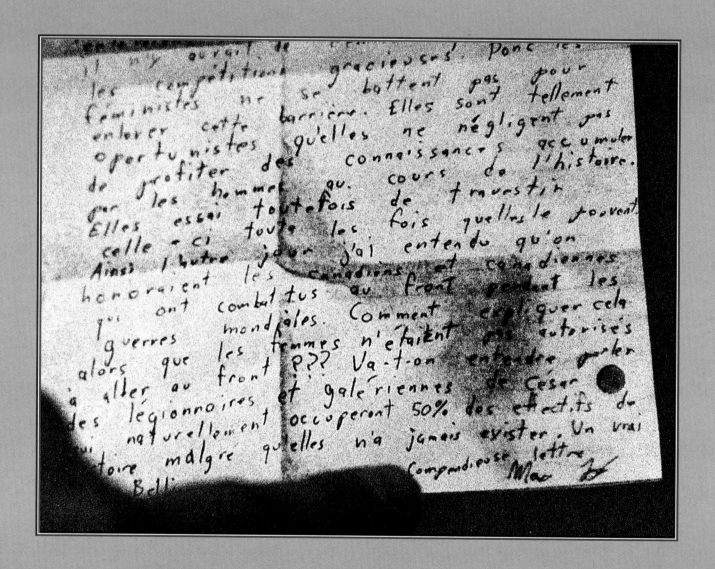

The final paragraph of the suicide letter police found in the
pocket of Lépine's parka rails in French against opportunistic
feminists who usurp male privileges.

was loud, obnoxious, disruptive, rebellious, resentful of authority. He rushed through his work, sometimes spilling food or breaking dishes. A favorite pastime was to build elaborate constructions with plastic cups, piling them higher and higher until the edifice toppled and the cups went rolling across the kitchen floor.

In September 1987, after 16 months on the job, Lépine quit—but he would insist, for some reason, that he'd been fired. At a high-school reunion where he'd hoped he would meet Jean Belanger, he encountered Gina Cousineau and, as she remembered the conversation, he "said he'd made one small mistake during his three-month probationary period and, bang, they told him to get lost. He told me that he'd been fired by a woman and that another woman had taken his place."

In February 1988, Lépine enrolled in a 15-month course in computer programming at the Control Data Institute, a privately run technical school in Montreal. His grades on the entrance examination had been very high, and the director of the institute considered him one of the most promising students there. Two nights a week, Lépine also took a chemistry course at a junior college, and there he met a woman, 28-year-old Sylvie Drouin, who found him interesting and asked him to be her laboratory partner. She didn't know quite what to make of him. "The first few weeks in the lab, he was very severe with me," she said later. "I was never correct. He was always right." At the same time, he seemed very insecure and distracted. "He was good at the theory, but at practical things, he was no good," Drouin recalled. "He was so nervous, he would make mistakes. His mind would wander."

Drouin visited Lépine at his apartment on de Bordeaux Street, seeking help with her homework for a computer course. But the relationship was frustrating. "He didn't teach me," she said. "He just wanted to solve the problems himself and hand them to me. If you follow him in his ways, things are fine. If you don't, there is nothing. He gets very cold and withdrawn."

In March 1989, just two months away from finishing his course at the Control Data Institute, Lépine dropped out, once again giving no reason. He didn't even tell Drouin that he'd left the computer school, but she sensed that something was wrong. "He slowly got more difficult to communicate with," she said. She continued to see him in chemistry class. On one occasion he came to school with a newspaper story about a policewoman rescuing someone from a burning building. He remarked to the instructor that he believed women should not be allowed on the police force. They lacked the necessary size and strength, he said. But the problem was not yet out of hand, he indicated, noting that he'd found the names of only six policewomen in newspaper stories. Evidently he'd been researching the matter.

As the course drew to an end, Drouin told Lépine that she'd been accepted at the engineering school of the University of Quebec. He replied that he would be attending the École Polytechnique in the autumn. When they parted, she had the feeling she would never see him again. His manner, she recalled, "was very strange, in a very hurried state, like someone with something very important on his mind. It was as though he had something to do that no one else could know about."

But now, driving south through a freezing drizzle toward the engineering school on the dark afternoon of December 6, he was at ease. He'd seen his mother for the last time a few days earlier; she detected nothing unusual in his behavior. He'd reconnoitered the École Polytechnique on December 1, December 4, and December 5. In his pocket was his letter, his last testament, a rambling, venomous explanation of why he had to act: Feminists, he wrote, "have always had a talent to enrage me." He blamed his female foes for wanting "to keep the advantages of women" and at the same time "grab those of men." Feminists, wrote Lépine, were "so opportunistic they neglect to profit from the knowledge accumulated by men through the ages. They always try to misrepresent them every time they can."

The letter ended with what its author called an "annex." It consisted of the names of 19 women, all apparently drawn from Lépine's reading of newspapers. Six were the policewomen he'd casually mentioned in his chemistry class. The list also included a union official, a sportscaster, and several other public figures. Beside some of the names were telephone numbers, indicating that the rabid antifeminist's research had gone beyond reading the papers.

The letter in Lépine's pocket left no doubt that his fondest wish would have been the execution of the women listed in his annex, but this aim was not to be. "The lack of time," he wrote, "has allowed those radical feminists to survive." There was enough time, however, for one symbolic blow against all feminists, and the École Polytechnique afforded him an ideal stage for such a venture: Of its 5,000 students, about 15 percent were women.

Lépine arrived at the University of Montreal shortly before 4 p.m. and parked close to the main entrance of the École Polytechnique. The engineering school was housed in a six-story yellow brick building just northeast of the university's main administrative building. Lépine left his car in a towaway zone; it hardly mattered—he didn't expect to need it again. Classes were still in session. This was the last regular day of the term, so the atmosphere was a little more hectic than usual. Eleven days of examinations would follow; then the students would leave for the Christmas break, some going home, others to vacations in sunnier climates.

Lépine was in no hurry. From about 4:00 to 4:40 p.m. he sat on a bench at the entrance to the registrar's office on the second floor. Holding the green plastic bag at his side, he stretched out his legs, making it hard for students to pass through the office doorway. From time to time he rummaged furtively in the bag, careful to conceal the contents. He spoke to no one. Finally, an employee behind a counter asked if she could help him. Without a word, he rose and left. He proceeded up a stairwell to the third floor, where he stood for a while in a corridor, leaning against the wall and holding the green bag. Then he made his way down to the second floor again. It was now about 5:10 p.m.

Most of this floor was devoted to offices, supply rooms, and lounges. There was only one classroom, C-230, reached through steel doors at the end of a long corridor. Lépine approached, pushed through the steel doors, and let the bag fall from the rifle. A few more steps down a narrow hallway brought him into the classroom, a large, echoing space with concrete-block walls.

In the room, Professors Yvon Bouchard and Adrian Cernea were conducting a class in mechanical engineering for about 60 undergraduates, nine of them women. Lépine entered as two students were giving end-of-the-term presentations on heat transfer. He walked quietly toward the two presenters, holding the semiautomatic rifle in both hands. Then he spoke. "Everyone stop everything," he said. He was grinning. Some of the students laughed. "We thought it was a joke," Professor Bouchard said later.

Lépine ordered the students to separate into two groups —women on the left, men on the right. No one moved. He fired a shot toward the ceiling to indicate that he was serious. As the echoes died away, so did the laughter. The

students stared in amazement at the cool, well-spoken intruder, who again demanded that the men and women separate. His voice was now much louder and harsher. The students tried to obey him, but they mingled in confusion for a moment. Lépine pointed to a corner of the room—at the far end, opposite the doorway—and commanded the women to go to it. When they'd gathered there, he told the men to get out of the room. They quickly left. But, as yet uncertain of what was happening, some of them paused beyond the doorway. They still hoped that the episode might be a joke and that the warning shot had been a blank.

Lépine now had the sort of audience he'd come to find— nine females who'd been admitted to a school that had rejected him, nine usurpers of a role that belonged to males. The muzzle of his rifle strayed casually over the group, pinning them in place against the concrete-block walls. "Do you know why you are here?" he asked.

"No," said 23-year-old Nathalie Provost.

"I am fighting feminism," said Lépine.

"Listen," Provost replied. "We're only women who are studying engineering." She tried to explain that they were not necessarily feminists. Marc Lépine wasn't listening.

He began to shoot the women, proceeding from left to right. The room became a hurricane of noise—gunfire hammering, moans and screams of terror and pain. Some of the women tried to dive away from his line of fire or find shelter behind the few pillars in the room. Lépine missed no one, but three of the students would survive. Nathalie Provost was among the wounded: One bullet grazed her temple, and others hit her in one leg. Josee Martin was hit in the right arm. France Chrétien took a slug through the right shoulder, and bullet fragments embedded themselves in her right side and buttocks. Her boyfriend was in the group of male students standing outside the door. He and Chrétien had planned to go to a seaside resort in Mexico for a New Year's holiday.

Six women died, some instantly, some sensing life ebb away as shot after shot rang out, growing ever more distant, blending into the encroaching darkness. Lépine fired at least 20 rounds of his high-powered .223-caliber ammunition before he was finished with this first stage of his war. The walls of the classroom slaughterhouse were splattered with blood, the floor strewn with shattered bodies.

When the men lingering in the hall outside heard the gunfire and the women's screams, they lost any hope that the whole affair was a joke. They sprinted through the steel doors at the end of the hall and down the main second-floor corridor, shouting that a madman was shooting people and that people should run for their lives. But a few of the male students eventually paused, halted by the thought of what was going on behind them. They stopped near some photocopying machines; a woman was there as well. Lépine emerged through the steel doors. From about 30 feet away, he fired at them. A man and the woman were hit. As he walked toward them, he spotted another female student, leveled the rifle at her, and fired; she too was wounded.

At 5:12 Montreal's emergency 911 number received its first call. In a breathless torrent of words, a student told the officer who took the call that a man had entered a classroom at the École Polytechnique, fired a shot, and forced the men to leave the room and the women to stay. At this point, said the caller, the killer was shooting randomly on the second floor. In the background, the officer heard groans and continuing gunfire. Two more calls came in less than a minute later, one of them from a security guard at the École Polytechnique. Police cars and ambulances went racing toward the campus, the wail of their sirens converging on Mont Royal at the city's heart. Ambulance attendants were told by police to exercise extreme caution and await the arrival of the police if they reached the scene first. Meanwhile, the telephoned cries for help continued to pour into 911, each punctuated by gunfire in the background.

Throughout the building where Marc Lépine was performing his executioner's work, the sound of shots, yells, and pounding feet alerted people to mortal danger. Three students were in the second-floor office of the school newspaper, the *Polyscope*, when the shooting began. At first they thought firecrackers had been set off. Then another shot rang out, and they heard a woman scream, "Help, help, I'm going to die!" The student-journalists double-locked the door and hunkered down on the floor, waiting for police to arrive. On the fourth floor a student burst into an office occupied by two engineers and slammed the door; they didn't protest. Alain Perreault, the 23-year-old president of the students' association, was on the third floor when the shooting started. He raced downstairs toward the association's second-floor office. On the way, he later recalled, he passed "one girl wounded badly in the eye, lying on the floor." Perreault reached the students' association office safely and barricaded himself in there, along with 30 others.

At the center of the spreading mayhem, Lépine remained the cool and skillful hunter. He held his gun at the ready and kept his back to the wall as he moved. He kept shooting, whenever there was a suitable target, and, all the while, he kept smiling. "It was, you know, a normal smile," a student remembered later. "Nothing crazy, just like he was having a good time."

Lépine was retracing his steps along the main second-floor corridor now. He stopped at the doorway of C-228 and saw a female student at the far end of the room. She was trapped. He aimed the rifle at her and pulled the trigger. The gun didn't fire. He tried a second time. When the rifle again failed to fire, he left, walking toward a stairwell where he began to reload. A male student hurrying down the stairway ran straight into him and heard him say in disgust, "Ah, shit, I don't have any more bullets." The student kept going. When he reached the bottom of the stairs, he saw three people lying in the hall ahead of him. He looked back at Lépine, saw him raise the rifle, and sprinted toward the main second-floor corridor and an escalator that led down to the cafeteria. A shot rang out. He couldn't tell whether it was aimed at him or not.

Lépine had unfinished business in C-228. When he returned to kill the coed who'd eluded him earlier when his gun failed to fire, he found the door locked. He shot at the lock three times, but it held. Giving up, he moved along the corridor to the main hall, stepping around the three people lying in lakes of blood. A woman was walking down the escalator from the third floor; it was out of commission. Lépine lined her up in his sights and fired. The impact knocked her down, and he turned away. She would live.

The gunman moved on toward Room B-218 in the Financial Services area. When he was about 20 feet from the office, he saw that a woman was closing the door. He hurried to stop her, but she managed to throw the latch. Still,

I *am fighting feminism.*

he could see into the room through a window by the door. She was moving away from him. He lifted his rifle and fired through the glass, spraying fragments into the room, putting a slug through the woman and killing her. She was not an engineer or an engineering student; Maryse Laganier was a finance-department employee, newly married.

Lépine was finished with the second floor. He took the escalator to the first floor, perhaps following a preplanned route toward fresh game. About 100 people had been in the first-floor cafeteria when the killing started.

From an office on the second floor, Paul Boileau, the 33-year-old manager of the student stationery store, had run downstairs as soon as he heard gunfire. Students rushing for the exits ran with him. Boileau darted into the cafeteria shouting, "There's a crazy guy upstairs shooting with a machine gun!" Most people heeded him and headed for a side door, but a few stayed at their tables and continued eating. "They thought it was a joke," Boileau said afterwards. "I was telling them it wasn't a joke, but they didn't believe me. Either that, or they thought they could protect themselves inside."

As Boileau and some other people ran from the cafeteria, Lépine appeared around a corner in front of them. "The guy was down the hall, coming really slowly," Boileau remembered. "He had his rifle in both hands, pointing up above his shoulder, like he could slip it down and fire really fast." Lépine could have shot them easily, Boileau said. He didn't bother. There were no women in the group. It was now about 5:20. Lépine had been on the hunt for almost 10 minutes. He entered the cafeteria, saw a woman standing near the kitchen, and took aim. Barbara Maria Klucznik and her husband, Witold Widajewicz, often ate at the École Polytechnique cafeteria because it was the least expensive eatery on campus. Once high-school sweethearts, the couple had arrived in Canada from Poland in 1987 and enrolled at the University of Montreal, he to work for a master's degree in neurophysiology, she to study nursing. Besides its usual appeal for students watching their pennies, the cafeteria had a special attraction that day: Free wine was being offered to celebrate the end of the term. "Red and white. Balloons were hanging. Everything looked like a party," Widajewicz later said.

At the moment when Lépine approached, Widajewicz was at the food counter, considering what to choose. His wife had already selected her meal and moved on to the

cashier to pay for it. Suddenly, chaos erupted around Widajewicz. People shouted, lunged, fought to get out of the cafeteria. Swept into the kitchen by the surging crowd, he lay on the floor with the others. Shots rang out repeatedly. Some of the women in the kitchen began to cry. A holdup, Widajewicz thought. Beyond the kitchen doors, his wife lay dead, felled by Lépine's first shot in the cafeteria.

The shooter ambled through the cafeteria, firing in different directions. He spotted two women in a storage area and killed them both. As he moved on he came across a man and woman, both students, hiding under a table. He ordered them to get up. They obeyed. Strangely, he paid no further attention to them. He left the cafeteria; his mission directed him elsewhere.

One of the dead in the cafeteria was 21-year-old Anne-Marie Edwards, who was studying to be a chemical engineer and had just won a place on Montreal University's alpine ski team. At that hour, her father was on his way home from work. His car telephone rang. It was his wife, calling to say that she'd heard a report of a mad gunman at the École Polytechnique. Edwards felt a cold dread. Later he would learn that the body of his daughter had been found slumped in a chair in the cafeteria.

As Lépine was leaving the blood-spattered cafeteria, the first police cars were arriving at the university. In the confusion, there was a certain amount of police bumbling. For example, the officers in the leading car went first not to the École Polytechnique, but to the campus's women's residence. This was because the frantic calls coming in to dispatchers kept saying that a gunman was shooting women. Quickly realizing their error, the officers raced toward the École Polytechnique, the tires of their cars screeching on the rain-slick pavement. They reached the building at 5:22 p.m., 10 minutes after the first 911 call. Within a few more minutes, police had surrounded the building and positioned themselves to cover the various exits. Fearing that there might be more than one gunman, they kept students and other civilians hundreds of yards away from the building.

In the early moments of the crisis, the police presence was sometimes too restrictive: When the first ambulance reached the scene at 5:24, it was stopped at a police roadblock. Some of the wounded walked out of the building on their own. The ambulance attendants radioed that there appeared to be many wounded. More ambulances were dispatched—eventually 13 in all.

The nature of the threat within the building was still unclear to the police. Students calling 911 described the gunman accurately, but they placed him in different parts of the building. One caller said the man was armed with a machine gun. The police delayed going into the building until more force could be brought in; they would not enter until 5:39 p.m., 17 minutes after the first cars pulled up in front of the École Polytechnique.

His affairs in the cafeteria concluded, Marc Lépine had started upstairs again around 5:22. He was next seen in the hall on the second floor, heading for the broken escalator that led up to the third floor. To terrified listeners all over the building, it seemed for a few brief moments that the shooting was over. But Lépine found more prey in a corridor on the third floor. Taking them by surprise, he brought down three students—two men, one woman. All were wounded, but not fatally.

A class was still in session at the end of a long hall on the third floor. The 26 people in Room B-311 had been aware of some odd noises earlier but had been too far away from the gunfire to identify the sounds as gunshots. Now they heard yelling and loud crashing sounds—breaking glass, perhaps. They looked at one another in confusion. On a platform at the front of the room, Roger Thiffault continued with the oral presentation he was giving. He shared the platform with two other students, Maryse Leclair and Eric Forget. Leclair, 23, was in the last year of her engineering studies and was regarded as one of the brightest students at the École Polytechnique—"brilliant, brilliant, always happy" said a school official later. Her father was the director of communications for the Montreal Urban Community police. His job would bring him to the École Polytechnique that night to brief journalists.

At 5:25 Lépine entered the classroom. He stepped toward the platform, saying, "Get out, get out." Presumably he was talking to the two male presenters, but they, like the others in the room, didn't immediately realize that they might well be facing death.

"At first," remembered Eric Forget, "nobody did anything. From a distance, the gun could have been a toy." But Lépine wasted no time in showing that it was real. He shot Maryse Leclair from a few feet away. As she went down, gravely wounded, he snapped off shots at students sitting in the front row. Thiffault and Forget dived for cover.

The room had two doors. Two women tried to scramble out the one nearest the platform; he killed them both, then spun and blasted away as students tried to escape by the other door. Many people were now cowering under their desks. Lépine strode up and down the classroom, shooting, reloading, shooting. Four people were hit, one fatally. The gunman climbed onto a desk and began walking along the desktops, blazing away in all directions.

On the platform, Maryse Leclair was pleading for help. A bullet had passed through her, fracturing ribs, tearing through the muscles of her chest and back, lacerating her lungs. Lépine sat down beside her. For the first time that day, he pulled his hunting knife from its sheath. He plunged it into her chest three times. She fell silent. Four people were now dead in the room.

Lépine put his knife on the professor's desk. He laid his baseball cap and two boxes of ammunition beside the knife. He took off his parka and wrapped it around the barrel of the rifle. Then he turned the gun in his hands and pressed the muzzle against his forehead. "Ah, shit," he said and pulled the trigger.

The coroner's report would describe the result as "a fatal, cranial, cerebral trauma caused by a firearm projectile of high velocity." The police would be more direct: Marc Lépine blew his brains out.

It was about 5:28. The professor in B-311 said that it was safe to get up. He said that the gunman had shot himself and told the students to avoid looking at him. The fire alarm, which had not been pulled until 5:25, was belatedly signaling that there was danger afoot and that the building should be evacuated.

At 5:39 police entered the building and began calculating the carnage. Maryse Leclair's policeman father went in as well, seeking the facts he would need when he talked to the press. He had no idea what awaited him there. "I turned the corner of that third-floor corridor," he said much later, after a yearlong silence, "and saw my daughter lying on the ground, on the platform at the front of the class. I turned that corner and saw the classroom walls with all their windows and I saw my daughter. That was a difficult moment and I'll always remember it: how she was lying on her back with her head thrown back. I'll never forget it."

The grief that followed Marc Lépine's war on women was widely shared. Montreal and the Province of Quebec declared a three-day period of mourning. Thousands of

Two hours after Marc Lépine committed suicide, officers of the Montreal Urban Community SWAT team enter the École Polytechnique to investigate persistent rumors of a second gunman. A suspect was arrested, but police soon determined that Lépine had carried out the bloodbath alone.

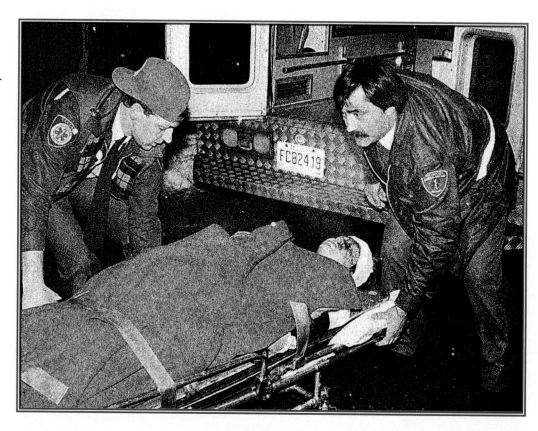

Medics load one of Lépine's wounded victims into an ambulance following the cessation of gunfire at the École Polytechnique.

people, forming a great ribbon of light, carried candles up Mont Royal to the campus in a silent vigil the night after the massacre. Thousands more gathered five days after the vigil for a funeral service in Montreal's Notre Dame Basilica.

Editorial writers and public officials expressed a range of opinions about the tragedy and what it meant or did not mean. The rampage was variously described as an explosion of purest insanity or, in the words of one prominent woman columnist, Francine Pelletier of the newspaper *La Presse,* as "a cold, rational, and calculated act." Pelletier was one of the "radical feminists" who were targeted for execution in Lépine's "annex." Leona Heillig of the Montreal Assault Prevention Centre said, "I think that what happened is an extreme example of the violence women live with all the time."

Lépine's boyhood friend, Jean Belanger, also had a comment. "I don't know whose fault it is," he said. "I guess mostly society's."

Fourteen women had died; 15 men and women had suffered injuries, some of them very serious. And a number of students were affected in invisible ways. They began to have nightmares, fail their courses, experience trouble in their personal lives.

Psychologists counseled hundreds of these troubled survivors during the months after the massacre. But the psychologists didn't get to everyone. In the summer of 1990, a young man named Sarto Blais, an engineer who had been at the École Polytechnique on the day of the killings, found that he could no longer bear to think about the classmates and friends who had died. He hanged himself. His mother and father, despairing at the loss of their son, committed suicide as well. The parents, a police spokesman said, "felt it was no use to live."

For his own perverse reasons, Marc Lépine had felt that way, too. But the poisons in his mind did not permit him to go alone. ◆

In the wake of the murders, an unidentified man takes down the cheery wish for a *"Bonne Année"*—French for "Happy New Year"—pinned up in the cafeteria of the École Polytechnique. Still sprawled in a chair behind him is the body of one of the three women Marc Lépine shot dead in the cafeteria.

I wish I had stayed in bed.
MICHAEL RYAN

War Game

6

It was late in the afternoon on an August day that had been uncommonly fine for England, with a sky so clear and a sun so bright that it was actually rather hot. For townsfolk in the village of Hungerford, it was a perfect day for a walk or a swim or a picnic in the woods.

Michael Ryan had been out in the lovely weather earlier, but now he was holed up in a drab, third-floor classroom of the John O'Gaunt School—his old school, the one he'd been so glad to get out of 11 years before. Now it was his sanctuary. It was an ugly, flat-roofed modern box of a building, reflecting nothing of the romantic history of the 14th-century duke whose name it bore. The door of Room Six was barricaded with a filing cabinet, a table, and chairs. The hideout's windows faced the countryside—not many targets out that way, except police sharpshooters who had the school surrounded. A room on the other side of the building would have been a sniper's dream, with a wide and unobstructed view of Hungerford's maze of streets. But Ryan was down to just one gun, his pistol, and he was almost through shooting. A few minutes earlier, in a gesture hinting at surrender, he'd tied a scrap of white cloth to his Chinese-made semiautomatic AK-47 assault rifle and tossed it out the window. But Ryan wasn't quite ready to give up. He had another hour and a half to go, and one target left.

He looked so harmless and nondescript, a short little dumpling of a man with thinning, dishwater-blond hair above a face as bland as pudding. He'd just committed the worst mass murder in England's history.

Lying 50 miles west of London, Michael Ryan's home-town of Hungerford has everything that a picture-book English country town of 5,000 should—all the attributes that entitle it to adjectives such as "quaint" and "charming" in the guidebooks. It even has a patron saint of sorts in John of Gaunt, duke of Lancaster and uncle of King Richard II. John is fondly remembered for granting Hun-gerfordians perpetual rights to hunt in his woodland, the Savernake Forest west of town. Hungerford's main thor-oughfare, the High Street, runs south from the A4, a major national highway. On the way it crosses the pretty little river Dun, a first-rate trout stream. Laid out perhaps 800 years ago, the High Street is shaded by large old trees and lined with antique shops, inns, and tearooms that are often filled with well-heeled Londoners.

The back lanes that sprout like random twigs from both sides of the High Street are dotted with ancient thatched cottages and timbered Tudor-period homes. Wiggling off toward the east from the High Street is Park Street, formerly Cow Lane. It leads to the 200-acre Hungerford Common, now more parkland than grazing ground, though a few cows still compete with picnickers and kite fliers. The common adjoins the War Memorial Recreation Grounds, where townspeople gather for football and cricket matches and swim in the public pool.

Michael Ryan, born May 18, 1960, grew up on the fring-es of the charmingly antique Hungerford. His family was working-class, however, and lived not in Tudor splendor or thatched quaintness, but in a squat and stolid 20th-century row house at 4 South View, a short dead-end street on the east side of town. Michael was the only child of Dorothy and Alfred Ryan. A building inspector for a local govern-ment agency, Alfred Ryan was 55 years old when Michael was born. His employees knew him as a rather dour man, a perfectionist who expected others to adhere to his own strict personal standards. By some accounts Alfred was as domineering at home as at work. But perhaps because of his advancing age and failing health, his control over his son appeared to wane once the boy became a teenager.

Some 20 years younger than her husband, Dorothy Ryan was a far more easygoing, sociable person than he—"a very nice lady" who "always had time for anybody," according to an old acquaintance. When Michael was a little boy, Dorothy worked as a "dinner lady" serving meals to the children at the Hungerford Primary School, just across the street from the Ryan home; Michael attended the school from the age of seven until 11. Around 1973 she got a job as a waitress at the Elcot Park Country House Hotel at Kimbury, a village three miles from Hungerford. She was popular with both the staff and the customers. When she finally passed her driver's test after 12 attempts—she simply couldn't seem to get the hang of motoring—the hotel owners broke out champagne for an impromptu celebration. Most people who knew Michael in his early years agree that he was a quiet boy, although they interpret his impassivity in different ways. Several relatives contend that he was quiet but happy. There were neighbors and schoolmates, however, who summoned up negative memories of a boy who was indeed quiet—but sullenly so. Standoffish with other children, the Michael they knew spurned schoolmates who tried to include him in their games, choosing instead to watch from the sidelines. He was a favorite victim of teases and bullies, who didn't let him forget how short he was for his age. Yet he never fought back, either verbally or physically; it seemed that he didn't know how.

Tourists and townspeople stroll along Hungerford's upper High Street, whose charming old buildings house churches, tearooms, antique shops, and inns. The street is also the site of a weekly market that draws a crowd of shoppers.

Michael did not make up for his playground failures in his school-work. He attended the John O'Gaunt School from the age of 11 to 16, and David Lee, the headmaster, recalled him as an unremarkable boy, "an anonymous sort of lad." Michael's grades were poor, and he had to do remedial work. He often played hooky to ride his motorcycle with Brian Meikle, a neighbor boy who was his best friend—perhaps the only close friend he ever had.

In 1976, shortly after his 16th birthday, Ryan finished his schooling at John O'Gaunt and enrolled in a technical college with the intention of becoming a building contractor. Unfortunately, he was no quicker a study at the technical school than he'd been at John O'Gaunt. "If you showed him how to use a chisel, you would have to say 'Now hit it,'" one teacher recalled. He noted that Ryan always sat off by himself and talked very little. Ryan dropped out without finishing the course and went to work as a gardener and handyman at a girls' school.

Some parents would have punished such lackluster performance by withholding money and presents, but not Dorothy Ryan. She doted on her boy and always tried her best to give him whatever he wanted—toys, styl-ish clothes, motorcycles and cars, the latest rock recordings. When Michael was old enough to graduate from a bicycle, he went in quick succession from a moped to a dirt bike to a string of cars. Dorothy Ryan took out loans to buy the cars and gave her son a credit card for gasoline and other such essentials. She paid the bills.

Among Dorothy's gifts to Michael was his first gun, an air rifle that he received on his 10th birthday. The boy often took the air gun onto the common to shoot at birds and cows—and, on occasion, at other children. When he was

18, he got a license permitting him to own a shotgun. From then on Ryan built up a constantly changing collection of both air rifles and shotguns, buying and selling weapons almost obsessively. He also bought a steel gun cabinet and bolted it to a wall in his second-floor bedroom. Along with guns, he collected military paraphernalia such as flak jackets and gas masks, as well as an array of survival gear.

In 1985, when Ryan was 25, his father died at 80 of cancer. One day shortly before his death, Alfred asked his son to put a bullet in a gun and leave it by the bedside. The horrified Michael refused. "Guns are not for that," he said. He went to his room and locked his gun cabinet.

Ryan reportedly promised his dying father that he would always look after his mother. According to several relatives, Michael fell apart emotionally after Alfred Ryan died, and Dorothy Ryan was worried enough about depression and deepening moodiness to mention her son's mental state to a close friend. For his own part, Michael didn't talk much about his feelings; indeed, he was as closemouthed in his twenties as he'd been as a boy, and acquaintances of long standing had trouble getting more than a hello from him. Sylvia Pascoe, one of Ryan's neighbors, said, "He kept to himself. It was very hard work getting a conversation out of him." She was able to draw Ryan out a little only on the subject of cars—he was a habitual tinkerer.

Although he never made much money at any job and was often unemployed, the gun-mad Ryan nevertheless found the wherewithal to keep adding to his collection of air rifles and shotguns. Presumably, Dorothy indulged her son's ex-pensive hobby. In late 1986, apparently ready for more variety, Ryan applied for an amendment to his gun license that would permit him to branch out into pistols. Under Britain's firearm laws, a person must seek permission when-ever he wants to buy almost any firearm other than a shot-gun. A police representative must determine that the appli-cant is not a threat to public safety and has a legitimate reason for owning a firearm, such as membership in a gun club. To the policeman who came to Ryan's house to in-terview him about broadening his gun license, Ryan ap-peared to meet the requirements. He had no history of psy-chiatric problems, and the only blemish on his record was a single speeding ticket. Moreover, he belonged to the Dun-more Shooting Centre, a gun club approved for pistol shooting. With the government's blessing, Ryan bought three handguns, including a 9-mm. Beretta pistol.

In April 1987, after a year of unemployment, Ryan got a government job clearing footpaths and mending fences near the river Thames, some 20 miles from Hungerford. He seemed to enjoy the outdoor labor, which earned him a modest £69–$115—a week. At first his supervisor and coworkers thought him to be an ordinary young man—shy, perhaps, but pleasant enough. Gradually, however, their impressions changed. Ryan would come to work with a loaded pistol tucked into the waistband of his pants and brag that he could get the other workmen any kind of gun or military equipment they wanted. Once he displayed the contents of his car's trunk to several of his mates: It was packed with an assortment of guns.

Ryan also brought homemade rockets and bombs to work—"Ryan Specials," he called them. One day he fired off one of his rocket specials on a footpath he and some other men were clearing in a field alongside the Thames. "It nearly gave me a heart attack," crew supervisor Charles Amor remembered. "It went up in the air, came down, and took off again straight towards some houses. I shut my eyes. It scared the life out of me, but then it dropped down onto the ground."

Ryan disclosed that he often used road signs for nighttime target practice—an illegal activity, day or night. When a coworker called him a liar, Ryan told him to take a look at a particular exit sign on a road just outside Hungerford. The man examined the sign—and found four bullet holes punc-turing its middle.

Most of the stories Ryan told, however, were self-aggrandizing fantasies. He claimed to have owned an antique shop and a gun shop. He'd earned a private pilot's license, he said, and he'd traveled to Venice on the Orient Express. He boasted of being a former paratrooper, when in truth he'd never served in Britain's armed forces in any capacity. Ryan's fondness for elaborate lies extended to his sex life. Unattractive to women, he nevertheless told a local antique dealer that he had married an Irishwoman and fa-thered a child. He broke off the relationship, he said, when he found her in bed with her elderly uncle. In another ep-isode he spread the word around Hungerford that he was getting married, even though no one had ever known him to have a girlfriend, much less a fiancée. Nor did he have any close male pals. Even his old friendship with Brian Meikle had faded following Meikle's marriage in 1980.

The most bizarre of Ryan's fictions involved a mysterious 95-year-old retired colonel who had supposedly taken him on as a kind of protégé. According to Ryan, the colonel had promised him an expensive car—a Porsche by one account, a Ferrari by another—and had invited him to visit his tea plantation in India. Weaving a romantic subplot, Ryan said he'd been engaged to the colonel's nurse but had called off the wedding when the young woman refused to buy his mother a gift. A peculiar fact: Although the story was pure invention—there was no colonel, no colonel's nurse, no tea plantation—Ryan's mother repeated it to a family friend as though it were true. As always, it seemed, her impulse was to protect her son at all costs.

When Ryan trotted out his fantasy life for his coworkers, they laughed in his face and accused him of lying. As the ribbing continued, Ryan became furious and threatened to shoot the men if they didn't stop calling him a liar. Fright-ened by the intensity of his anger and remembering his stash of guns, the men backed off. In the heat of the moment at least, mousy-looking little Michael Ryan seemed capable of carrying through on his threat. "He was serious about it," Amor said later. "He was gritting his teeth in temper."

In the wake of Ryan's alarming explosion of rage, Amor decided it was time to report to his superior Ryan's habit of carrying a loaded gun. Whether this had anything to do with Ryan's quitting his job is unclear, but on July 9 he told the supervisor that he'd found a better-paying job and left. In fact, Ryan had no other job to go to; instead, he went back on unemployment, collecting $180 a month.

A few days before quitting his job, Ryan received gov-ernment permission to buy two semiautomatic rifles. Cer-tain things that might have changed the mind of the po-liceman conducting the obligatory interview remained Ryan's dirty little secrets—the threats he'd made against his coworkers, the signs he liked to shoot up, the pistol he tucked in his pants. To all appearances the applicant had followed the rules to a T, including joining the Wiltshire Shooting Centre, which had facilities for rifles. Ryan quickly purchased the guns he had applied for—an American World War II M-1 carbine and the AK-47 assault rifle.

Ryan had not gone shooting at either of his clubs during May and June. Now his interest picked up sharply, and during July and August he frequently signed in at the Wilt-shire club, which was housed in an abandoned railway tun-nel in Devizes, some 23 miles from Hungerford. Ryan might have found a special appeal in "practical shooting," a new

A slight, somber-looking Michael Ryan (center), about 11 years old, poses with other students of the Hungerford County Primary School for a picture. "He was very introverted," a classmate recalled. "A bit of a mystery."

Michael Ryan boasted to his disbelieving coworkers about the four bullet holes (circled) that he put into this road sign at a major interchange north of Hungerford.

reported later that he shot poorly during the practice, missing most of the targets.

The following day, he would make up for that medio-cre performance.

August 19, 1987, was a Wednesday, the day of Hungerford's weekly market, when stalls set up along the High Street draw crowds of shoppers. Dorothy Ryan drove away soon after breakfast to shop and run errands; she was not due at her waitressing job until later in the day.

Michael Ryan had his own plans for the day. He climbed into his most recent automotive extravagance, a sporty metallic silver Vauxhall Astra GTE, and drove to the A4 highway just north of Hungerford. There he turned west toward John of Gaunt's Savernake Forest, seven miles from Hungerford. He had three of his guns with him—the Beretta pistol, the M-1 carbine, and the AK-47 assault rifle.

The forest was a favorite retreat of his. On his visits there, Ryan once confided to some fellow workers, he liked to pretend that he was on military maneuvers. During this

sport the Wiltshire club was offering its members. Participants fired at life-size drawings of human beings, some of which looked like terrorists. The stated aim of the sport was to "kill the enemy."

To other club members, Ryan came across as a polite young man who liked to wear Dutch paratrooper's boots, which he kept well-polished. An average marksman, he could hit a dummy terrorist with a rifle shot at 300 feet. Given the intensity he brought to the shooting, it seemed Ryan might have done better. Most members enjoyed the camaraderie of the club, but he did not. He arrived, did his shooting, and then was gone, with a minimum of chitchat.

On August 18 Ryan made his last visit to the Wiltshire club. To Andrew White, one of the club's owners, Ryan appeared restless and preoccupied, not quite himself, when he stopped to pay the fee for two targets. "He was rubbing two pound coins together in his hand, fidgeting with them between his fingers," White recalled. "Then he just picked up his rifle bag and disappeared." Ryan shot at targets with his AK-47 for an hour before calling it a day. Witnesses

In the summer of 1987 Ryan often visited the Wiltshire Shooting Centre, located within an abandoned railway tunnel that muffled firing-range noise. A provisional member of the center's gun club, Ryan never completed the probationary period required for full membership.

solitary game — he would always played alone — he would sneak up on unsuspecting picnickers, spy on them for a while, then creep back into the woods. The police later found a survival hut made from broken branches just yards from a picnic area in the forest; they speculated that Ryan had built it.

While Ryan made his way toward the woodlands, others were preparing to go there too. In the village of Burghfield Common, 35-year-old Susan Godfrey packed up the picnic lunch she and her two children, four-year-old Hannah and two-year-old James, would eat in the forest before going on to visit her parents. Her husband, Brian, was at work. A vivacious woman, the five-foot-tall Godfrey worked week-ends as a nurse. On weekdays she often took her children on outings to nearby public parks. On this bright, balmy day she parked her car on one of the many isolated lanes that wound through Savernake Forest's 6,000 acres. On a grassy spot not far from the car, she and the children spread out a groundsheet and set out their lunch. Shortly before 12:30, the meal done, Godfrey began packing the car. Hannah, found unharmed later that day with little James,

SUSAN GODFREY

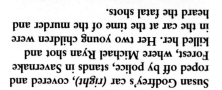

Susan Godfrey's car (right), covered and roped off by police, stands in Savernake Forest, where Michael Ryan shot and killed her. Her two young children were in the car at the time of the murder and heard the fatal shots.

told the police as best she could what had happened. A man walked up to her mother as they were about to leave, Han-nah said. He was carrying a gun. Ryan said something to Godfrey, who then led the children to her car and strapped them into their seats. Ryan and Godfrey walked to a clear-ing in the woods, about 100 yards from the car.

Although no one can know what went on between Ryan and Godfrey, one possibility is that he intended to rape her. But if so, his scheme went awry; an examination would show that Godfrey had not been assaulted sexually. What-ever occurred, sometime after reaching the clearing Godfrey apparently tried to run back to her car. Perhaps in a rage, perhaps fearful that she'd identify him to police, Ryan fired his Beretta at the retreating woman's back over and over, wounding her 13 times. She fell dead 240 feet from her car.

Hannah knew what had happened and decided that she and James must go find their father. They got out of the car, and when a woman came upon them walking through the woods Hannah took her hand. ''A man in black has shot our mummy,'' the little girl said.

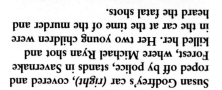

Some 300 yards away from the Godfreys' picnic site, a 14-year-old boy was in his yard feeding his cats when he heard a rapid series of shots. Knowing a thing or two about guns, he instantly recognized the sound of a semiautomatic weapon. He did not, however, report the gunfire to police; the army, he thought, must be practicing in the forest. His chore done, he went back indoors.

Leaving Susan Godfrey dead and her children alone in the car in the forest, Ryan roared back along the A4. About 12:35 p.m. he pulled into the Golden Arrow service station in Froxfield, a crossroad village some two miles west of Hungerford. Standing inside at the cash register, Kakaub Dean recognized him when he pulled up at the pump. He was one of her regulars, stopping in several times a week. He usually bought just a few liters of gasoline.

This day, however, Dean's customer didn't follow his routine. He drove in from the west instead of from Hungerford, and he filled his tank—something he'd never done before. He took a five-liter can from his trunk and filled that, too. After Ryan returned the hose to the pump, he

patted his clothes as if looking for his wallet and glanced nervously at another customer. As soon as the other customer drove off, Ryan busied himself with something—something Dean couldn't see—in the trunk.

Dean was busy for a few moments ringing up Ryan's purchase, and when she looked through the window again, he was standing near the pump with a rifle. The muzzle was pointing at her. Before Dean's disbelieving eyes Ryan placed one foot forward, crouched slightly, positioned the butt of his carbine against his right shoulder, and fired. The bullet drilled a one-inch hole through the window and ricocheted off a wall and the ceiling before landing on the floor.

Dean dropped to her hands and knees behind the counter. From her hiding place, she heard the door open and Ryan enter. The footsteps stopped, and she heard four distinct clicks. Apparently the weapon had jammed and wouldn't fire. "Please, please don't kill me," Dean begged. Without saying a word, Ryan wheeled around and left the store. When she was sure he was gone, Dean, shaking with fear, dialed the national emergency number, 999, and reported

the incident to police. As it turned out, authorities already knew something was wrong at the Golden Arrow. A witness—perhaps someone who drove up to the pumps while Ryan was inside—had called the police two minutes before Dean to report what looked like an armed robbery at the station. The Thames Valley Police now sent three patrol cars to the A4 to keep a lookout for the gunman.

But Ryan was no longer on the highway. Shortly after 12:45 p.m, Margery Jackson, a neighbor of Ryan's, was walking home along South View when he pulled into his driveway. He jumped out of his car and ran toward the house. Jackson thought he looked upset. Victor Noon, the Ryans' 54-year-old next-door neighbor, said hello to the young man. Scarcely slowing his pace, Ryan replied, "Oh, hello. All right, are you?" and disappeared into the house, slamming the door behind him.

Within minutes Noon heard gunfire from inside the house. Noon couldn't have known it at the time, but Ryan had shot the family dogs, an aged mongrel and a black Labrador retriever that had been his special favorite.

When Ryan emerged from his house he had a bag loaded with ammunition and was wearing a sleeveless flak jacket and a black headband. The attire brought him as close as he could come to the rakish soldier of fortune look that he so admired in movies and magazines. He gathered up survival gear—a rucksack, waterproof trousers and jacket, a ski mask, a gas mask, a canteen, a bottle of brandy, and a first-aid kit—and packed his car.

The sequence of Ryan's actions over the next few minutes went unobserved and can only be guessed at, but by now he was clearly a desperate man. A physician who steeped himself in the case would later speculate that Ryan, having just committed a murder on impulse, decided between Saver-nake Forest and the Golden Arrow that he would drive to some remote place to hide out—hence the gasoline and the survival equipment. He tried to kill Kakaub Dean, this theory went, because she could identify him.

If indeed Ryan had some survivalist plan for escape, it didn't make much sense. A more rational person might have concluded that in a small and heavily-populated country such as England, the best chance of refuge lay in the anonymity of a city. Yet Ryan took with him equipment suitable for standing off a siege in wild terrain. He was behaving as though he'd slipped out of reality and into some Rambo fantasy that now had to be played out to the end. The

survival gear was one of several signs that he'd snapped somewhere along the line and had descended into madness. Wherever he may have been heading, Ryan came out of his house in his commando clothes and climbed into his Vauxhall, only to find that it wouldn't start. He dealt with this new crisis by shooting the car, firing four bullets from his Beretta into its trunk. And if he'd meant to use the can of gasoline from the Golden Arrow to refill his car during his escape, it could now be used for something else—to set his house on fire. Ryan took the can into the house, emptied its contents on the living-room floor, and struck a match. The room burst into flames, which would soon spread throughout the house and to several adjacent homes.

Slinging the carbine and the AK-47 over his shoulders, Ryan set off on foot. He headed down South View, Beretta in hand, in the direction of the school playing field at the lane's dead end. At the house next door to the Ryans', Roland Mason, a retired lineman for an electrical company, was in his garden creosoting the fence. His wife, Sheila, a charwoman at a store in Hungerford, had just stepped outside. Spotting the pair, Ryan shot Roland in the neck and Sheila in the face. The Masons died instantly.

Fourteen-year-old Lisa Mildenhall was in her family's back garden when she thought what she heard were fire-crackers. She ran around to the front of the house to investigate the noise and saw her neighbor, Michael Ryan, with a rifle under his arm. Ryan smiled at Lisa, who didn't realize that anything was wrong until he dropped down on one knee and lifted the rifle to his shoulder. Four bullets fired at point-blank range hit the girl's legs.

Somehow, Lisa was still able to walk. Stunned, and uncertain about what had happened, she stumbled into the house and asked her mother, "Mummy, have I been shot?" When she saw her daughter's bloody legs, Jenny Mildenhall started crying and rushed off to fetch her neighbor Sylvia Pascoe, who had first-aid training. Pascoe managed to stop the gush of blood from an artery torn open by a bullet. The swift action saved the girl from bleeding to death.

As Pascoe was tending to Lisa, Ryan roamed up and down the street, shooting indiscriminately at anyone within range. Seventy-seven-year-old Dorothy Smith went to her door to see what all the noise was about and saw him—but he looked so peculiar that she didn't recognize him at first, even though she'd known him for 20 years. "Is that you making that noise?" Smith demanded. "You are frightening

The Golden Arrow service station in Froxfield shows evidence of Michael Ryan's visit: a bullet hole in the kiosk window *(inset).* Ryan stopped to buy gas, then shot through the window at cashier Kakaub Dean. He missed her.

everybody to death up here. Stop it!" Ryan turned his head and looked at her. "He had a terrible vacant look in his eyes and a funny sort of grin on his face," Smith said. "He looked to me as if he was brain-dead." As Ryan walked away, the feisty old woman yelled after him, "You stupid bugger!" Moments later, Margery Jackson, the neighbor who'd seen Ryan come home, was hit in the back by a bullet as she was going in her front door. Crawling to the telephone, she called her friend George White. She told him that she had been shot and asked him to fetch her husband, Ivor, from his bricklaying job in Newbury, eight miles away. White assured her he would go for Ivor immediately.

Out on the Hungerford Common, 51-year-old Kenneth Clements was taking an after-lunch stroll in the bright sunshine, his dog at his side. With him were his son, Robert, and several other family members. They were on a footpath leading to South View when a woman rushing past warned them that a man with a gun was nearby. Kenneth Clements remarked that it must be nothing but kids messing about and strode ahead. The rest of the family, however, heeded the warning and stopped—all but Robert, who was worried about his father and in a moment went after him.

Kenneth Clements was a few yards ahead of his son when the sound of gunshots ripped through the air. Ryan suddenly appeared from behind a hedge. He held the AK-47 in shooting position. Robert Clements immediately leaped over a nearby fence for cover. But his father, who suffered from a lung disease, couldn't move very fast. The elder Clements raised his arms to Ryan in a gesture of surrender. Ryan ignored the gesture and shot the older man, killing him instantly. When Kenneth Clements's body was retrieved hours later, one hand still grasped the leash of the dog. The animal, trembling, sat by its dead master's side.

Ryan was now at the edge of the town common. If he had any thought of escaping from Hungerford on foot, this was the time to try it, to take off across the common for the countryside beyond. Instead, he retraced his steps along South View. It was now 12:50 p.m., and police were fielding a frantic barrage of calls from Ryan's neighbors. The officers who had been sent just minutes before to search for him on the A4 were ordered to head for Hungerford and South View. "We believe the bloke in connection with the Froxfield job is there with a weapon," the radio dispatcher said. "Person in this area discharging a shotgun. One person injured at this stage. No further details."

The officers in the first two cars to arrive agreed to block both ends of South View in hopes of containing the gunman. Constable Roger Brereton was to cover the intersection of South View and Fairview Road by himself, while Constable Bernard Maggs and Sergeant Peter Ryan in the second car were to prevent an escape across the common by way of South View's dead end. None of these men was armed. In Britain, police officers go about their daily business without weapons. In the event of a shooting incident—and only after police are sure they aren't dealing with a false alarm—specially trained armed officers are called in.

When Ryan saw the police car at the entrance to South View, he wasted no time. He shot at Brereton first with the pistol, then switched to the AK-47. The car passed the Ryans' house and crashed into a telephone pole. Using police code for "officer in distress," Brereton shouted into his radio, "Ten-nine, ten-nine, ten-nine. I've been shot!" Ryan kept shooting. A bullet hit Brereton in the back of the neck. He slumped over onto the passenger seat and died, radio in hand. The time was 12:58 p.m.

Ryan continued west on South View, shooting and wounding Linda Chapman and her daughter Allison, who had just driven into the lane in a Volvo. Chapman managed to shift the car into reverse and got away. Then an ambulance, responding to a 999 call, came down Fairview Road to its intersection with South View. Neither the driver, 37-year-old Linda Bright, nor her partner, 31-year-old Hazel Haslett, had any inkling of the danger they were venturing into; they thought they were responding to a domestic shooting. Because South View was too narrow for the ambulance to turn around easily, Bright backed her vehicle into the street. She saw Ryan first. He was standing a few yards in front of the ambulance, a rifle raised to his chest. "There's a man with a gun!" she screamed. A bullet smashed through the windshield. Flying glass cut Haslett's arms and legs. The two women ducked, and Bright floored the gas pedal and sped away. Ryan fired again at the retreating vehicle. As soon as she'd maneuvered the ambulance safely around a corner, Bright grabbed the radio. "This is a priority message," she gasped to the dispatcher at ambulance control. "We are being shot at! There's a man gone berserk!"

The two policemen sent to cover South View's dead end arrived in time to hear the shots that killed Officer Brereton. They came upon Robert Clements, who told them, "That's me dad lying there in the path" and indicated that the killer had gone off in the direction of South View. Constable Maggs and Sergeant Ryan went to investigate. They were within 100 feet of Roger Brereton's car when Maggs saw a man rear up on the other side of it. It looked to the constable as though the man was reloading a pistol. Maggs and Peter Ryan had scarcely taken cover in a rose-bordered garden when they heard the crack of four or five bullets going past them. The two officers slipped into a neighboring house, where they warned the residents to stay away from the windows. Once he had gathered his wits, Maggs crept outside again to take stock of the situation. He saw Michael Ryan walking eastward toward the common. He also saw, for the first time, the gunman's AK-47 and realized the kind of firepower Hungerford was up against. Maggs returned to the house and called 999 to report to the police dispatcher; neither Maggs nor his partner had a portable radio.

The fourth police officer, Constable Jeremy Wood, had now arrived in Hungerford. As Michael Ryan approached the common, he spotted Constable Wood in his car. Robert Clements was with him. Ryan fired at them, but they managed to elude his bullets and drive a quarter-mile across the common to the shelter of a stand of trees on the far side. At 1:12 Wood radioed a report of the attack and requested that armed local police and the Tactical Firearms Unit (TFU) of the Thames Valley Police be summoned. Without weapons, there was no way to stop Michael Ryan's bloody rampage. But Wood's wait for the heavily armed specialists of the TFU would be a long one, for the entire squad was on a training range 38 miles away. Not until 2:20 p.m. would the last of its 15 members arrive in Hungerford.

After calling 999, Constable Maggs went outside again, just as Margery Jackson's husband, Ivor, and their friend George White turned into South View in White's Toyota. As Maggs

watched, Ryan fired the AK-47, killing White instantly and seriously injuring Jackson. The car swerved and crashed into Constable Brereton's car. Although he had three bullets lodged in his chest and one just behind his right ear, Jackson had the presence of mind to slump down and feign death. He would survive. Ryan stopped shooting and walked past the car and out of Maggs's sight, toward Fairview Road.

At the corner of South View and Fairview Road, 84-year-old Abdur Khan, a retired London restaurateur who'd come to England from India as a boy, was in the garden of his bungalow weeding his runner beans. Maggs heard a shout, then

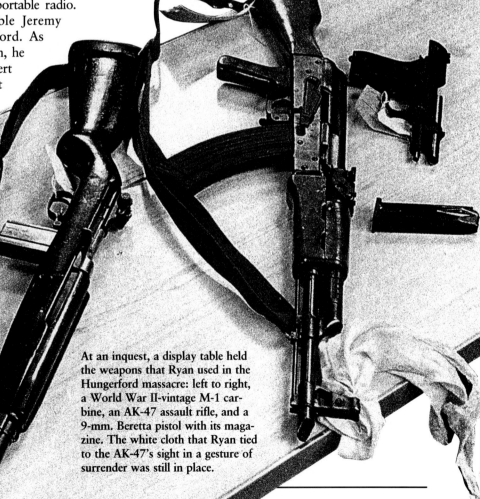

At an inquest, a display table held the weapons that Ryan used in the Hungerford massacre: left to right, a World War II-vintage M-1 carbine, an AK-47 assault rifle, and a 9-mm. Beretta pistol with its magazine. The white cloth that Ryan tied to the AK-47's sight in a gesture of surrender was still in place.

several shots. Ryan had killed Khan as the victim's 81-year-old wife, Maureen, watched helplessly from inside their house. Ryan also wounded a man walking along Fairview Road. Maggs rushed back inside to call in a new report. By now, the telephone system was so clogged that several minutes passed before he got through to headquarters. An inspector instructed him to sit tight and wait until a police helicopter with a sharpshooter on board arrived.

After shooting Khan, Ryan reversed his direction again and walked back toward the common. He had passed George White's Toyota and Constable Brereton's police car when Dorothy Ryan drove into South View. She brought her car to a screeching halt behind White's Toyota. She must have been horrified by the devastation she saw: injured and dead bodies, crumpled automobiles, flames shooting up from her house and those of her neighbors—and, worst of all, her son in the street with his guns. Jackson heard Dorothy Ryan open the door to the car he was in and say softly, "Oh, Ivor." Then she shut the door gently and ran down the street shouting, "Michael, Michael! Stop it!"

But she could not make Michael stop. As Dorothy ran toward him, her son lifted the Beretta and aimed. Dorothy screamed and cried out, "Don't shoot me!" He fired twice. One bullet hit her in the front of her leg, the other in her abdomen. Dorothy fell forward onto the ground. Michael walked over to his injured mother, placed the Beretta less than four inches from her back and fired twice more. She was the eighth fatality of the day.

Leaving his mother's body in South View, Ryan doubled back and ran to the playing field, passing the dead Kenneth Clements along the way.

In Clarks Gardens, a little lane immediately south of Ryan's, 70-year-old Betty Tolladay was outside her house when she heard gunfire nearby. The commotion annoyed her, and when she glanced across the playing field behind her house she spotted a man with rifles—surely the culprit.

"Kindly stop that racket!" she shouted as Ryan walked past her garden. He smiled at her strangely. Then, to the elderly woman's utter astonishment, Ryan took aim and fired one bullet in her direction. It struck her in the groin, knocking her down. Ryan kept going. Tolladay dragged herself into her house and dialed 999. She had to wait over four hours for an ambulance, since the police had by now banned emergency workers from entering the area. Tolladay was one of the lucky ones; she survived her wound.

DOROTHY RYAN

Ryan's mother, Dorothy, arrived at her South View home on the day of the killings to find it in flames. Leaving her car in front of the house, she squeezed past the bullet-riddled automobiles of victims George White and Constable Roger Brereton to confront her son. He shot her dead and left her body sprawled facedown in the narrow lane (inset, right).

POLICE ROADBLOCK

POLICE COMMAND POST

1 ROLAND MASON

2 SHEILA MASON

3 KENNETH CLEMENTS

4 ROGER BRERETON

5 GEORGE WHITE

6 ABDUR KHAN

7 DOROTHY RYAN

8 FRANCIS BUTLER

9 MARCUS BARNARD

10 DOUGLAS WAINWRIGHT

11 ERIC VARDY

12 SANDRA HILL

13 JACK GIBBS

14 MYRTLE GIBBS

15 IAN PLAYLE

In this aerial view of Hungerford, diamonds mark the spots where 15 of Michael Ryan's murder victims fell. He shot seven near his house on South View and eight more along the route he took to the John O'Gaunt School. The roadblock indicated at top center is set up beside the High Street, just south of its intersection with the A4 highway. The open ground to the east is the Hungerford Common.

Francis Butler was walking his dog on the War Memorial Recreation Grounds bordering the south side of the playing field. The 26-year-old Butler would ordinarily have been at work on a Wednesday, but he'd taken the day off to be with his wife and two young children. He wasn't a block from his house when he encountered the gunman. Ryan shot him first in the leg, then in the chest. The second shot was fatal. Ryan had been carrying the M-1, but it was useless, having jammed at the Golden Arrow. He now threw the carbine on the ground near Butler's body and walked on.

At 1:18 p.m. two armed policemen from the Thames Valley Police joined Constable Wood at the makeshift command post across the common. Wood had been straining for a glimpse of the gunman, and at 1:20 p.m. he spotted him near the war memorial's cricket pavilion. Four hours would pass before police would again catch sight of Ryan. They would try to keep track of him through the logjam of phone calls from terrified residents. But many callers had trouble getting through quickly, and as a result, many of the sightings they reported reached the police well after Ryan had moved on—around the corner, down another street. People trying to phone family members and friends to warn them about the gunman had just as much trouble getting through. Thus many of Hungerford's townsfolk went about their business as usual, ignorant of the deadly mayhem so close at hand, only a little out of earshot.

A stone's throw from the spot where Ryan killed Francis Butler, swimmers at a Memorial Grounds pool heard shots. Someone went to investigate and returned with alarming news of a gunman standing over a person lying on the ground. Two lifeguards and an airline stewardess rushed the 20 swimmers out of the water and into the locker rooms. Hearing another series of shots, the stewardess and the lifeguards ran from the pool to see if they could find victims and offer first aid. On nearby Bulpit Lane they spotted a taxi that had come to a halt; the driver was motionless.

Cabby Marcus Barnard had been on his way home between fares to visit his wife and their first child, five-week-old Joe. One of Hungerford's best-known and most popular residents, Barnard often gave free rides to the town's elderly citizens. Ryan sprayed the taxi with bullets from the AK-47. One struck Barnard in the forehead, shattering the left side of his skull. He slumped forward over the steering wheel, dead. His wife heard the shots from their house, 50 yards away, but she would not learn

Francis Butler, 26, lies dead beneath a makeshift shroud in the Hungerford War Memorial Recreation Grounds. Hearing shots, several staff members from a nearby swimming pool rushed to Butler's aid. When a neighbor shouted that his killer was doubling back in their direction, they fled, leaving their first-aid equipment behind.

for hours that her husband had been the target. The stewardess had brought oxygen equipment from the pool, but Barnard was past help.

Kenneth Hall, a passerby, reported later that he saw Ryan throw the AK-47 on the ground and stomp away, as if he'd had enough shooting. But after a few steps Ryan seemed to change his mind, for he retrieved the rifle. The next person to be raked by its fire was John Storms, an appliance repairman who'd just stopped his van on Priory Avenue, a short distance from Bulpit Lane. Hit in the face, Storms crouched down under the steering wheel. He heard two more cracks of a gun and felt the van shake, but he wasn't hit again. He survived.

Guessing about the gunman's whereabouts, the police had set up three roadblocks to keep people away from the area where they thought he might be—the Hungerford Common. Their assumption was that Ryan would make an attempt to escape across the common. But Ryan didn't do the reasonable thing. After shooting John Storms, he continued north onto Priory Avenue, toward the center of Hungerford. And some motorists, forced to make detours because of the roadblocks, drove directly into his deadly path.

One of these unfortunates was Douglas Wainwright. He and his wife, Kathleen, had come to Hungerford to visit their son, a local policeman who lived on Priory Avenue. A roadblock at the north end of town forced them to go the long way around, down the High Street. The Wainwrights could see the smoke rising from the houses burning in South View, and they made the very sensible inference that the trouble was a fire.

Sensible but fatally wrong, and no one stopped them to warn that a killer was on the loose. After several blocks the Wainwrights turned east toward Priory Avenue. They were less than 100 yards from their son's house when two bullets ripped through the windshield. Douglas slammed on the brakes, and Kathleen saw a man with a pistol standing just beyond her husband's open window. The gunman fired eight rounds into the car. Hit in the head, Douglas Wainwright groaned and toppled over on the seat. Blood trickled down his face, and Kathleen knew he was dead. She'd also been hit: One bullet penetrated her chest and another blew off the ends of two fingers.

Ryan walked to the front of the car and started to reload his gun. Kathleen was terrified that he was about to fire at her again. Gathering all her strength, she unlatched her seat belt, got out of the car, and crouched down behind it. But the bullets she feared never came. Ryan walked away, still reloading his pistol, and several neighbors rushed out of their houses and dragged Kathleen Wainwright to safety.

About this time, Rosemary Henderson was turning her car onto Priory Avenue. As she made the turn, she saw a man in the street pointing a gun at her. Odd, she thought— and kept going. Suddenly, she felt something small and hot in one hand. She spread her fingers. A 9-mm. bullet fell to the floor. In a freakish happenstance, the bullet in penetrating the car had apparently lost just enough velocity by the time it reached Henderson to fall into her hand without hurting her. Moments later, Kevin Lance drove into Ryan's range. Shot in the arm, Lance jumped from his van and ran away before Ryan had a chance to hit him again.

At the same roadblock that had shunted Douglas Wainwright to his death, 51-year-old Eric Vardy, a driver and handyman for a nurses' training school, and his passenger, Stephen Ball, were waved on by the same policeman. Probably a pub fight, Vardy speculated; nothing to worry about. The two followed the Wainwrights' tracks and turned onto Priory Avenue.

Ball saw a man—it was Kevin Lance—clutching his arm and running fast down a narrow side street. Suddenly gunfire came out of nowhere, shattering the van's windshield. Ball heard three more shots, and the van swerved across the road and into a hedge. Vardy had collapsed onto the steering wheel. He would die later from wounds in his neck and side. Ball, miraculously, suffered no serious injuries.

At 1:30 p.m. Ryan crossed the gardens of Orchard Park Close, firing into the houses as he went. Reaching Priory Road, a busy thoroughfare forking off the High Street, he fired a single shot from the Beretta at a passing red Renault. The driver, 22-year-old Sandra Hill, screamed as the bullet tore through her

The blanket-covered body of Douglas Wainwright slumps behind a shattered windshield. One of several motorists who detoured around police roadblocks only to cross Michael Ryan's path, Wainwright, a retired security guard, was killed by a shot to the head. Police still stalking the gunman tossed the temporary cover over the body.

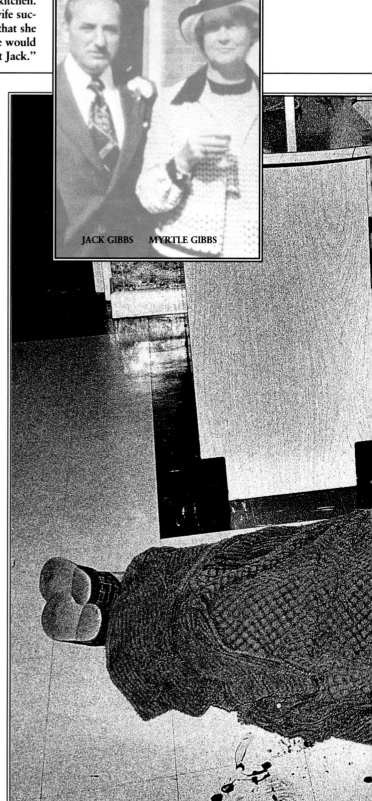

Jack Gibbs, 66, threw himself between his wheelchair-bound wife, Myrtle, and Michael Ryan when the killer burst into their kitchen. Gibbs died on the spot *(below);* his wife succumbed two days later. "It is a blessing that she died," neighbor Sylvia Dodds said. "She would not have wanted to survive without Jack."

JACK GIBBS   MYRTLE GIBBS

right shoulder and into her chest. Carl Harries, a soldier on leave visiting his parents, ran toward her car. Seeing Harries, Ryan raised his gun, but the soldier dived over a hedge before Ryan could take proper aim. Ryan moved on, and Harries quickly returned to the unconscious Hill and lifted her out of the car. She was bleeding badly, and a terrible gurgle escaped her lips. There was nothing to be done; an artery near her heart had been lacerated. Harries cradled the dying Hill in his arms.

Joyce Anderson had just returned to her house on Priory Road after doing her shopping at the Hungerford market when she saw a gunman walking her way. In his path two brothers, aged six and nine, were playing, oblivious to the danger slouching toward them. Anderson rushed outside, grabbed the boys, and hurried them into her house, locking the door behind them. At about the same time, Jack and Myrtle Gibbs were in the kitchen of their Priory Road bungalow preparing lunch and a pot of tea. Jack, 66, had been the president of a large heating company before his retirement. He devotedly cared for his 62-year-old wife, Myrtle, who was confined to a wheelchair. Some impulse propelled Ryan to the Gibbses' front door. Blasting off the locks, he burst into the house and went to the kitchen. A witness heard a woman shout, "What the hell do you think you are playing at?" followed by shots from inside the house. Ryan emerged from the front door. When he'd gone a safe distance, the Gibbses' next-door neighbor went in to find the old couple in their blood-spattered kitchen. Myrtle, who'd been shot four times at point-blank range, was sobbing over her dead husband. He had flung himself across his wife's wheelchair, trying to shield her as Ryan opened fire. His effort was in vain; Myrtle would die two days later.

Ian and Elizabeth Playle and their two children, six-year-old Richard and 18-month-old Sarah, were on their way home after a shopping trip to the nearby town of Swindon when they came upon a roadblock as they neared Hungerford Common. Several men were gathered at the roadblock, but none stepped forward with a warning. Thus ignorant of the horror in Hungerford, the Playles took a detour—to Priory Road. As they drove along, Elizabeth Playle heard a peculiar whirring sound and turned to ask her husband what it was. Blood was gushing from his neck. According to a witness, Ryan had fired once at the Playles' car, then shrugged as if he thought he'd missed. Carl Harries, the soldier on leave, hurried to the car and saw Eliz-

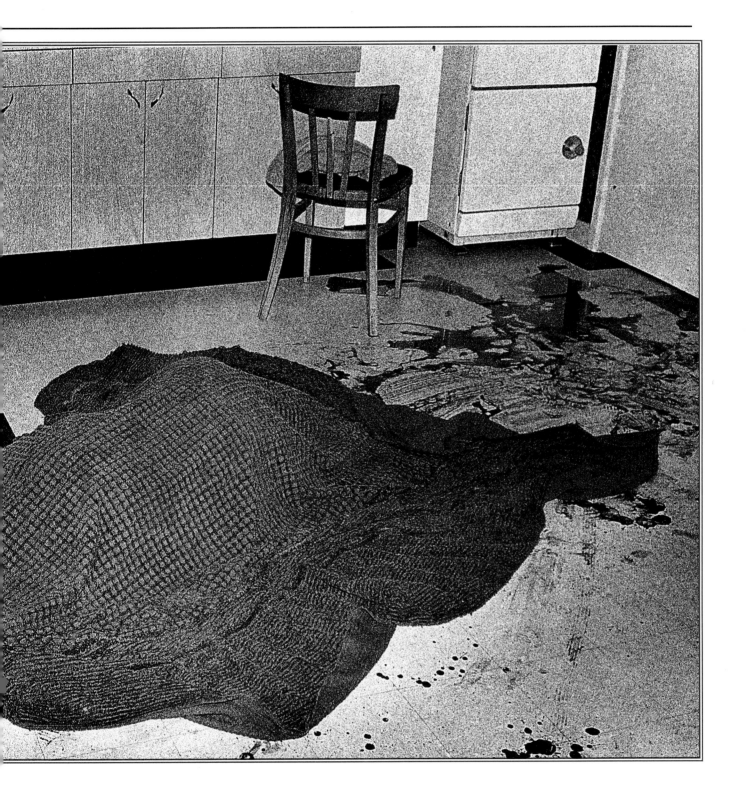

abeth Playle holding a cloth to her husband's neck. She was screaming, "He's gone, he's gone!" Harries tried cardiopulmonary resuscitation, but Ian Playle's injury was fatal. He was the last stranger Ryan would murder that day.

At 1:45 p.m. the police helicopter at last arrived. As it flew over Hungerford, the police aboard broadcast warnings for people to take cover. This was how many of the townsfolk, especially the shoppers crowding the market in the High Street, first learned about the shootings. As it turned out, the warnings came too late to save anyone, for Michael Ryan was nearing the end of his bloody tour.

Hearing first gunshots and then the broadcast from the helicopter, William Noon hurried to Priory Road to check on his grandchildren. He found them playing in the family's garden and rushed them into the house. Noon was just crossing the threshold himself when he was hit first in the shoulder, then in the eye. He survived.

Noon's neighbor Thomas North witnessed the shooting. He watched as Ryan ran along the road. Ryan saw North too—and did something bizarre. He pointed his gun at North, and grinned. "Bang!" he said. He didn't shoot. Seconds later, he fired at a house farther along the street.

The last stop on Ryan's tortuous two-mile spree was dead ahead. Caretaker John Miles, who lived in a cottage on the grounds of the John O'Gaunt School, had just seen two children bicycle past shouting frantically about a man shooting people in the streets when Ryan appeared at 1:50 p.m. Carrying the Beretta in his left hand and the AK-47 over his right shoulder, he walked into the school. He didn't bother to look back to see if anyone was following. With his two teenage children in tow, John Miles ran into his house and called out a window to two groundskeepers nearby to take cover, then dialed 999 to report seeing the gunman.

Police officers aboard the low-flying helicopter surveyed Hungerford and were able to pick up portions of Ryan's course, marked as they were by wrecked vehicles and by victims who still lay where they'd fallen. There were 30 victims so far—15 dead, 15 wounded. Afraid that ambulances would come under fire, the police had not allowed medics to answer calls for help. The killer had disappeared from view. Among the dozens of locations where callers reported seeing Ryan, the school emerged as a likely spot; besides Miles, Bert Watley, who lived across Priory Road from the school, also saw Ryan and called the police. But confirming such reports was a dangerous and painstaking

Carrying a gas mask and wearing a bulletproof vest and police radio, an armed member of the Tactical Firearms Unit gears up to secure Hungerford. By the time the armed police went into action, Michael Ryan was already holed up in the John O'Gaunt School.

business. Taking ground a little at a time, the TFU, at last present in full force, made its way through the terror-stricken town, kicking in doors, securing gardens, searching houses to make sure the gunman was not hiding within, perhaps with hostages. By 4 p.m. the TFU had the school surrounded. At 4:40 they heard gunfire inside the building. They were in the right place at the right time at last.

When Sergeant Paul Brightwell of the TFU heard on his radio that a shot had been fired from a school window, he dashed through the neatly manicured gardens of several houses on Priory Road to the school grounds. He crouched down beside Police Constable Anthony Bates, who had his gun trained on a third-floor window. Ryan had just tossed his AK-47 out that window. Shouting from a safe distance, Brightwell asked him his first name.

"Mind your own business," Ryan yelled back.

"What weapons do you have with you?"

"One 9-mm. pistol and ammunition."

So he still had a gun—and, Ryan volunteered in a moment, a grenade as well. Brightwell was anxious to keep Ryan talking, in one place, lest he move around the building and start killing again, shooting through the windows. For 83 minutes Brightwell and Ryan kept up their shouted conversation.

"I want to know how my mother is. Tell me about my mother," Ryan yelled.

"I will try to find out about your mother. Just bear with me."

"I must know about my mother. Tell me or I will throw the grenade out of the window."

"Don't do that. I am trying to find out about your mother, believe me." Hungerford was still in chaos, and Brightwell had not yet heard that Dorothy Ryan was dead.

At one point Brightwell tried without success to coax Ryan down a staircase. Then their conversation resumed.

"I had an M-1 carbine which I left in the park," Ryan said. "It was on a gravel path near the body of a male I shot near the swimming pool. There should be a 30-round magazine with it."

"Thank you for that, Mr. Ryan."

"Also there is my dog. Has anybody found that? It is a black Labrador. I shot it. I had my eyes shut the first time and I just winged it."

"Will you come out?"

"I am not coming out until I know about my mother."

Once again Brightwell tried to get the gunman to leave the building, but Ryan stayed put. Asking about his mother again, the killer moved nearer the events of the day:

"What are the casualty figures?"

"I don't know," Brightwell answered. "Obviously you know you shot a lot of people."

"Hungerford must be a bit of a mess."

"You are right. They know you have been through," Brightwell said. "How many do you think you have shot?"

"I don't know. It is like a bad dream."

The killer couldn't stop thinking about his mother:

"She is dead, isn't she? That is why you won't tell me. I am throwing the magazine of the pistol out."

The magazine fell to the ground.

"I still have one round left."

"Why do you have that?"

"It's obvious, isn't it?"

Ryan returned to the subject of his dog, asking Brightwell to see that it got a decent burial. Then there was another agonized outburst about Dorothy Ryan:

"What about my mother? She is dead. I know she's dead."

Time was slipping by. It was now 6:24 p.m. Brightwell still had no information about Dorothy Ryan.

"If only the police car hadn't turned up," Ryan wailed. "If only my car had started."

After a brief exchange about the number of armed officers at the scene, Ryan repeated his terrible refrain:

"How is my mother? I didn't mean to kill her. It was a mistake."

"I understand that."

"How can you understand? I wish I had stayed in bed."

Ryan asked whether he might be sentenced to prison for life, then suddenly shouted to the sergeant:

"It's funny. I killed all those people, but I haven't the guts to blow my own brains out."

"Don't do anything silly, do you understand?"

For the last time, Ryan said that he wouldn't come out until somebody told him about his mother. He fell silent; the conversation was over.

He had the guts after all. Putting his pistol to his right temple, he fired the bullet he'd saved into his brain. Sergeant Brightwell noted the time of the muffled shot. It was 6:52 p.m. Michael Ryan was dead. ◆

The High Street's cheerful market-day bustle gave way to chaos as ambulances clogged the road waiting

Acknowledgments

The editors thank the following for their valuable assistance:

Charles Amor, Thatcham, Berkshire, England; Anthony Aslanes, Massillon, Ohio; James Aslanes, Massillon, Ohio; Jack Aubry, *Citizen,* Ottowa, Canada; Special Agent Steve Band, FBI Academy, Quantico, Va.; Andrew Barnard, Director, Wiltshire Shooting Centre, Devizes, England; The Hon. Peter Beer, New Orleans, La.; Peter Bloodworth, Newbury, England; Bernard Clarke, Newbury *Weekly News,* Newbury, England; Ivan Delp, New Orleans, La.; Irivrine Eggerson, New Orleans, La.; Sam Garcia, San Diego Police Dept., San Diego, Calif.; Arthur Goodnough, Massillon, Ohio; Stewart Hookey, Berkshire Ambulance Service, Wokingham, England; The Hon. Moon Landrieu, New Orleans, La.; David Lee, Aldbourne, Wiltshire, England; Officer David McCann, New Orleans Police Dept., New Orleans, La.; PC Bernard Maggs, Thames Valley Police, Berkshire, England; Holly Marshall, Austin History Center, Austin, Tex.; Robert Morgan, Manager, Dunmore Shooting Centre, Abingdon, England; Agent Andrew Nash, FBI Field Office, New Orleans, La.; Sylvia Pascoe, Hungerford, England; Robert Ressler, Spotsylvania, Va.; Colin Shepherd, South West News Service, Bristol, England; Dr. Richard Shepherd, Guy's Hospital, London; Paul Suttle, Apple Creek, Ohio; Thames Valley Police, Kidlington, Oxfordshire, England; Greg Weston, *Citizen,* Ottowa, Canada; Oscar White, Canton, Ohio; Dr. Marvin Ziporyn, Chicago, Ill.

Bibliography

Books

Altman, Jack, and Marvin Ziporyn, *Born to Raise Hell.* New York: Grove Press, 1967.

Cox, Bill G., et al., *Crimes of the 20th Century.* New York: Crescent Books, 1991.

Grier, William H., and Price M. Cobbs, *Black Rage.* New York: Basic Books, 1968.

Herndon, Peter, *A Terrible Thunder.* Garden City, N.Y.: Doubleday, 1978.

Leyton, Elliott, *Hunting Humans.* New York: Pocket Books, 1986.

Marighella, Carlos, *Manual of the Urban Guerrilla.* Transl. by Gene Hanrahan. Chapel Hill, N.C.: Documentary Publications, 1985.

Nash, Jay Robert, *Bloodletters and Badmen.* Vol. 3. Philadelphia: Lippincott, 1973.

Tobias, Ronald, *They Shoot to Kill.* Boulder, Colo.: Paladin Press, 1981.

Periodicals

"Accused Slayer 'Always Wanted to Be Known.'" *World Journal Tribune,* Nov. 13, 1966.

" 'All American Boy.' " *Newsweek,* Aug. 15, 1966.

Ansell, Kay, "Knight Planned to Kill Himself with Last Bullet, Court Told." *AGE,* Apr. 19, 1988.

"Arizona Slayer of 5 Convicted." *New York Times,* Oct. 25, 1967.

Attwood, Alan, and Philip Chubb, "Bloody Sunday." *Time,* Aug. 18, 1987.

Aubry, Jack, "Haunted by Lépine." *The Gazette,* Dec. 2, 1990.

Beach, Patrick, "Roommate Recalls Killer as Egomaniac Frustrated by Women." *Des Moines Register,* Nov. 4, 1991.

Berger, Joseph, and Anthony Mancini, "The Man Who Never Smiled." *New York Post,* Feb. 28, 1977.

Berry, Jim:
"Slayer of Whitman Shocked by Ordeal." *Austin American,* Aug. 2, 1966.
"What Each Man Did." *Austin American-Statesman,* Aug. 7, 1966.

"Berserk Gunman Kills 6 Friends." *New York Times,* Oct. 25, 1967.

Bigart, Homer, "Portrait of a Killer." *New York Times,* Oct. 25, 1967.

"Bloodbath on Market Day." *Daily Mail,* Aug. 20, 1987.

Booth, William, "Texas Killer Said to Have 'Problem with Women.' " *Washington Post,* Oct. 18, 1991.

Brisbane, Arthur S.:
"Father of Mass Murderer, Son's Violence Is Inexplicable." *Washington Post,* July 21, 1984.
"Huberty Was an Angry Man Searching for a Better Way of Life." *Washington Post,* July 20, 1984.

"Brother of Killer Slain in Bar Clash." *New York Times,* July 5, 1973.

Buchignani, Walter, "Victim Tried to Reason with Killer." *The Gazette,* Dec. 9, 1989.

Buckie, Catherine, and Peter Kuitenbrouwer, "Student Journalists Hit Floor During Gunfire." *The Gazette,* Dec. 7, 1989.

Burton, Anthony, "Killer: Wanted the World to Know My Name." New York *Daily News,* Nov. 14, 1966.

Burton, Anthony, and William Federici, "Youth Lines Up 7, Kills 5 — and Laughs." New York *Daily News,* Nov. 13, 1966.

Caputo, Philip, "Death Goes to School." *Esquire,* Dec. 1989.

Casteel, Chris, "Edmond Killings Defy Explanation." *Sunday Oklahoman,* Aug. 24, 1986.

Castlebury, Glen, "What Happened: The Terrible Sequence of Tragedy." *Austin American-Statesman,* Aug. 7, 1966.

Castlebury, Glen, and Jim Berry, "Sniper in U. T. Tower 'Fortress' Shot after 90 Minutes of Terror." *Austin American,* Aug. 2, 1966.

"College Friends Knew Him as Easygoing Nice Guy." New York *Daily News,* Aug. 2, 1966.

"Cop Used to Date Slain Nurse." *Chicago Tribune,* July 15, 1966.

Crabill, Steven, "Post Office Siege Lasted Four Hours." *The Record,* Oct. 11, 1991.

Cummings, Judith, "Neighbors Term Mass Slayer a Quiet but Hotheaded Loner." *New York Times,* July 20, 1984.

"Doctor's Dilemma." *New York Times,* Aug. 8, 1966.

"Doctors Will Study Tower Sniper's Brain." *Killeen Daily Herald,* Aug. 4, 1966.

Doucet, Clarence, "No Trace of Sniper Found After Police Comb Hotel." *Times-Picayune,* Jan. 9, 1973.

Evans, Derro, "Whitman Had Year to Live." *Austin American,* Sept. 9, 1966.

Evans, Derro, and Sara Speights, "Sniper on the Tower." *Austin American-Statesman,* Aug. 6, 1966.

Federici, William:
"Arizona Mass Killer of 5 May Be Pro." New York *Daily News,* Nov. 14, 1966.
"Dad Kept Doc." New York *Daily News,* Nov. 15, 1966.

Filkins, Dexter, and Martin Merzer, "Kentucky Native Jailed in Fla. Deaths." *Lexington Herald-Leader,* Apr. 25, 1987.

Flynn, George, and Ed Jahn, "A Quiet Upbringing, but a Rage to Kill." *San Diego Union,* July 20, 1984.

"Forty-Eight Minutes." *Australian Her-*

ald, Nov. 4, 1988.

Foster, Howard, "Ryan Boasted That He Was Never without a Gun." *The Times*, Sept. 25, 1987.

Franks, Zarko, "Massacre at High Noon." *Houston Chronicle*, Aug. 7, 1966.

Freed, David, " 'Going Hunting Humans,' Slayer Told Wife." *Los Angeles Times*, July 20, 1984.

Frink, Cheryl Coggins, "Fliers Brave Fire in Attempt to Halt Frenzy of Killing." *Austin American-Statesman*, Aug. 1, 1986.

Geiger, Peter, and Terry Oblander, "Ex-Massillon Man Was a Gun-Obsessed 'Loner.' " *Akron Beacon Journal*, July 19, 1992.

Gooding, Richard, "The Victims of Hatred." *New York Post*, Feb. 28, 1977.

Greene, Bob, "The Voice of Richard Speck." *Chicago Tribune*, Dec. 8, 1991.

Gregory, Peter, "Knight Dreamed of Being a Hero: QC." *AGE*, Oct. 29, 1988.

"Gunman Massacres 20 in Restaurant." *Akron Beacon Journal*, July 19, 1984.

"Gunman's Arrest After Siege Recounted." *Miami Herald*, Mar. 22, 1989.

Hall, Jerry:
"The Last Night: Wife and Mother Killed." *Austin American-Statesman*, Aug. 7, 1966.
"Tower Sniper 'Ate Drugs Like Popcorn.' " *Austin American*, Mar. 7, 1967.

Hamilton, Graeme, and Andrew McIntosh, "Lépine Was Recluse and Noisy at Night Neighbor Says." *The Gazette*, Dec. 8, 1989.

Hayes, Thomas C., "Gunman Kills 22 and Himself in Texas Cafeteria." *New York Times*, Oct. 17, 1991.

Heinreich, Jeff:
"Students Ignored Warning About Gunman—Witness." *The Gazette*, Dec. 15, 1989.
"Veteran Cop Breaks Year-Long Silence Over His Daughter's Murder." *The Gazette*, Dec. 1, 1990.

Helmer, William J.:
"Blood-Soaked Textbooks." *Texas Observer*, Aug. 19, 1966.
"Madman on the Tower." *Texas Monthly*, Aug. 1986.

Henderson, Nat, "Wife, Mom Killed in 'Mercy.' " *Austin American*, Aug. 2, 1966.

Henderson, Nat, and Derro Evans, " 'Everyone' Loved Him." *Austin American*, Aug. 2, 1966.

Hilliard, Brian, "The Hungerford Massacre." *Police Review*, Oct. 9, 1987.

Holden, Wendy, "It Is Like a Bad Dream, I Wish I had Stayed in Bed." *Daily Telegraph*, Sept. 30, 1987.

"I Never Really Believed That He Would Do Anything Like This." *Washington Post*, July 21, 1984.

Ingram, Carl, and Robert A. Jones, "Gunman Had Attended School He Assaulted but Motive Remains Unclear in Attack." *Los Angeles Times*, Jan. 19, 1989.

Jones, Garth, "Sniper's Bullets Kill 12 in Austin." *Dallas Morning News*, Aug. 2, 1966.

"The Julian Knight Story." *Australian Herald WeekEnd*, Nov. 4, 1988.

"Just One of the Boys Who Gave, Took Lumps." *Dallas Daily News*, July 18, 1966.

Keller, Loren, "Letters Reveal Anger, Violence behind Killings." *Daily Iowan*, Dec. 5, 1991.

Krebs, Albin:
"Father Shocked by Son's Charge." *New York Times*, Aug. 8, 1966.
"The Texas Killer." *New York Times*, Aug. 2, 1966.

Kuehler, Marilyn, "All Forces Join in Fight Ending in Sniper's Death." *Daily Texan*, Aug. 2, 1966.

Kuempel, George, "Sniper's Terror Reign with 15 Dead, 34 Wounded." *Daily Texan*, Aug. 2, 1966.

Lamey, Mary, "Nothing Prepares You for Such Savagery." *The Gazette*, Dec. 8, 1989.

"Lépine Planned to Kill 19 More Note Suggests." *The Gazette*, Nov. 24, 1990.

Leusner, Jim, and Dan Tracy, "Retired Librarian Accused of Brevard Mass Murder." *Orlando Sentinel*, Apr. 25, 1987.

Lillard, Dorothy, "Tower's History Tragic." *Dallas Morning News*, Aug. 2, 1966.

Long, Phil, "Neighbors Feared Hate-Filled Loner." *Miami Herald*, Apr. 25, 1987.

McBroom, Patricia, "Tumor Found Innocent." *Science News*, Aug. 22, 1966.

MacDonell, Rod, et al., "Killer's Father Beat Him as a Child." *The Gazette*, Dec. 9, 1989.

McLaughlin, Peter, Larry Cole, and Paul Meskil, "A Cowan Note." *New York Post*, Feb. 28, 1977.

McLemore, David, "Sniper's 20-year-old Legacy Haunts Austin." *Dallas Morning News*, Aug. 1, 1986.

Malcolm, Andrew H., "Kansas Home-town Baffled by Violent End to Life of Mark Essex." *New York Times*, Jan. 11, 1973.

Maraniss, David, "Mourning Town Tries to Understand Killer Who Feared Illness." *Washington Post*, Aug. 22, 1986.

Martin, Frank L., III, "One Terrorist Dead; Possibly Two Others at Howard Johnson's." *Times-Picayune*, Jan. 8, 1973.

"Mass Murder on Campus." *U.S. News & World Report*, Aug. 15, 1966.

"Mass Slayings, Many Sites." *New York Times*, Aug. 21, 1986.

"Massacre in Melbourne." *Time Hong Kong*, Aug. 24, 1987.

"Massacre." *Today*, Aug. 20, 1987.

Mathews, Jay:
"Gunman Said He Resented Enterprising Immigrants." *Washington Post*, Jan. 19, 1989.
"Legacy of Schoolyard Turned Killing Ground." *Washington Post*, Jan. 14, 1990.

Mathews, Tom, and Susan Agrest, "The Nazi of New Rochelle." *Newsweek*, Feb. 28, 1977.

Mead, Andy, Valarie Honeycutt, and Sharon M. Reynolds, "Ex-Lexington Resident Charged with Killing 6." *Lexington Herald-Leader*, Apr. 25, 1987.

Montgomery, Paul, "Sniper Told about Deaths in Note 'to Whom It May Concern.' " *New York Times*, Aug. 3, 1966.

Moon, Jule, and Gwyn Smith:
"What Can We Learn?—I." *Daily Texan*, Sept. 20, 1966.
"What Can We Learn?—II." *Daily Texan*, Sept. 21, 1966.
"What Can We Learn?—III." *Daily Texan*, Sept. 22, 1966.

Morain, Dan, and Louis Sahagun, "Escalating Hate Reportedly Consumed Gunman." *Los Angeles Times*, Jan. 20, 1989.

Morain, Dan, and Mark A. Stein, "Unwanted Suitor's Fixation on Woman Led to Carnage." *Los Angeles Times*, Feb. 18, 1988.

"Neighbors Tell of Awakening to Tragedy." *Chicago Tribune*, July 14, 1966.

"New Mass Slaying: 4 Women, Child." New York *World Journal Tribune*, Nov. 13, 1966.

Norris, Alexander, and Paul Wells, "Trapped Students Cowered as Lépine Fired at Will." *The Gazette*, Dec. 8, 1989.

"An Obsession with Firearms, a Short Course in Rejection, a Sniper Stalks." *AGE,* Nov. 11, 1988.

Ourlian, Robert, Mike Martindale, and Rebecca Powers, " 'Everybody Knew This Had to Happen.' " *Detroit News,* Nov. 15, 1992.

Parker, Laura, "Jacksonville Gunman Shot 4 Others Before Rampage at Finance Company." *Washington Post,* June 20, 1990.

Porter, G. Bruce, "The Mass Killers." *New York Post,* Aug. 6, 1966.

"The Quiet One." *Time,* Sept. 12, 1949.

"The Real Story of Austin's Mass Killer." *U.S. News & World Report,* Aug. 22, 1966.

Reeves, Phil, and Nick Cohen, "Witnesses to a Trail of Terror That Claimed 14 Lives." *The Independent,* Aug. 20, 1987.

"The Revolt of Leo Held." *Time,* Nov. 3, 1967.

Ricketson, Matthew, "I Wanted to See What It Was Like to Kill." *Australian,* Apr. 19, 1988.

Salpukas, Agis, "Essex, Called a 'Loving' Man, Buried Amid Militant Symbols." *New York Times,* Jan. 14, 1973.

Schumach, Murray. "Cowan Was 'Nice Man' to Some in New Rochelle, But to Others 'Real Prejudiced' Backer of Nazis." *New York Times,* Feb. 15, 1977.

Scott, Austin:
   "Epithets Cover Walls of Sniper's La. Shack." *Washington Post,* Jan. 13, 1973.
   "Harassment in Navy Turned Essex to White Hatred, 'Black Rage.' " *Washington Post,* Jan. 13, 1973.

Scott, Marian, "Rifle Bullet Snuffed Out Dream of a New Life—Victim's Husband." *The Gazette,* Dec. 12, 1989.

Scott, Marian, Jeff Heinrich, and Peter Kuitenbrouwer, "Campus Massacre." *The Gazette,* Dec. 7, 1989.

"Season of Savagery and Rage." *Time,* Feb. 28, 1977.

"A Short-Tempered Loner Who Liked to Get Even." *Akron Beacon Journal,* July 20, 1984.

Singleterry, Wayne, "Edmond Killer Painted as Lonely, Sullen Man." *Daily Oklahoman,* Aug. 21, 1986.

"Slaughter in the College of Beauty." *Time,* Nov. 18, 1966.

"Slayer of 6 Is Buried." *New York Times,* Oct. 29, 1967.

Smothers, Ronald, "Florida Gunman Kills 8 and Wounds 6 in Office." *New York Times,* June 19, 1990.

"Sniper's Rites to Be Saturday." *Times-Picayune,* Jan. 11, 1973.

Terry, Don, "Portrait of Texas Killer: Impatient and Troubled." *New York Times,* Oct. 18, 1991.

Tessler, Ray, "Accused Killer's Story of Sunnyvale Rampage." *San Francisco Chronicle,* July 15, 1988.

Tessler, Ray, and Colleen Gillard, "Sunnyvale Killer's Love Fantasy 4-Year Ordeal for Woman." *San Francisco Chronicle,* Feb. 18, 1988.

Thomas, David, "The Search for Michael Ryan." *You,* Aug. 7, 1988.

Thomas, Robert McG., Jr., "Supervisor Sought by Cowan Hid under a Desk as Killer Searched." *New York Times,* Feb. 15, 1977.

Thompson, Elizabeth, "Policeman Finds His Daughter among the Victims of Bloodbath." *The Gazette,* Dec. 7, 1989.

Todd, Jack, "Killer Smiled, Then Told Men to Leave." *The Gazette,* Dec. 7, 1989.

Tu Thanh Ha, "Polytechnique Toll Continues to Climb." *The Gazette,* July 17, 1991.

"12 Minutes of Murder." *Life,* Sept. 19, 1949.

"24 Years to Page One." *Time,* July 9, 1966.

"Two States of Mind." *Time,* Nov. 3, 1967.

"Under the Clock, a Sniper with 31 Minutes to Live." *Life,* Aug. 12, 1966.

Wainwright, Loudon, "Who the Gentle Victims Were." *Life,* July 19, 1966.

Wallace, Diana, and Marcey Bullerman, "Acquaintances Talk About Lu." *Daily Iowan,* Nov. 4, 1991.

Ward, Pamela, "Survivors Shaken by Shooting Spree." *Austin American-Statesman,* Oct. 17, 1991.

Weston, Greg, and Jack Aubry, "The Making of a Mass Killer." *Ottowa Citizen,* Feb. 11, 1990.

Whitcraft, Chris:
   "The Psychiatrists: Right before and after the Tragedy." *Austin American-Statesman,* Aug. 7, 1966.
   "This Was Charles Whitman." *Austin American-Statesman,* Aug. 7, 1966.

White, Jerry:
   "Secret File Describes UT Sniper." *Austin American-Statesman,* July 6, 1986.
   "Whitman Writes of Murders." *Austin American-Statesman,* July 6, 1986.

Williams, Al, "Victims' Blood Bathed Top Floor of Tower." *Austin American,* Aug. 2, 1966.

Wilmoth, Peter, "Jailed for 27 Years, a Killer Bows." *AGE,* Nov. 11, 1988.

Woodbury, Richard, "Ten Minutes in Hell." *Time,* Oct. 28, 1991.

Woodin, Heather Sloman, "Gang Lu Planned for Months." *Cedar Rapids Gazette,* Dec. 5, 1991.

Wright, Scott W., "23 Die in Killeen, 20 Hurt in Attack at Busy Cafeteria." *Austin American-Statesman,* Oct. 17, 1991.

Wrolstad, Mark, "Hennard's Odyssey Contradictions, Paranoia Marked Troubled Path of Hot-Tempered Loner Who Killed 23 in Killeen." *Dallas Morning News,* Nov. 24, 1991.

"Youth, 18, Slays 4 Women and Child in Beauty School." *New York Times,* Nov. 13, 1966.

Other Sources

Blumberg, Joe M., and Russell N. de-Jong, et al., "Report to the Governor: Medical Aspects, Charles J. Whitman Catastrophe." Austin, Texas: Sept. 8, 1966.

Committee on Post Office and Civil Service, House of Representatives, "A Post Office Tragedy: The Shooting at Royal Oak." Washington, D.C.: U.S. Government Printing Office, June 15, 1992.

"Hungerford—the Lessons." Television script. Thames Television (London), Jan. 1, 1988.

Lépine, Marc (Letter). *The Gazette,* Nov. 25, 1990.

Lu, Gang (Letters):
   Cedar Rapids Gazette, Dec. 5, 1991.
   Des Moines Register, Nov. 2, 1991.

San Diego, Calif., Police Department Investigator's Report, Case #84-050362, July 18, 1984.

Shepherd, Richard Thorley, "The Hungerford Massacre." *The Medico-Legal Society,* Vol. 57, Part 4. London, 1989.

"The Shooting Incidents at Hungerford on 19 August 1987." The Report of the Chief Constable to The Thames Valley Police Authority at Their Meeting Held on 17 November 1987.

Sourour, Teresa, "Coroner's Report." Coroner's Office, Montreal, Canada, May 10, 1990.

Testimony of Bonita Sue (Harris) Cantaloupe at trial of Robert Benjamin Smith (Transcript). *Time Law,* 1967.

Testimony of court-appointed psychiatrist, Dr. Kent Durfee at trial of Robert Benjamin Smith. *Time Law,* 1967.

Index

189

Picture Credits